A BIRD OF CURIOUS PLUMAGE

By the same author

PRINCESS CRISTINA IN 1843
from the painting by Henri Lehmann

A BIRD OF CURIOUS PLUMAGE

Princess Cristina di Belgiojoso
1808–1871

———◆———

CHARLES NEILSON GATTEY

The great political or social agitator
is most often a bird of curious plumage,
all of whose feathers, even the queerest,
play their part in his flight.

HENRY JAMES
(referring to Princess Cristina) in
William Wetmore Story and his Friends

Constable London

First published 1971
by Constable & Company Ltd
10 Orange Street, London WC2
Copyright © 1971 by Charles Neilson Gattey
ISBN 0 09 457720 X

Set in Monotype Bembo
Printed in Great Britain by
Cox & Wyman Ltd.
London, Fakenham and Reading

To Dorothy Muller

ACKNOWLEDGEMENTS

For helping me in the research for this book in Italy, France and Switzerland my grateful thanks are due to Mrs Dorothy Muller and Miss Berta Rahm and to the staff of the Museo del Risorgimento e Raccolte Storiche, Milan; the Museo Nazionale del Risorgimento Italiano, Turin; the Biblioteca, Lugano; the Istituto per la Storia Del Risorgimento Italiano, Rome; the Istituto Mazziniano, Genoa; the Società Toscana per la Storia del Risorgimento, Florence; and the Bibliothèque Nationale, Paris.

For assistance with the Belgiojoso family records and tracing various pictures and portraits I have to thank Princess Paola Bruni Belgiojoso, the Marchesa Marianna Brivio Sforza Trivulzio, the Marchesa Ludovica Niccolini Valperga di Masino, and the Contessa Vittoria Valperga di Masino.

C.N.G.

CONTENTS

ILLUSTRATIONS

xi

FOREWORD

Princess Cristina di Belgiojoso was probably the most intriguing and original Italian woman since the Middle Ages. She organised the first military nurses' corps – four years before Florence Nightingale did the same in the Crimea. Certainly Melchior de Vogüé of the Académie Française was right when he wrote: 'Above all her caprices, all the showiness of her life, one sincere passion rose up. No other Italian of her sex has contributed more to the resurrection of Italy: none other has served her country with more zeal and tenacity.'

Henry James, who knew and admired Cristina, based his *Princess Casamassima* on her. Hers was 'a strange, pale, penetrating beauty, without bloom, health, substance, that was yet the mask of an astounding masculine energy,' he recorded. She reminded one 'that the great political or social agitator is most often a bird of curious plumage, all of whose feathers, even the queerest, play their part in his flight.'

Princess Cristina puzzled her contemporaries. One called her 'a character replete with contradictions' – and another *'une femme qui a été aimée et qui n'a pas aimé.'* She has been accused of having stolen Liszt from Marie d'Agoult and Alfred de Musset from George Sand. There were probably only two men she ever really loved – her husband, Prince Emilio, and her young secretary, Gaetano Stelzi, whose body she stole from its grave, had embalmed and kept in her villa. Its discovery during her absence sparked off a scandal that led to her leaving for Asia Minor, where she travelled extensively and had an extraordinary escape from being murdered.

No biography of Princess Cristina has been published in English since H. R. Whitehouse's short study appeared in 1906. It is only

xiii

in recent years that the letters and documents in the Belgiojoso
family archives have become accessible, presenting a quite new
light on various aspects of her life, and the present biographer has
made extensive use of the information they contain. All quoted
matter not referred to in the Notes is from this source.

CHAPTER I

NAPOLEON III's FIRST LOVE

It is one evening in early autumn, 1828. The auditorium of La Scala, Milan, then the largest theatre in Europe, is crowded for the opening of the new season. Even the thirty-nine boxes belonging to the aristocracy, often inherited by unmusical sons from musical fathers and as a result left empty, are tonight crowded with the fashionable élite and have ermine tippets draped over their fronts; all except one – that belonging to young Prince Emilio di Belgiojoso. It is surprising, for not only is he an appreciative patron of the opera but has himself what is admitted even by his enemies to be the finest voice in Italy.

Suddenly the door in the back of the box is flung open to admit the Prince's girl wife, Cristina. Her face is phantom white and she is dressed in full mourning. She stands for a moment, deliberately displaying herself, before moving slowly to sit on a gilded chair next to the one her husband should have occupied. So the rumour is true, excited spectators whisper to one another, the Princess has finally broken with Prince Emilio. Could this mean that he has returned to his former mistress, once Byron's inamorata, the Countess Guiccioli? This theatrical way of drawing attention to herself was to be repeated many times during the first half of Cristina's life.

Born in Milan on 28 June 1808, in the palace of her patrician father, Jerome Trivulzio – whose family had lived in Lombardy since the twelfth century – she was christened in the Church of Sant' Alessandro and given the usual hard to remember string of names – Maria Cristina Beatrice Teresa Barbara Leopolda Clotilde Melchiora Camilla Giulia Margherita Laura. Three years before her birth Napoleon had come to the city and in the cathedral there had startled the congregation by uttering the words, 'God gave it to me – woe to him who touches it!' as he placed on his own head the Iron Crown of Lombardy, which according to tradition was fashioned from a nail of the True Cross. Among his supporters ennobled soon after was Jerome Trivulzio, who included among his ancestors a Marshal of France and whom he had created a count.

The first King of Italy had left in Milan as Viceroy his stepson, Eugène Beauharnais. The new Count was attached to the latter's court, where the Countess became a lady of honour to the Bavarian Princess chosen as a bride for the Viceroy.

Jerome Trivulzio died suddenly when his daughter Cristina was only four years old. A hard man, he was not long mourned by his attractive twenty-one year old widow, who a year later married the Marchese Alessandro Visconti d'Aragona, one of the leaders of the Liberal party in Lombardy.

Little is known of Cristina's childhood save for a letter she wrote in 1842[1] contradicting assertions made by a practitioner she had consulted at a time when phrenology was the fashion: 'You say that I must have been very gay and lively as a child, but that I am now subject to fits of depression. The contrary is true. I was a serious, quiet girl. I don't know where the gay, equable nature which I now enjoy comes from; what has happened in my life should have made me just the opposite. The more I consider the matter the more grateful I am to God.

'You also say that I must have been full of ambition and have striven to attract attention. In fact I was so timid that I would often burst into tears in my mother's drawing-room when anybody tried to talk to me. According to you, I must have been very fond of admiring myself in the mirror. This is quite wrong. As a girl I decided that I was positively ugly and I still think so. Far from gaining any pleasure at regarding my reflexion, I was often punished when young because I preferred old clothes to new ones, and would put them on back to front rather than have to look in the mirror.

'You add that I must have been completely selfish. Immediately after the birth of my first half-brother I was told to amuse him, and my hours of recreation would be spent without a murmur of protest on my part pushing his small perambulator and playing with him. '"You loved reading romantic novels." I never read any novels before my marriage except those of Miss Edgeworth. "You loved looking at pictures of battles." Again incorrect. As far back as I can remember I have always detested anything to do with war and the shedding of blood. You say that from an early age I kept aloof from other children. But I never met any children apart from my half-brother.'

Thanks to her stepfather, Cristina received a far better education than most of her sex did at that period. She excelled at drawing, which she was taught by a talented, warm-hearted woman, Ernesta Bisi, who remained her lifelong friend with whom she corresponded regularly.

Following the Congress of Vienna in 1815, Lombardy had been returned to Austria and under the repressive hand of Prince Metternich, champion of absolutism, all change was forbidden. It was he who said contemptuously: 'Italy is but a geographical expression.' The Nationalist movement, the *Conciliatore*, was outlawed. The introduction of machinery was discouraged. Count Hartig, the Governor, even forbade gas to be used for lighting the streets of Milan or steam-boats to be allowed on the Po.

But the forces set free by the French Revolution could not be destroyed, and opposition driven underground led to the birth of secret societies. The most active of these was the *Federazione*. Its object was to free Italy from all foreign domination and form a confederation with an Italian prince as its titular head. The Marchese d'Aragona became a leading member. A rising to overthrow Habsburg rule was plotted, but the Austrian police had their spies and swooped beforehand on the conspirators. Thanks to the presence of mind of the Marchesa Visconti d'Aragona, who burned her husband's incriminating papers before the police could reach them, he was acquitted for lack of evidence at his trial, which dragged on for two years.[2] Had he been found guilty the penalty would have been death.

3

Cristina loved her stepfather and this was a time of tension and anxiety for her. When he came home he was a nervous, physical wreck, alternating between fits of deep depression and violent irritability. His wife began to tire of him. She was still beautiful and vivacious, and had not the temperament to be a nurse. She found consolation in an affair with a handsome penniless Sicilian libertine of high birth, the Duke of Cannizzaro,[3] whom Cristina disliked intensely on account of this.

Living in such an atmosphere of family discord, the girl grew very unhappy. Then, when she was only fifteen, she fell in love with the exceptionally handsome Prince Emilio Barbiano di Belgiojoso d'Este, eight years older than herself. His contemporaries have recorded that he was tall, with fair wavy hair and 'caressing eyes.' His total lack of vanity allowed him to appeal to women without arousing male jealousy. Rossini had been his music master.

The Prince gathered round himself many young companions, imitators of his vices, artists, musicians, men about town, *madamine*, ballet dancers and women of easy virtue. His robust health defied excess, but not his fortune. He had mortgaged all he could when he met Cristina. Her adoration amused him, but he realised that marriage with this most sought-after young heiress would solve his financial difficulties. His intimate friend, the Comte d'Alton-Shée summed up his character thus: 'Emilio suffered from a Byronic intemperance, an insatiable craving for sensual distraction. He thought life should be entirely devoted to satisfying one's personal pleasure to the full. Endowed by nature with all the gifts for seducing women, he went about doing so without scruples or remorse.'

There was much opposition from Cristina's relatives against the match, especially as some hoped she would marry her cousin, Giorgio Trivulzio. But she took no notice of their protests, though she was much distressed on receiving a long and scurrilous poem denouncing Emilio as a dissipated spendthrift and listing his many amours, which is said to have been read to her on her wedding morning, 24 September 1825.

To marry, the Prince had in fact given up his *maîtresse en chef*, the Countess Guiccioli, with whom Lord Byron had once lived. Cristina received a dowry of 400,000 Austrian lire, and the couple spent their honeymoon in Emilio's ancestral home, the Palazzo Belgiojoso in Merate. But it soon proved an unfortunate marriage. From letters written by Cristina to Ernesta Bisi we learn how Emilio neglected her more and more to have a succession of love affairs. They were reconciled from time to time when he needed her help to pay off his mounting debts.

The famous Ball of Romanticism held in Milan on 30 June 1828, saw the Prince and his wife together dressed as courtiers of Francis I of France. They were judged the most striking couple present. Then later in 1828 came a breach that lasted several years, caused by his attempting to bring his new mistress, Signorina Ruga, to live under the same roof with them. Cristina wanted to apply for an annulment of the marriage, but Emilio begged her not to do this, so they separated by mutual consent instead.

Bitterly she wrote to a friend that she 'had seen the world, also more than seen it.' She now found consolation for her husband's neglect in politics. She became a member of the *Giardiniere*, as the women supporters of the *Carbonari* were styled. Bianca Milesi who led them instructed the young Princess, teaching her passwords, secret signs, and the art of disguise. Their policy was to drive the Austrians out of Lombardy and to unite the whole country under a king, ruling democratically. But their organisation was poor, and the peasants saw no point in risking their necks to join a secret society that offered nothing to improve their living conditions.

Cristina was soon taking part in subversive activities. The Marquis de Floranges, in his *Souvenirs*, relates how one evening in an outer suburb of Milan he was almost knocked down by a donkey that had strayed into his path:

'A youth in rags was astride its back. "You idiot!" I cried. "Why don't you look where you are going?" I was so angry that I gave him a blow. He almost fell off the beast, and as he struggled to keep his seat I saw him full face in the light of a street lantern. I stood amazed as I recognised the vagabond to be the Princess Belgiojoso. I thought for a moment that I was having a nightmare.

5

My curiosity soared. I seized the false mendicant and pulled her towards me.

'"Cristina!" I exclaimed. She struggled furiously to free herself from my grasp, and taking out a knife stabbed me first in the shoulder and then in my side. I fell onto my knees and fainted like a ninny. My beautiful assailant then leapt back onto her mount and galloped away.'

Dressed in this fashion, Cristina went round the slums of Milan stirring up the poor against the Austrians and inciting them to prepare for the day when they might stage a mass revolt and eject the foreigners. Her conduct did not escape the notice of Count Hartig, the Governor, and he briefed two master spies to follow her everywhere, and their lengthy reports on her activities were preserved in the secret archives of the Lombard-Venetian Government in Milan.[4]

Shortly before their separation, the Prince had purchased from a Signore Grassi of Milan Lord Byron's carriage, which the poet had sold him before leaving for Greece. As Cristina had paid for this with her own money, she retained and used it for much of her future travelling. A very comfortable vehicle with room for two to sleep inside, and seats at the back for servants, it was still inscribed with the Byron armorial bearings. In this she travelled in December 1828, to stay in Genoa. She felt she had to make a break with her unhappy past. She was well received in the sea port and was soon very much involved in the plots of the *Carbonari*, whose agents disguised as her servants she conveyed about the country in her carriage.[5]

By 1829 the temporarily quiescent revolutionary movements in the peninsula were beginning to ferment again. Lord Malmesbury, in his *Memoirs of an ex-Minister*, wrote that 'conspiracies were universal.' When Cristina arrived in Rome towards the end of April, the Liberals in the Papal States were being encouraged by the belief that the French Government might at last put pressure on the sick and ageing Pope Leo XII to act less repressively towards them.

Through having been at the court in Milan of Eugène Beauharnais, Cristina's mother had remained on excellent terms with the Bonapartes, and had given her a letter of introduction to Queen Hortense, daughter of Josephine Beauharnais and step-daughter of Napoleon, who had married the Emperor's brother, Louis, King of Holland, and who now lived surrounded by the relics of her great past in the Ruspoli Palace.

Cristina was warmly received by the Queen, who was busy plotting to restore Napoleon I's son to the French throne and her eldest son, Prince Napoleon Louis, to his father's kingdom of Holland, whilst his brother, Louis Napoleon, was to lead frag-mented Italy to liberty and unite it under his kingship. This last plan appealed to Cristina. Lord Malmesbury, who was in Rome at the time, wrote in his memoirs that she was 'the leader of the conspirators.' In a letter to Ernesta Bisi she cryptically refers to having been visited by nearly all the 'best artists' in Rome. That city's branch of the *Carbonari* was known as the Artists. Prince Louis Napoleon (the future Napoleon III) had joined them when only fifteen, and had taken their solemn oath pledging himself for life to the cause of Italian unity.

Cristina was at the height of her singular beauty and the Prince fell in love with her.[6] If she had not already had a husband, they might possibly have married, for then his sights were on the throne of a united Italy, and an alliance with a descendant of one of the oldest families in Lombardy would have been immensely popular. It is interesting to speculate what would have happened if his elder brother had not died, thus making him the Bonaparte pretender to the French throne, and if Cristina instead of Eugénie Montijo had become his wife.

After visits to Naples and Leghorn, on behalf of the *Carbonari* where she stirred their supporters with her fire, Cristina went to Florence, which experienced travellers then considered to be the gayest city in the world. Accounts of her social success in Rome had preceded her and she was enthusiastically received. She took part in the productions directed by the famous English actor, Charles Matthews, a protégé of Lady Blessington. In Shakespeare's *Henry IV* she enchanted everybody with her performance as Lady Percy.[7]

The Comte d'Alton-Shée, in his *Mémoires*, wrote that at one of

7

the balls in Florence given by Prince Camillo Borghese (widowed husband of Pauline Bonaparte) he noticed appear 'amidst a gathering of the most elegant and best looking women present a strange beauty: her black and red gown was both simple and bizarre. She had fine black hair, naturally wavy, worn without any ornaments, a broad forehead like that of a young Faust, admirably drawn eyebrows, large widely separated eyes like those of some ancient statue, their mysterious look giving to the upper part of her face an air of ascetic spirituality; whilst the perfection of her nose, the delightful smile and the attractive dimple showed feminine grace in all its charm. Her complexion was pale and matt. She was hardly twenty years old and seemed to have come back to life for the second time. I asked her name: Princess Belgiojoso.'

Cristina had other qualities. She was alert, capable of making quick decisions, and despite her periods of ill health and her slight build, she had almost masculine strength. She was an excellent swordswoman and a crack shot, and rode astride. The shy, introspective girl, firstly through her unhappy home life and then through her disastrous marriage, had learned much about the ways of the world, and chiefly that it paid to create an effect and draw attention to oneself. Superficial observers were thus misled into believing that she was merely a beautiful shallow *poseuse*. This convenient mask enabled her to work in secret for the great cause of her life, that of Italian unity.

Prince Napoleon Louis Bonaparte and his wife suddenly arrived in Florence, having had to leave Rome on account of his being involved in a plot to overthrow the Pope's temporal powers. A few months later Prince Louis Napoleon was also banished from Rome, and all three spent the summer in a villa at Serravezza. It was reported that a large quantity of arms was smuggled ashore near Livorno in 1830 and hidden in the villa, with Cristina directing the operations.[8]

In February she travelled to Lucca to visit in college her half-brother Alberto, and whilst there wrote to the Austrian Minister in Florence, Count Bombelles, for the renewal of her passport, which he granted, allowing her to visit Switzerland and France.[9] By now she was very much involved in the revolutionary move-

8

ment. Under pretence of visiting doctors and obtaining treatment, she went in early April, as an emissary of the conspirators of Florence,[10] to Geneva, which was rapidly becoming a great international centre on account of its geographical position and enlightened government that allowed absolute freedom of political opinion.

Here were gathered many of the exiled supporters of Napoleon, visionaries who hoped to build a new world in the future, sovereigns without thrones, generals without armies, ministers without portfolios, revolutionaries who had fled from their countries to escape the firing squads. Cristina met them all. Here, too, she made the acquaintance of Giuseppe Mazzini, the young Genoese patriot, and listened with sympathy if not agreement to his opinions. He had no use for the *Carbonari* and had started his 'Young Italy' party. It was so named because only people under the age of forty were allowed to join it. Those above that age he believed were too set in their ways to want completely to destroy the royal régime and aristocratic structure of society and replace it with an egalitarian republic as he proposed.

Cristina left Geneva for Lugano on 28 June 1830. Pausing in Berne, she wrote an urgent note to the Austrian Minister, Baron de Binder, requesting him to extend the validity of her passport so that she could pass the winter at Hyères. This request was granted; in fact, the passport was renewed without limit of time or route, so that she could legitimately go abroad or to France as she pleased.[11]

The young Princess next left for Lugano, capital of the Canton of Tessin, hoping to meet her mother there. That town was then the classical rendezvous for exiles and their relatives remaining in Italy. Vittoria Visconti d'Aragona applied for a collective passport for herself, her children and a number of friends, including Ernesta Bisi, so as to visit Cristina.

However, things were not fated to go smoothly. Just at this time there had been an uprising of the Liberals in the Canton. The old government was overthrown, a new democratic constitution brought into existence, to the delight of the people and the political exiles. On learning of this Baron Torresani, the Milan Chief of Police, forbade the granting of a passport to anyone except Cristina's mother. He saw no reason why the others should want to visit Lugano, which he described as of no interest to travellers and a focal point for refugees of all countries and their revolutionary plots. He added that he was not satisfied about the Princess Belgiojoso's own absence abroad, and called it irregular and unauthorised as she had not obtained her passport through his office.[12]

Austrian spies had reported to him that mob rule prevailed in Lugano (which was a travesty of the facts) and that the Princess Belgiojoso was conspicuous by 'her blatant support of these ultra-democratic reformers. She most shamelessly expressed approval of the revolution and indulged in improper attacks in her conversations against the Austrian Government. She did not limit her conduct to voicing her opinions, but also became a close friend of the head of the Liberals, the lawyer Luvini-Perseghini, and there is reason to suspect from her long visits to him that she may be engaged in subversive activities.[13]

Count Hartig, Governor of Lombardy, wrote to Prince Metternich on 22 October 1830: 'The Princess Belgiojoso who has been some time now in Lugano is constantly surrounded by the most important Swiss Liberals and refugees. On the 18th she gave a Ball to celebrate the new Constitution, to which she invited those known for their radical views. On the same day an allegorical ballet was performed in the theatre. The spectators applauded the lawyer Luvini when he stood up in the Princess's box to thank her for her support. I consider that her conduct deserves some form of light censure.'[14]

Metternich agreed. Torresani now sent a special messenger to Cristina to inform her that her stay in Switzerland was illegal and ordering her to return to Milan within a week. She, however, produced the passport issued by the Austrian Minister in Florence and countersigned by his opposite number in Berne. She further discomfited the messenger by disclosing that she was also a Swiss citizen, and produced a certificate to this effect issued by the new government of the Canton of Tessin in accordance with a decree of 1808, when in return for services rendered by her father he and his descendants had been given the right to the protection of the Swiss Republic.

Once this was reported back to Vienna, Metternich tried to intimidate the Swiss with diplomatic threats into expelling the Princess and other plotters, but without success. Cristina herself, however, soon tired of a peaceful uneventful life. Armed with her Swiss passport she crossed Piedmont to Genoa. Austrian spies reported back to Milan what she did there, exaggerating and passing on all gossip, particularly if it were slanderous, for they knew this was expected in the cases of persons in the Austrians' black books.[15]

Piedmont was then being ruled by the reactionary King Charles Felix, who regarded most of the Lombard exiles in Genoa as republicans and undesirable aliens. So when the Austrian Minister at Turin asked for the Princess to be extradited to Milan the King agreed.

Cristina was staying in a house with her friend the arch-conspiratress, Bianca Milesi, when news came that the police were on their way to arrest her. Bianca disguised her as a sailor, and whilst the *sbirri* were hammering on the front door the Princess climbed over the back wall and fled through the narrow streets to the docks and boarded a ship for Leghorn, where she was sheltered by an active member of the revolutionary movement, Baron Poerio, who sent her to see the Neapolitan patriot, La Cecilia, with a note of introduction that read: 'She is one of the most charming and beautiful women in Italy. The Austrian tyrants are pursuing her and she seeks a refuge in revolutionary France. The Committee at Leghorn through her can establish communications with our exiled supporters in France.'

La Cecilia fell immediately under Cristina's spell and was for many years associated with her. He helped to smuggle her aboard a French ship bound for Marseilles. When she reached the port in the spring of 1831, it was full of exiles from all parts of Italy. Being young, beautiful, separated from her husband, very wealthy, and attached to the revolutionary party, she immediately excited interest. Like all women of her social standing, she had been accustomed to travelling with several servants as well as a secretary.

Here in France she engaged in the latter capacity a thirty-three year old refugee lawyer, Pietro Bolognini, who was the leader of the Italian colony in Lyons. A spy, Svegliati, reported all he could glean about Cristina to his superiors in Milan. He alleged that young Bolognini was living in the house she had rented, that she was 'madly in love with him' and wore his miniature suspended from a chain round her neck.

In February came news of the popular uprising in Modena against its petty tyrant, Duke Francis IV, who fled the town. This was followed by insurrection in Bologna, which soon extended in a remarkably peaceable and methodical way throughout Romagna, the Marches and parts of Umbria. An assembly of representatives from the liberated provinces met in Bologna on the 26 February 1831, and declared the Pope's temporal powers to be at an end. They formed a Federation of the United Italian Provinces. Very active in all this were the two young Bonaparte princes.

In a few days it seemed as though the impossible had happened. The tricoloured flag now flew from the upper Tiber to the lower Po. The insurrectionary fever spread to the province of Emilia, and its Duchess, Marie Louise, was soon in flight from Parma. Everywhere new provisional governments were springing up.

These events were received with joy among the exiles in Marseilles. Cristina gave practical help to the revolutionary cause by contributing 35,000 Austrian lire for the arming and provisioning of those desiring to return and fight in Italy. The Austrian spies in their reports, with customary exaggeration, gave the amount as 100,000 lire, alleged all volunteers leaving for Savona wore cockades supplied and made by Cristina, and that she had become 'the very soul' of the anti-Austrian plotters, sitting at the piano like the Goddess of Liberty improvising revolutionary battle songs. They mentioned her generosity to exiles and claimed that when she would give them no more, they attacked her in the cafés and called her 'a Messalina'. The truth was that these men included many ex-jailbirds, embezzlers and swindlers of all kinds, who were inclined to turn viciously on those who began by helping them, then saw through them and stopped doing so.

When visiting the home near Marseilles of a prominent French Calvinist the Princess had first met in Geneva, his guest, Augustin Thierry, a historian, was introduced to her. Though young the latter was losing his sight and was also in danger of becoming paralysed. Throughout her life Cristina always went out of her way to help such people. Soon she was acting as his guide. Born in 1795, he had been the secretary and adopted son of the Comte de Saint-Simon, the founder of French socialism, and edited with him in 1819 the periodical, *L'Organisateur*, in which their views for the reform of society had been propounded. They gained few converts, and Saint-Simon becoming wretchedly poor committed suicide. Since then, however, his followers had grown and were now demanding the communal ownership of goods, the abolition of the rights of property and the enfranchisement of women.

Thierry himself since the death of Saint-Simon had turned his attentions to the study of history. In 1825 his *History of the Conquest of England by the Normans* had been greeted with enthusiasm, and he gained further standing for his *Lettres sur l'histoire de France*. Through her association with him, Cristina was to become increasingly sympathetic towards socialistic ideas.

Her new friendship was interrupted by bad news. Metternich, the Austrian Chancellor, feared that the new Liberal governments south of the Po might lead to rebellion in the northern territories controlled by his country. The deposed rulers' appeals for help provided him with the necessary pretexts for intervention. By the end of February Austrian troops had brought back the Duchess Marie Louise to Parma. In early March they restored Francis IV in Modena. Next they invaded the Romagna, and the provisional Government was forced to withdraw from Bologna to Ancona and soon capitulated, despite the fierce resistance put up by General Zucchi and his army of seven thousand volunteers. The latter eventually sailed from Ancona (the usual exit port for refugees) but were seized by an Austrian squadron and taken to the prisons of Venice, where they then faced death or lifelong imprisonment. Among them was Colonel Vincenzo Bolognini, father of Cristina's new secretary.

On hearing this, Augustin Thierry offered to give her a letter of introduction to influential people in the French Government. In early April she left for Paris with young Bolognini to see if they could not get them to intercede for his father's life.

CHAPTER 2

LAFAYETTE'S LAST LOVE

Paris, after the revolution of 1830, became the Mecca of all Liberals. Here the Princess learned that a decree had been issued in Milan that unless she went back within three months and surrendered her person to the police she would be declared civilly dead and her property confiscated; and in order to try and force her to do this, sources of income under Austrian jurisdiction were blocked to her. But all such threats achieved was to make her an active partisan of Mazzini.

Cristina had scarcely any money with her, for she had given most of it away in Marseilles. Her jewels she had left with Bianca Milesi in Genoa when she had so narrowly escaped arrest. With the enthusiasm of youth, she began to plan an important role for herself. She would devote all her energies to the task of making as many leading Frenchmen as she could supporters of the cause of Italian independence.

On reaching Paris in April 1831, the young Princess stayed first in the Hotel de Bath, then, owing to the need for eking out her slender resources, she moved to a top floor garret in the outlying suburb of Clichy. She presented Thierry's letter of introduction to François Mignet, who was in charge of the Foreign Ministry's archives and who had gained success as editor of the Radical paper, *Le National*. Later he was to win lasting fame for his *Histoire de Marie Stuart*. Extremely intelligent, he knew everybody who mattered, not only in the world of politics but also in that of the salon, where his distinguished appearance, perfect manners and personal charm made him a favourite guest. His impressive brow, carefully arranged fair hair, and hands like those of a bishop appealed to society women. Cristina and he were immediately

15

attracted to each other. A bachelor still at thirty-four he had lived since they were students together with the lawyer politician, Adolphe Thiers, author of the widely-acclaimed *Histoire de la Révolution Française* and founder of *Le National*. This hook-nosed little man with the piping voice was destined to become the first President of the French Republic in 1871 and was as assertive as Mignet was gentle.

For a woman like Cristina, who enjoyed playing at the game of love but who was sexually frigid, François was the ideal friend, and this became one of the closest friendships of her life. The elegant historian introduced her to Thiers and to the great Lafayette who had gained a political triumph in his seventy-fifth year thanks to the revolution of 1830.

As a result of his part in setting the Citizen King, Louis-Philippe, on the throne, Lafayette, the hero of two revolutions, now wielded immense political power. It was he who invented the tricolour cockade by adding white to Paris's colours of red and blue, and who offered it to Louis XVI, saying prophetically: 'Take this. Here is a cockade which will go round the world.' The tricolour had now become the emblem of the Italian Nationalists.

Austrian spies continued to watch Cristina and to send back highly coloured reports to Milan such as: 'The Princess leads a strange life, modestly living in one of the unfrequented suburbs of Paris. She goes regularly to meetings of the Chamber of Deputies and to listen to the lectures of the Saint-Simonians. Usually one sees her only with young Bolognini. She also visits old Lafayette, who has done the utmost to ruin her with her husband.'[1]

Apart from their avant-garde ideas, the Saint-Simonians were weirdly clothed. The men, long-haired and bearded, wound knee-long black scarves round their necks. Over skin-tight vermillion trunks and vests, they wore loose white mini-tunics reaching half-way down their thighs. Knee-high black boots, gauntlets and hats, all made out of black leather, completed their costume. The women's uniform consisted of short skirts over trousers. The fact that Cristina associated with such people as well as Lafayette, whom French royalists ranked as little better than Robespierre and Marat, made many of them regard her with suspicion. They nicknamed her *Citoyenne Couperet*, linking her with the knife of the guillotine.

The knowledge that Pietro Bolognini accompanied her everywhere gave rise to rumours that she was his mistress, rumours which even reached her lawyer friend Luvini in the Tessin, who wrote to her on the 4 May 1831: 'I hope that despite the distractions of Paris you remain my true friend.' If she came back to Lugano he would receive her 'with transports of joy.' He had been led to understand that what had kept her in Paris was an affair of the heart. 'Is this true? I cannot believe this, remembering what you once said to me.' He signed the letter – 'one who loves you.'

Describing her first few weeks in Paris, Cristina wrote later in her *Souvenirs dans l'exil:* 'For the first time in my life I prepared my modest meals with my own hands. One morning when I was thus engaged, M. de Lafayette returning from the Chamber of Deputies came up my rickety stairs. Recognising the sound of his stick, I ran to open the door and I led him into my kitchen. There, equally inexperienced in the culinary art, we helped each other to cook the meal. This led to much laughter but not much to eat. The exquisite manners of the Marquis forbade him to allow me to work in his presence. A duel in politeness resulted, during which we heatedly disputed who should use the grill and who should use the oven. Protesting against his insubordination, I complained about the inconvenience of having for my scullion the hero of two worlds!'

In April 1831, at her request Lafayette put all his energies into persuading the French Government to intercede with Austria to show clemency to the prisoners of Ancona. He even arranged for the Princess to address the French Chamber of Deputies on the subject.

Soon another important political personality was visiting her: this was hot-headed Adolphe Thiers, who excelled at omelettes and washing-up, whilst Cristina was best at making ragouts. She even became friendly with Thiers' rival, the austere Conservative François Guizot, who was yet another historian.

In this way Cristina persuaded many of the most important men in French political life to support the cause of Italian liberation.

When she found that Louis-Philippe was beginning to take matters of foreign policy under his personal direction, she tried to be presented to him. Through her friendship with the Austrian Ambassador's wife, she eventually received an invitation to the Tuileries. This read:

> The Queen has done me the honour of telling me last night, my dear Princess, that she will be charmed to receive you on Sunday evening. Would you therefore be good enough to call on me before 8.30 p.m. Will you then accompany me in my carriage; yours can follow if you wish.
>
> I am delighted to have this opportunity of paying you again my respects,
>
> Thérèse Apponyi née Nogarola.

Following the visit, Cristina became friendly with Queen Amélie and met the King, but failed to win his co-operation as he wished to remain friendly with Austria. As a result she became his enemy and also that of the House of Orléans.

She had arrived in Paris with only four thousand lire. As this sum diminished, Lafayette became extremely concerned about her future. He knew she was too proud to accept a loan, so he tactfully suggested instead that she should come and stay with him and his wife at their country place, La Grange, which she did. Unfortunately, after only one week she was thrown from her horse when riding in the forest and was obliged to return to Paris to have treatment for an injured knee. She had only six hundred lire left, and to conserve her resources, ate very frugally. Bolognini used to bring her game, pretending that friends had made him a present of it.

A journalist friend, Alexandre Buchon, editor of *Le Constitutionel* suggested that the Princess might contribute articles on Italian politics, and also translate some from English newspapers into French. In this way she began her career as a journalist. The articles, written anonymously with such vigour that readers thought them by a man, were brilliantly successful and gave the *Constitutionel* the reputation of being the best informed paper in France on Italian matters.

PRINCE EMILIO
DI BELGIOJOSO
by Francesco Hayez

CRISTINA
TRIVULZIO
IN 1824

LAFAYETTE IN HIS LAST YEARS

Meanwhile Lafayette had been busy campaigning in the General Election which returned a right-wing majority, strengthening the King's position and weakening that of Lafayette and his party. Impressed with Cristina's talent as an artist, Buchon suggested that she should draw from life the portraits of the new Deputies which he would then publish for sale in album form. The idea appealed to her, because she thought that through personal contact in this way she might be able to persuade them to support the cause of Italian unity. So Buchon announced the project in his columns, stressing the fact that every portrait would be by '*Une Princesse Ruinée*', as he believed such snob appeal would prove irresistible bait for both the Deputies and the public.

Whenever Lafayette was away from Paris he would correspond almost daily with Cristina. His letters show that the man who in 1789 had resisted the charms of Marie Antoinette had been captivated by the young Italian.

In a letter from La Grange, dated 10 July 1831, he wrote: 'If one's feelings could be valued, my dear Cristina, I do not think you are getting a bargain out of our affection for each other. The difference in our ages is such that by attaching yourself to me you are preparing yourself for a great misfortune – I am sure to die long before you . . . I feel the need to be first in your affection. That is allowable, I hope, for you are a woman who does not love her husband, is separated from him, and has no children or a living father. In such a situation a foster father stands a good chance of gaining the first place in your heart, and it is as a foster father that I regard myself. My love for you will have so much influence on the rest of my life . . .' He goes on to say that he does not like the idea of her going out at six o'clock in the morning to draw the Deputies' portraits, especially in view of the trouble she was having with her knee. He begged her to see a doctor he had recommended. 'What concerns me, dear friend, more than anything else is your health. I send you from the bottom of my heart a thousand tokens of affection.'

Next day he was writing to her again: 'I wish you would see M. Jules Croquet, one of the most highly regarded surgeons in

Paris. I am enclosing a note I have written for you to show him.'
What he thought would do her good would be for her to come
back again for a few days to La Grange. If her project to draw all
the members of the Chamber of Deputies were an obstacle, then
she should abandon it. He called it a speculative undertaking
which might land her in difficulties.

Next day he added a stronger warning. Without wishing to
speak ill of her associates, there was 'a very fine fellow, no doubt,
whom I have seen throw himself into many enterprises; once he
exploited connections with some Greek Prince with a view to
marrying his sister . . . and about you he is saying that the million
francs you came to Paris with were down to six hundred till he
persuaded you to write articles for the *Constitutionel*. He is also
spreading other tittle-tattle harmful to your reputation . . . Don't
let your kind heart get you too much involved in other people's
affairs. And apart from this you are in the middle of a whirlpool
of your compatriots and others whom I esteem, but who take up
too much of your time and have no regard for your need to rest.
All these thoughts upset me. You are so necessary to me that I in
my turn believe myself necessary to you, my very dear
daughter . . .'

Lafayette's references to her being constantly approached by
Italian exiles was well founded. Once they learned of her friendship with him and other influential personalities, they gave her no
peace. One required special treatment for a leg injured by torture
in Spielberg. Cristina, through Lafayette, had him sent to one of
the best surgeons in Paris. Another wanted his son to be educated
for nothing. Lafayette arranged this, too. A refugee tailor begged
for work – Lafayette assured Cristina that he would see to it.
Only the poor troubled to thank her. Literary and political exiles
took what she did for them for granted. Some were to say that
she kept a mass of exiles round her only to satisfy her craving for
popularity.

A few days later, not having received an answer to his last two
letters, Lafayette feared that he had offended her and wrote again,
expressing his admiration for 'your noble character, your con-
tempt for wealth, your devotion to liberty, your fatherland and

your friends. I more than anyone else have applauded your determination to owe everything to your own exertions. I have shared your ideas, your plans. I have tried to co-operate with you.' He hopes that what he has written has not vexed her – or wounded her even, thus doing himself irreparable harm. '. . . I was intending to give you some interesting news about my family, but I am too upset today – and I will limit myself to assuring you once more of my fond though blundering friendship.'

Next day he heard from her. We learn from his reply to this that she had reproached him for pointing out the hardships of poverty instead of encouraging her to endure it, but in a further letter received on the 17th she completely forgave him, and told him that her knee was better. In answer he wrote: 'The moment is approaching when I shall once more be near you – I shall be in Paris between three and four in the afternoon. When can we meet?' He ends by expressing his delight at her having signed her letter: 'Your loving daughter.'

On 22 July he wrote again that although he disliked writing letters, corresponding with her was a joy at all times. Regarding the project upon which she was engaged, he was glad to hear the members of the Chamber of Deputies were now visiting her to sit for their portraits, so she would not have to tire herself with travelling. But wasn't it too large an undertaking to draw the faces of five hundred Deputies? Why not limit her work to forty of the most prominent? There were pictures in existence, too, of many of them. Could she not copy these?

But this would not have suited her plans. She wanted to meet all the Deputies she could, so as to try and win through friendship their sympathy for the Italian patriots. To this end she deliberately set about making her attic studio intriguingly colourful and bizarrely romantic.

The Marquis de Floranges describes in his *Souvenirs*[2] a visit he paid there:

'Having directed myself by asking passers-by and fruit and flower street-sellers, of which there were a number in this quarter installed under huge umbrellas, I arrived before a tall house and ventured into the malodorous retreat of the concierge whom I could hear from afar grumbling, coughing and spitting. 'Is it here, my good man, where the Princess di Belgiojoso resides?' I enquired.

'"Princess?" he replied, blowing his nose. "Princess, well, you can call her that, if you like. Anyhow, she lives on the top floor, poor lady. And you'd be doing a good deed in going to look after her, for I don't think she's likely to live long. It wrings my heart to see a young person like her so thin and wan. She can hardly have a drop of blood in her, if you ask me."

'I was out of breath when I reached the fifth floor. I saw facing me a narrow door to which was fixed a card bearing no name but only the words: "*La Princesse Malheureuse.*" Below this held by a nail hung a letter addressed to myself. I opened the envelope and read: "I have gone to try and sell some fans I have been painting. The bread of an exile is hard to earn. Enter without fear into my abode. There are neither bolts nor chains on the doors of those banished from their native land, for they have nothing worth stealing."

'I raised the latch. I went into this strange woman's lair. My uneasiness grew. It seemed as though I had wandered onto the stage of a theatre and was taking part against my own wishes in some melodrama. I half expected to see a proscenium arch instead of a fourth wall and the public beyond it. The perfume of Cristina which I well recognised pervaded this false garret. I say "false" because all looked as if it had been deliberately arranged for effect. It was "misery" such as would appeal to some lyrical poet. A small painting on an easel portrayed the oval and aristocratic face of the Princess. But it made her seem paler and thinner than when I last saw her.

'Further away a gaping skull reposed on an open book, which on approaching I noticed was printed in Hebrew – yes, Hebrew! Further away still was a guitar with broken strings, tubes of paint and a palette. A sharp-bladed stiletto lay in a prominent position on a table, and scattered around were sheets of paper covered with Cristina's handwriting and full of erasures. Not content with conspiracy, with being beautiful, with being able to play the guitar, defend herself with a dagger, paint fans, and let all

Paris know that Austria was persecuting her, she was also reading Hebrew and writing a book – and what a book! There were piles and piles of paper, I assure you there were.'

In common with other writers of reminiscences, the Marquis de Floranges in his old age undoubtedly let his imagination run away with him and one must regard the correctness of this description with reservations, for it was not until at least eight years later, following the death of her mother, that Cristina embarked on the writing of her four volume essay on Catholic Dogma.

Like the friendly concierge, Lafayette went on worrying about her health and also about her finances. He wrote to her to say that the most sensible thing for her to do, whilst waiting for the day when she could use her frozen assets in Lombardy, would be to borrow two or three thousand francs – 'which would be easy to negotiate as the loan would be well covered.' This would solve her temporary financial difficulties. So that the trouble of raising such a loan would not interfere with her work, would she allow him to arrange it all? But this proved unnecessary as her jewels which she had left with a friend in Genoa were brought to her. The spies reported that she received 150,000 francs from their sale. This was a great exaggeration. In reality she received a fifth of this sum, but it enabled her to move from her garret in October 1831, to a modest apartment on the fourth floor of 7 Rue Neuve de la Ferme des Mathurins, which was much more central, being near the Madeleine.

All this while Cristina was concerned about the fate of Bolognini's father and the other Italian prisoners of war held by the Austrians in Venice, and to please her Lafayette was doing what he could to prod Louis-Philippe to make representations to Austria for them to be released and sent into exile in France. On 25 July he wrote to her: 'I have just come from the Royal concert ... The King promised to take prompt action to see that they were sent from Venice to Marseilles.' Shortly afterwards he was able to give her the good news that the prisoners had actually been released, and that the French Government would give them asylum.

When the expiration of the three months' period laid down in the edict threatening confiscation of Cristina's possessions drew near, Lafayette asked the French Foreign Minister, Count Sebastiani, for his good offices on her behalf. The Count had met and had been charmed by her. He decided the best approach would be to make use of her genuine ill health as an excuse for not returning to Milan. On 3 May he wrote to Prince Metternich in Vienna:[3]

'Will you allow me to ask for your indulgence in favour of a lady in whom I am extremely interested and to whom I am much attached? Princess Cristina de Belgiojoso is one of six persons who, following an order signed in Milan by Baron Torresani, have been summoned back to Italy within three months, failing which they have been threatened with the confiscation of their property. Your personal moderation gives me reason to hope that you will be willing to exempt from this severe measure a young woman whose state of health makes it necessary for her to live away from Italy for some years. I dare therefore to hope that you will permit her to live in France without being exposed to the loss of her fortune through the confiscation of her possessions.

'I attach much importance to the granting of this request. In allowing it you would be doing me a personal favour. I am always so eager to be agreeable to your Highness that I hope in return you will not refuse one of the things I desire the most.'

Writing on 17 May to Count Anton Apponyi, Austrian Ambassador in Paris, from 1828 to 1852, Metternich mentioned that he had received this letter from Sebastiani, and that at the same time the French Ambassador in Vienna had received a despatch from the French Foreign Minister instructing him to make similar pleas in person on behalf of Prince Belgiojoso and several other male Milanese who had been ordered home by Torresani. 'The laws, *Monsieur l'Ambassadeur*, are executed in our country without consideration of the rank of the individual concerned, and complete equality before the law forms part of the foundations of our government. The law requires that the Emperor's subjects obtain passports before they proceed abroad; if they do not return when recalled they are given a time limit, after the expiration of which failure to comply leads to their being classed and treated as émigrés.'

Madame de Belgiojoso, Metternich claimed, came under this category. When she had gone to Genoa, the Imperial Government had withdrawn her passport. But determined to enter France, she had eluded the vigilance of the authorities. Concern over the well-being of this young lady had made her own family desire her repatriation. Ignoring all their appeals, she had remained in Paris. The dispatch continued:

'Each day she continues to do so, she further jeopardises her reputation and her fortune. It is for persons interested in her fate to urge her to return home. I have replied along these lines to Count Sebastiani in the enclosed letter.

'The other persons this Minister has pleaded for through the French Ambassador are young men who have allowed themselves to be misled and corrupted by Italian exiles and refugees, and who will end by completely ruining themselves.With the exception of Prince Belgiojoso, whose fortune is not very considerable, they belong to some of the richest landed families in Italy . . . It is for those who are interested in the welfare of these young people to make them realise that they are doing themselves real harm which they will later regret . . . His Imperial Majesty cannot be expected to exempt individuals who have no plausible reasons for not complying with regulations which everybody else has to observe.

'Will you please convey these views to Count Sebastiani, and tell him from me that, as often as he finds himself in the position to require my personal intervention with the purpose of giving good advice to French refugees and exiles here in Vienna, I shall be pleased to do so in exchange for his giving similar advice to the Italians in Paris.'

Metternich attached to his despatch a confidential report on Cristina's mode of life, received from Torresani in Milan and based on information obtained from the spies who had been watching her. One passage reads: 'The Emperor has ordered the Governors of Lombardy and Venice to recall all Italian subjects abroad without permission. Far from exempting Madame de

Belgiojoso from this general order, all the circumstances in her case make it particularly applicable. The opinions which she flaunts, her inexcusable conduct, the kind of people with whom she associates in Paris, as well as the need to preserve an illustrious family from the shame of criminal proceedings, have made it the duty of the Government of Lombardy to order her return. M. the Prince Emilio di Belgiojoso has also left the country and is living in the Canton of Tessin, where he is taking part in treasonable plotting. He, too, has been recalled.'

When Count Apponyi handed Metternich's reply to the French Foreign Minister he was surprised by the latter's complete volte-face. After reading the note he said: 'Cristina Belgiojoso? What do I care about her? I could say I don't even know her.' This, Apponyi thought, was rather a remarkable statement, coming from someone who had written that she was a person to whom he felt much attached. Sebastiani went on to tell Apponyi that the pressure in favour of the Princess had come from Rome. This was an obvious lie, made because he did not want to reveal to Metternich that the request had originally come from Lafayette, and that the Government was still under the influence of a revolutionary whom Metternich hated. Later Apponyi learned from Sebastiani that on hearing of the Austrian Chancellor's reply Cristina had said she was willing to go back to Lombardy, but that her ill health still made her unable to undertake so long a journey – and that she also feared if she complied she would be shut up in a convent. 'If this were to happen, she said she would die,' Sebastiani told Apponyi.

Cristina was to take the same line for another nine years, always declaring her intention of returning to Milan but at the same time offering good reasons for postponing the journey. Evidently she had been advised by a shrewd lawyer to adopt such tactics, and thanks to this method she played a successful game of evading the issue.

On 15 June in the following year, 1832, the Austrian authorities in Milan issued an edict offering free pardon to all Italian subjects illegally abroad, on condition they immediately came home. In a despatch dated the 31 July Count Apponyi informed Metternich that Cristina had called on him to say she was willing to comply as soon as her health permitted. She had handed him a petition addressed to Prince Metternich, which he was enclosing together with medical certificates from several doctors, confirming that she was unfit to undertake any long journeys. Whilst wishing to avail herself of the offer made in the edict, she also asked permission to delay her return until she recovered. He had no doubt about the serious state of her health – and that she needed to remain in a more temperate climate than that of Lombardy. It is interesting to note that some years later when Cristina was spending the winter in her home at Locate, she wrote to Alfred de Musset suggesting that he should join her as the climate in her part of Lombardy was better than that of Paris!

Apponyi described the Princess's conduct up till then as being that of a foolish young woman led astray by bad companions, who, taking advantage of her inexperience, had tried to involve her and her fortune in their revolutionary plots.

'I reproached her for having lowered herself in this way. She replied that she had only been trying to amuse herself. It was also natural for anyone to prefer to live in Paris instead of Milan.

'The straitened circumstances in which the Princess at present finds herself, oblige her to live on the top floor in a poor district, and on account of her ill health to go everywhere in a fiacre. She will, I am sure, agree to all the conditions laid down, before she can once more enjoy her fortune. She told me that so long as she received her whole annual income, she would be willing for the time being to forego having control of her capital.'

In August 1832, against the advice of her doctors, Cristina travelled to Geneva to meet her mother and her three half-sisters. Lafayette wrote her daily letters whilst she was away, saying how much he missed her and enjoining her to take care of her health. 'I realise that through the joy of seeing again your mother, you have not had time to discuss with them your financial problems. It would be extremely unwise if you were not to ask her to help you. Everybody has admired how you have put up with poverty without complaining, but now that you have the chance of arranging something, you must take it.'

Not only Lafayette but also the Austrian spies were very interested in what she did in Geneva. One report to Torresani alleges that she had rented a villa in the town's outskirts and that she was 'living with a young Frenchman who is her present favourite lover.' Her maid, Maria Longoni, was dismissed by her and returned home to Milan where she said that she had left because the Princess, being half-consumptive, was extremely bad-tempered and spent most of the day in bed.

At the end of August she travelled back to Paris. Her mother had agreed to make her an allowance. It was thought possible to obtain Vienna's authorisation of this. Thanks to Count Apponyi's co-operation it was arranged, and finally in April 1833, fifty thousand lire were paid to Cristina through the Austrian Embassy in Paris, after she had renewed before the Ambassador her promise to return to Milan as soon as her health permitted.

Cristina now gave up her fourth floor apartment and rented a far finer one in the house of the Duc de Plaisance, 1, Place de la Madeleine. This consisted of a hall, a dining-room with the walls painted to resemble green marble, a drawing-room with two windows and mirror-panelled doors, and walls papered in red, a bedroom with white satin walls, and a bathroom.

Lafayette was delighted at the move, and he was particularly pleased to receive a letter from the Marchesa d'Aragona, in which she said she had heard a great deal about him from her daughter – and would he, in her own absence, take her place in looking after the girl.

Augustin Thierry, with whom Cristina had regularly corresponded, wrote that he hoped her improved circumstances would be the end of her unhappiness. 'To see you happy might, I feel, restore my failing sight. You are really wonderful, a true friend, and I can never be grateful enough for what you have done for me.'

Whilst Cristina was in Switzerland, some of the Italian patriots freed from their Venetian prison were allowed to leave Toulon and come to Paris, having obtained permits to do so, thanks to Lafayette's efforts. None had any money and all needed to earn their living. Cristina was tireless in her endeavours to help them to do this, and in the case of Professor Orioli of Bologna she arranged for him to give a series of lectures in her home for which he received payment. She saw to it that they were all well attended. These highly successful lectures were the beginning of Cristina's famous Paris salon.

CHAPTER 3

THE WORLD OF THE SALON

The most famous salon in Paris at that time was that of Madame Récamier, then in her old age. It was not long before Cristina was honoured with an invitation to call. She has left her impressions of the old lady and Chateaubriand. The drawing-room at *L'Abbaye-aux-Bois* was always dimly lit and the thick curtains drawn to keep out the noises of Paris. 'The twelve chairs and six *bergères* which furnished the salon were reflected in a polished parquet floor without rugs or a carpet. Madame Récamier lived in this sanctuary, seated in a large *bergère* beside her fireplace. In the semi-obscurity she looked like a white cloud, from which came neither thunder nor lightning but only a sweet voice.'

Cristina was among the few much envied people who were invited to M. de Chateaubriand's readings of his famous work, *Mémoires d'Outre-tombe*. But she declined the invitation. Later, in her *Souvenirs* she explained why.

'I was never any good at feeding vain people with compliments. They are always fishing for praise, and if you politely comply with a small compliment they immediately protest their unworthiness to receive it, in the hope that that will encourage you to pay them even greater compliments.

'Now M. de Chateaubriand expected us to go on complimenting him despite his protests. I took him at his word and never again paid him a compliment, and that made me rather unpopular with him. There was another way in which I disappointed the great man. Not once did I ever express a desire to be present when he read aloud from his *Mémoires d'Outre-tombe*.

'One day when we were alone together, Mme. Récamier in her charming way adroitly steered the conversation onto the subject of reading aloud. She had heard that I myself was fond of entertaining my friends in this manner. I realised that in her tactful way she was throwing me a life-line, so that I might pull myself out of the cultureless swamp into which she believed I was fast sinking. She was opening a door so that I might escape from my dungeon and bask in the sunshine of M. de Chateaubriand's brilliance. But I saw only danger ahead and the prospect of having to listen to reading after reading and being obliged to add my quota of compliments. So I hurriedly stammered that to tell the truth reading aloud bored me.

'I can still hear Mme. Récamier's stifled sigh and see the look of pain on her face which seemed to say: "I have done all I can, but there is no way in which I can bring home to that woman what she is missing. I give it up".'

Cristina also wrote:

'Madame Récamier did not usually admit guests to her salon before four o'clock in the afternoon. As for reasons of health I spent every summer in the country outside Paris, my visits to the capital were governed by the railway timetable.

'As a result I could not call on Madame Récamier between four and five, which was her receiving hour. So, kindly as she always was, she made an exception in my favour and admitted me into her sanctum during the hour reserved exclusively for M. de Chateaubriand. I made many people envious when I disclosed that I was admitted to the Abbey between three and four.

'Many a time have I been asked in tones betraying an ill-disguised curiosity how that mysterious hour was spent. I would pretend not to hear the question, for I did not mind appearing to have been let into a great secret not to be revealed to ordinary mortals. Who knows what wild flights of fancy the uninitiated indulged in as a result? If I insist on remaining silent, perhaps in a few years' time I shall read that Madame Récamier and M. de Chateaubriand conspired for one hour a day during fifteen years in favour of the elder branch of the Bourbons, or that it was Madame Récamier who wrote Chateaubriand's books and that she spent the sacred hour telling him all what he was supposed to have written during the previous twenty-four hours. I want to

tear aside the veil, and rout the romancers. What then did Madame
Récamier and Monsieur de Chateaubriand do between three and
four o'clock? They drank tea!

'What surprised me about this was not that two friends should
every day for fifteen years drink a cup of tea by the fireside, for I
feel capable of behaving in the same way, but that after a fortnight
this tea drinking should not have become a habit. I should do it
automatically, barely aware of what I was doing. But these two
illustrious friends were different. To see them, one would think
that they were drinking tea together for the first time in their lives
and that they needed to take mutual pains to be in complete
harmony during this important ritual of tea drinking.

'"Would you like some tea, Monsieur de Chateaubriand?"

'Every day for all those years he answered: "Yes, but serve
yourself first, Madame."

'"Shall I add a little milk?"

'"A few drops only."

'"May I offer you a second cup?"

'"I cannot allow you to take the trouble."

'And so on for half an hour.

'Seated by a pedestal table, I observed and sadly admired. I even
envied that happy disposition which belongs almost exclusively to
the French, and which belonged much more to the French of the
eighteenth century than today, never to deviate from the con-
ventions and rules of etiquette prescribed by society. Thanks to
this care, the most insignificant acts, the most trivial and common
things acquire and retain through the repeated ritual a certain charm
which lends them an appearance of freshness.

'I, on the contrary, and those who resemble me take everything
with both hands; we turn it this way and that, over and over
again; we sometimes break things as children break their toys to
see what they contain. We analyse every feeling; we fear exaggeration and affection; and for all that, does not reality often remain
hidden from us? Why tear away the finery and the flowers with
which one would adorn it? . . .

'Place me for one hour every day for a month before a tea table
in company of whoever you wish. The first day I shall behave and

speak like Madame Récamier; the second day I shall offer tea to my companion with a gesture and without saying a word. At the end of the week we shall take our cups without a glance at each other; and at the end of the month, unless one of us is afflicted with a violent passion for the Chinese beverage, we might well through other distractions forget to meet.'

In her fine new apartment in the Place de la Madeleine, Cristina herself held her own salon. At first it was the assembling point of all Italians of note in Paris. At the end of July 1833, Vincenzo Bellini arrived in the capital, where he was to owe much of his success to the patronage of the Princess, whose mother had taken him up to please her own lover, the Duke of Cannizzaro. She wrote to Cristina: 'I highly recommend Bellini to you and shall be grateful for all the assistance you can give him. Possibly he will stay some time in Paris. Do what you can to make the critics favourably disposed towards him.'

Over a year later, on 2 October 1834, the Marchesa informed her daughter: 'Bellini is enchanted with you. He writes that you are the only person in whom he can confide.'

The sensitive, idealistic Bellini had become closely attached to Cristina, confiding his innermost thoughts to her. She wrote in her *Souvenirs dans l'exil*: '"It needs a great deal of courage," he would say, "to attempt something new. There are people who enjoy breaking in a horse, sailing on a ship making its maiden voyage, wearing new boots. As for me, I detest equally doing all those things, and even more the role of the seducer. I want everyone to get at least half-way to gaining their heart's desire." I can still hear his youthful voice as he spoke. I can still see his fair, curly hair, his pink and white colouring, his gentle and gracious manner, his elegant appearance. His whole personality was in harmony with his tender and dreamy music. What a pity he died young.'

Although Cristina had parted from Emilio, she never ceased to love him. When they had separated he had presented her with a list of his debts, which she very generously had paid. But he kept her dowry, and during her poverty in Paris never sent her the interest on it which was legally due to her.

At the family conference in Geneva the Marchesa had attempted to reconcile the couple, and Cristina as a result allotted him an apartment of five rooms near her own at 1 Place de la Madeleine. In a letter dated 3 July 1833, to Ernesta Bisi she wrote that she did not regret having agreed to an apparent reconciliation, that he was grateful to her for having given him an apartment for which she paid the rent and that he was behaving extremely pleasantly towards her.

Emilio now led a very gay life, keeping fit by frequent visits to the *Ecole de Natation* at Pont Royal, after which he would dine with his fellow lions Lord Henry Seymour and Major Fraser at the Café de Paris. He was so fond of swimming in the Seine that he never went near it without taking a bathing costume with him.

He failed, however, to exercise more discretion in his extra-marital activities. Cristina's absence in the country led to his using the apartment in her house for a particularly wild party. In a letter to a friend he wrote:

'This morning I had a disagreeable visit from Mme. S. to warn me that on her lawyer's advice she intends to bring an action against me for the alleged rape of her daughter, Clarisse, on the grounds that I lent my house and assistance for the purpose. *Bellissimo!* I was in my bath and she was like a fury. I wanted to turn her out, and she kept asking to see my wife. In the end I told her I had to go hunting and to call again on Friday. She gave me her address, Faubourg Montmartre 33.

'My dear friend, please discuss the matter with Belmont and advise me what to do. If I'm not wrong, one of our friends raped the girl first in his place before Ricardo did so here. If we can prove that, it ought to stop the old tigress from attacking me. I shall be back on Friday. Emilio.'

It seems that Clarisse's mother was persuaded with money to drop the matter, but this did not make the Prince change his way of life. Shortly afterwards, in early August, a similar scandal caused him to leave for Switzerland. On 11 September he wrote to d'Alton-Shée from Bellinzona that although only absent from Paris a month, he had been so busy that he was astonished at himself and wondered if he really were the same Emilio of forty days previously. He had seen the fête at Vevey, had walked through the Oberland, had admired the waterfalls and the Alps until he had had enough of them. He had spent a fortnight with his parents. 'I have plotted like a madman, and at the present time it is the only occupation remaining to me as it rains all day in this beautiful town of Bellinzona, as my family is near, and as I have for all resources only the wife of a cobbler whom I share with my manservant. O *tempora!*'

But soon after this he received the welcome news from Paris that the Danish diplomat he had wronged had secured a transfer to London and had left with his tearful wife. So back the Prince sped to the French capital. Despite this behaviour Cristina, who never ceased to be fond of her wayward husband, allowed him to continue living in the apartment she had allotted him and also to attend her receptions, where his devil-may-care charm and his singing thawed the disapproval of those who criticised her for being too forgiving.

Liszt once wrote to Cristina that the Prince had the finest and most agreeable baritone he knew, and that he wished Emilio would get so much into debt that he would have to embark on a professional career in order to earn his living.

In November 1835, yet another amorous entanglement made him leave again for Switerland. This time he went to stay with the Bonapartes at Arenenberg on Lake Constance, from where on 5 December he wrote to d'Alton-Shée: 'Here one eats and drinks well and often. One laughs a great deal and hunts occasionally, and there are deer, hares, and above all rabbits without end. I shall remain here for twenty more days. Paris beckons and it should be safe for me to return by then. I am leading the life of a monk, and frankly it does not suit me. Just think, my dear friend, how lecherous I shall be when next we meet. Major Fraser is always the same – except that he has changed a dozen times the shape of his moustache.'

It is not surprising in view of this that Cristina should seek solace in the company of other men, principally Lafayette and François Mignet, who attended all her parties and rented a house for her in the country when she found the summer heat too trying.

In the preceding year, 1834, Lafayette's health had begun to fail. All through his final illness Cristina stayed at La Grange in the room which had been allotted to her so as to nurse the old man and keep him company. J. Cloquet, in his *Souvenirs sur la vie privée du général Lafayette* wrote: 'A lady as noted for her beauty as she was distinguished by her charm, wit and kind heart, the Princess Cristina de Belgiojoso (née Trivulzio) looked after Lafayette with the greatest devotion. He had so to speak adopted her as one of his children. . . . I often found this excellent woman at his bedside; her knowledge, as sound as it was varied, and her attractive voice charmed him and made him forget for a while his sufferings. Lafayette often spoke to me about this lady's rare merit, her noble character and her generosity in helping her unfortunate compatriots.'

Camillo Ugoni wrote to young Bolognini: 'Kinder than ever, that Princess like a real angel closed the eyes of our patriarch of the patriots. One can say that goodness is the beauty of the plain, and makes the beautiful even more beautiful. The latter was true of the Princess as she nursed him during his last illness.'

After Lafayette's death on 20 May 1834, Cristina fell into a state of deep depression, and she began to take an increasing interest in religion. She learned Hebrew, folio-sized Bibles were to be found in all her rooms, while strewn about were sheets of paper bearing her handwriting and all to do with theology. It was not until some nine years later that the purpose of all this was revealed.

Cristina had an implacable enemy in Torresani, the Chief of Police in Milan, and it annoyed him that she had been allowed on the grounds of ill health not only to remain in France, but to receive money as well. He kept urging Vienna to put a time limit on her stay. Fortunately for Cristina Count Apponyi was favourably disposed towards her, and he forwarded her periodical applications for clemency to Prince Metternich with approving comments. She was certainly in bad health at this time, aggravated by sorrow at Lafayette's passing. To show willing, however, she applied to Apponyi on 19 June for a passport, stating that she was intending to set out shortly for Milan but that on the way she would pause for a while to take the waters of Bourbon, which her doctors had prescribed and which she hoped would give her the strength to complete the journey.

But she added: 'If, despite my sincere efforts. I do find it impossible to continue on my way, I hope that I will receive some credit for my willingness, and that with your accustomed kindness you will report sympathetically on my case.' On 6 September she wrote direct to Prince Metternich to say she had to abandon her journey and return to Paris. She enclosed more medical certificates.

Some two weeks earlier, on 21 August, Count Hartig, Governor of Lombardy, had written to Count Apponyi stating that the previous month the latter had transmitted a new petition from the Princess di Belgiojoso, asking permission for 50,000 Austrian lire to be sent her from Milan so that she could extend her stay in France until her health permitted her to return home. He had submitted the matter to the government over which he presided, and they had unanimously rejected her request. Would the Ambassador convey this to the Princess, informing her that she was free to appeal to the Chancellery in Vienna.

This Cristina did, but December came and no decision reached Apponyi. So on the 10th of that month she wrote to him asking if he would apply for an urgent ruling, mentioning that owing to lack of funds she was in an embarrassing financial position.

The Ambassador wrote to Metternich on 17 December, forwarding her letter. The Chancellor replied on 17 January 1835, that since 20 September the Emperor had been considering the matter and had just decided to order the unfreezing of all the Princess's assets, and had also authorised the Government in Milan to send a passport, prolonging her stay abroad for a year in any foreign country that the state of her health should render it necessary for her to reside in. 'In this way everything that was illegal regarding Madame de Belgiojoso's absence from her native land has been pardoned.'

But though Cristina had made her peace with the Austrians, she was secretly no less determined than before to continue her fight for Italian independence. Her success in Paris with the politicians encouraged her in the belief that the best way she could serve that cause would be by using her restored riches for propaganda purposes. She decided to create a salon on a grand scale that would attract all whose help she needed – statesmen, diplomats, authors, journalists, poets, painters and musicians. Her success playing the part of 'La Princesse Malheureuse' in her garret had taught her that it paid to appear startlingly different from anyone else To be really popular one must appeal to the Romantics who reigned in the 'thirties, and she could not help but do that with her natural pallor and thinness suggesting that she had been racked by some great passion or sorrow, which had drained the redness from her cheeks.

The Vicomtesse Alix de Janzé in her *Etude et Récits sur Alfred de Musset* states: 'The Princess was a beauty ideally suited to the romantic period. . . . She was the personification of all the qualities the school admired.'

Cristina installed herself in a magnificent house in the Rue d'Anjou-Saint Honoré, with Emilio lodged in a separate and comfortable apartment over the stables, and here from 1835 to 1842 she held sway over one of the most famous salons in Paris. At her soirées there were often as many as six hundred people present. Outwardly she played the part of an eccentric patroness of the arts to confuse the Austrian spies, who never ceased to watch her. Behind this bohemian cloak her house became the nerve centre of the Italian freedom movement in France. Here exiles were brought into contact with leading French statesmen and also received help when in need. For example, on 28 March 1837, Cristina organised a charity bazaar in her house. She persuaded famous authors, actors, actresses, and politicians to let her have their autographs to auction, and painters like Delacroix, Scheffer, Grenet and Delaroche to give some of their pictures for her to sell. This event became the talk of Paris and was followed two days later by a concert under her patronage when Liszt, Chopin and Thalberg among others entertained the company. All the money thus raised went to aid impoverished Italian *émigrés*.

In Cristina's salon the coming Risorgimento was discussed and planned and French support gained. As Gabriel Hanotaux has written: 'She was with more passion what Madame du Deffand had been in the eighteenth century with more wit, and what twenty years earlier Madame Récamier had been with more majesty. She was a centre of attraction. No one did more than she for the cause of a united Italy.'

Cristina was to write later that in her role of literature-loving hostess she must have read all the books published in France of that period. 'I did more and worse than this. I knew the authors. How many tenth-rate imitators of Byron flocked to my salon because I was a woman, and a woman only could understand them! I learnt to tell from the very first line these would-be poets uttered, from the way they opened their mouths and contorted their lips, what was coming.'

Arsène Houssaye wrote of her at this time: 'She had a Byzantine pallor, black hair like raven wings, beautiful luminous eyes, great windows in the façade of a small palace, with lids like magnolia petals.'

Her enemies said she strove to look beautiful and gay, because she was neither beautiful nor gay. Houssaye agreed that she was not really gay, but insisted that she was undoubtedly beautiful to those possessing the eyes of an artist. He called her the Muse of Romance. Gossips said that she overworked her intelligence through taking a fashionable drug, *datura stramonium*. 'The Princess was like a startling new book which one could take in only a little at a time . . . At first she amazed one, then soon she charmed you. She had the penetrating feminism of the Milanese, but unfortunately the apostle masked the woman. She wanted to reform the world.' Stendhal had the same impression, and according to Balzac based his character of the great female artist and republican, the Duchess of San Séverins in his *La Chartreuse de Parme*, on Cristina.

Describing her house in the Rue d'Anjou, de Beaumont-Vassy, in *Les Salons de Paris*, wrote: 'The walls were hung with black velvet spangled with silver stars. The sofas and the chairs were upholstered with the same material. Next to the salon was her bedroom, which formed a complete contrast. Everything was in immaculate white, the hangings, the furniture, even the ornaments. And so as to better harmonise with the rest, the clock and the candelabra were of silver. This room resembled a fairy queen's palace set next to some sombre sorcerer's abode.'

The American, George Ticknor, in his *Life, Letters and Journals* states: 'Her house and her style of reception savour strongly of her native Italy.' This explains perhaps why Parisians, unaccustomed to this kind of décor, were often astonished by it.

Théophile Gautier, who had only a superficial acquaintance-ship with the Princess, wrote an ill-disguised satirical study of her and her home in *Souvenirs romantiques*:

'You may perhaps have met somewhere that celebrated blue stocking known as the romantic Marquise. She is beautiful, so all the artists assure us. Her apartment reminds one of a suite of catafalques, and appears to have been decorated by a high class undertaker. The drawing-room is hung with violet damask; the dining-room with black velvet. The furniture is of ebony, old oak or rosewood. Crucifixes, holy water stoups, Bibles, skulls and daggers are to be seen everywhere in this cheerful interior. Some Zubarans, real or faked, representing monks and martyrs, hang from the walls, and terrify the visitors with their contortions and grimaces. This catacomb-like colour scheme is intended to show up the waxen cheeks of the lady who looks more like a ghost than the mistress of this establishment. She does not live there. She haunts it.

'But don't think, dear Roger, after this somewhat funereal beginning that your friend has been the prey of some Lamia. The Marquise is after all quite a beautiful woman. She has regular features, although a little Jewish, which induce her to wear a turban more often and earlier than she should. She would look only pale if instead of making up her face white she rouged it. She has fine aristocratic hands, rather frail, rather thin, and wearing rather too many bizarre rings, and her foot is no larger than her tiny shoe, which is rare – for women in choosing their footwear have given the lie to the geometrical axiom: the lesser cannot contain the greater.'

Like de Beaumont-Vassy, Gautier describes Cristina's bedroom as having white hangings which gave it 'the appearance of being the chapel of a dedicated virgin.' The bed he says was made of ebony inlaid with ivory and stood on a three-stepped dais like a cenotaph.

Actually Cristina's scheme of décor as described by Gautier was similar to that affected by several Romantics at this time. Charles Lassailly, who created a sensation with his novel, *Les Roueries de Trialph*, in 1833 and who was engaged by Balzac to 'ghost' write for him, used a skull as a candlestick. Roger de Beauvoir, the Beau Brummell of Paris, had his bedroom in the Rue de la Paix hung with black velvet and its windows paned with stained glass. Alphonse Karr, the journalist who first coined the phrase, *'Plus ça change, plus c'est la même chose'*, also draped his bedroom with black and had violet-coloured glass fixed into the window frames as well as decorating the walls with skulls. The young bohemians calling themselves the *'Bousingos'* hung daggers on their walls labelled, 'Beware – this is poisoned.' They drank out of skulls which they pretended belonged to former mistresses.

Count Rodolphe Apponyi, cousin of the Austrian Ambassador, Count Anton Apponyi, and his attaché-secretary, disliked Cristina intensely on account of her anti-Austrian activities, and whenever he mentioned her in his published memoirs[1] he denigrated her. Beginning in 1836, he wrote: 'The Princess, besides her claims to being a second Sappho or Corinna, does her best to look like a spectre; she is deathly pale. The way she does her hair and the turbans she wears heighten this effect. Her gowns are excessively *décolletée*, and invariably white, giving one the illusion that she is floating in a mist. . . . Her staring black eyes are always looking about her in a somewhat sinister manner. The rest of her face is expressionless. Her pale, thin lips seem capable only of emitting a sigh of sorrow. All her movements and her whole bearing are in harmony with the role which she is playing. How sad to find a woman becoming so eccentric.'

On Thursday, 8 June, that same year, he records that he and his wife had to dinner Cristina's mother, the Marchesa Visconti d'Aragona.

'She has come to Paris with her cicisbeo, the Duke of Cannizzaro, and her youngest daughter who is ugly but witty. The Marchesa is well-preserved for her years. She is well-groomed,

41

too, and although she is a grandmother all her gowns and hats are pink. Her skin is still very white and her face having grown plump appears unwrinkled. She hides her double chin by means of a wide ribbon adorned with bows artistically and coquettishly arranged.

'She has visited Paris to try and persuade her daughter, the Princess Belgiojoso, to sell her possessions in Milan to the Duke of Cannizzaro. The Princess would then become independent and could remain permanently in Paris with all her young and old poets and novelists who wallow in sentiment whenever they write a line or open their mouths.

'It is not surprising that having surrounded herself with un-disciplined young people, the Princess behaves like them and gives herself superior airs, ignoring the rules of polite society. The evening she, together with her mother, half-sister and the Duke, dined with us, there were present Mr Hannage from the English Embassy, the Swiss chargé d'affaires, and the Comte d'Harcourt, all of whom the Princess had not met. The invitation was for 6 p.m. Everyone arrived punctually except her party. We waited over an hour, then at last at a quarter past seven we ordered dinner to be served. We were eating the second course when she entered with her relations and friends. Do you think she would have apologised? Not a word. She just told us that she had lost the invitation card and had thought we dined at seven.'

Later he states: 'I went recently to see her at home. I found her seated on a Renaissance-style sofa in a similarly furnished study. It was in the morning. She was wearing a white dressing-gown. I caught a glimpse of a sort of red velvet bodice which she had on beneath it. On her head was an immense turban which reminded me of that worn by Michael Angelo's Sibyl. M. Mignet was standing behind the sofa, leaning nonchalantly on its carved oak back; M. Liszt, the pianist, in an open-necked black velvet blouse, with his long sleek hair falling on his shoulders and a beret in his hand, was seated on a stool in front of the Princess. . . .

'I was so taken aback by this extraordinary scene that I had diffi-culty in starting up a conversation. The Princess, loving to surround herself both with young bohemians and the most distinguished savants, presents an odd mixture of tastes which inspires in turn admiration and pity.'

Elsewhere Rodolphe Apponyi writes: 'Alfred de Musset, one of the Princess's most intimate friends, lolls on the sofa, puts his feet on the table, wears his hat on in the salon and smokes cigars. Is it surprising that the Princess, being surrounded as she is by such unconventional young people, starts behaving like they do and regards herself as above the rules of society?'

Later on in his memoirs, the Count accuses Cristina of 'aiding and abetting political small fry who seek a cure for the world's ills through Communism.' When visiting her salon on the 26 March 1839, he found that she had invited there 'the lion of the desert, Bou Maza' who, following the French conquest of Algeria, had been brought to Paris under detention and who was present with Captain Richard, the officer in whose custody he was. 'This social gathering made me think of the one which took place in the Valley of Jehoshaphat. I saw there Robespierre's former secretary. Can you image such tolerance? The only excuse I can suggest in favour of her is that she is mad.'

Kathleen O'Meara, in her book of Parisian recollections describing those she met in a salon she frequented, wrote: 'Another picturesque visitor was the Princess de Belgiojoso, who made one think of a Léonore of the Renaissance . . . It is said that entering late in a drawing-room where a musical soirée was in progress, she remained motionless on the threshold so as not to interrupt the singer. Her gown of pleated white silk, her necklace of jet, her immobility, and above all her astonishing pallor, gave the illusion of a beautiful phantom. Someone murmured: "How beautiful she is." Another whispered back: "Yes, she must have been very beautiful – when she was alive!"'

The Comtesse d'Agoult, who became Franz Liszt's mistress, detested Cristina because he was such a fond admirer of hers. She wrote in her *Mémoires*:[2] 'No woman understood better the art of effect. She searched for it assiduously. At one time it was in having a negro servant and in studying theology; another in the handsome young Arab she had sitting beside her in her carriage so as to intrigue those frequenting the Bois de Boulogne. Pale, almost alarmingly thin, with flame-like eyes, she cultivated the appearance of a spectre. For the sake of effect she fostered the belief that she possessed a cup and a dagger that had once belonged to Lucretia Borgia.'

The Duchesse de Dino (afterwards the Duchesse de Talleyrand) wrote in her *Journal*[3] for March 1836: 'The Princess Belgiojoso is more striking than beautiful: she is extremely pale, her eyes are too far apart, her head too square, her mouth large and her teeth discoloured; but she has a good nose, and her figure would be pretty if it were somewhat fuller; her hair is jet black, and she wears startling dresses; she has intellect, but wants balance, and is full of artistic whims and inconsistencies; her manner is intentionally and skilfully natural, sufficiently to hide her affectation, while her affectation seems to counterbalance a certain innate vulgarity, which her flatterers style an untamed nature. Such is my impression of this personage, with whom I have but the slightest acquaintance.'

Cristina made a more favourable impression on the British Ambassador's wife than she did on the Duchesse de Dino. Lady Granville wrote to her sister, Lady Carlisle: 'Yesterday at Madame de Bourke's I met Princess Belgiojoso – *distinguée*, pale, big eyes like saucepans, small hands, gracious manners, most intelligent, with a spirit like a demon.'

Regarding the Duchesse's criticism of the Princess's teeth, Alfred de Musset in contrast wrote to Caroline Jaubert that he found Cristina irresistible when she smiled. 'Her teeth are like orange buds and her mouth is like a satin-skinned red fruit.'

On Wednesdays, musicians and singers displayed their gifts in Cristina's salon. She was intensely fond of music. When she attended the Italian Opera in Paris, she would be so emotionally stirred by the performance that friends would have to half carry her to her carriage after the final curtain had fallen. Should the Prince not accompany her, she would wear for her visit the garb of an order of nuns known as the Grey Sisters.

On Saturdays came the turn of literature, history, theology and politics. The poets then repaid their hostess's hospitality with sonnets in praise of her. She would be stretched out on a sofa, smoking a hookah, wearing round her head a circle of her favourite flowers, fuchsias. Between each puff she would insert a pair of silver tongs into a silver-gilt cup, and drawing out a thin slice of orange, place it on her tongue to freshen her mouth.

Here are some typical laudatory verses, unpublished and unsigned, found among her papers in the family archives:

Sonnet d'un républicain farouche á Madame la Princesse de Belgiojoso, Mai 1836

> *Voyez ces habitants de la molle Italie*
> *Que de Winterhaltêr nous traça le pinceau*
> *Dans son Décameron: quel magique tableau!*
> *Que la nature est la vaporeuse, embellie!*
>
> *Entendre Rubini, Thalberg, Damoreau*
> *Ou le cor de Gallay qui tour à tour s'allie*
> *Aux chants d'amour, de guerre ou de mélancolie,*
> *C'est connaître des arts ce qu'ils ont de plus beau.*
>
> *Mais il est une chose et plus douce et plus belle,*
> *Et qui n'a point encore trouvé de coeur rebelle,*
> *Charme indéfinissable on te résiste en vain!*
> *Cette toute-puissance inconcevable, étrange,*
> *Et qui semble à nos yeux faire apparaître un ange,*
> *C'est de Belgiojoso le sourire divin!*

After they had listened to the verses and the music and had tired of conversing, Cristina and her guests would dance in the dining-room, a long gallery-like apartment decorated with sculptures in stucco and Pompeiian paintings. The 'lions' waltzed with frenzy. The Princess would circulate among her guests and from time to time whirl past with one of them.

Very occasionally there was a mishap, as when Victor Cousin the philosopher waved his arm about stressing some point and one of the Princess's hounds bit it, mistaking it for the stick with which he and his mistress played – so Prosper Mérimée records.

Did Cristina, with so many admirers to choose from, take a lover? A. J. Pons, Sainte-Beuve's secretary, wrote in *Sainte-Beuve et ses Inconnues*, published in 1879: 'The Princess Belgiojoso after several years of platonic love from the learned and handsome Mignet dismissed him and took a lusty mason for lover. This caused a great scandal. One of her friends scolded her for this strange lapse of taste. "Eh, my dear!" retorted the impatient Italian. "He at least doesn't think."' But nobody else records such a story, and in all the voluminous correspondence in the Belgiojoso family archives there is nothing to suggest promiscuity on her part.

Arsène Houssaye probably assessed the position correctly when he said in his *Confessions*: 'She would invite you to the banquet of love and welcome you with adorable grace, but would fly away just when one was about to sit down to enjoy the meal.'

CHAPTER 4

HEINE, LISZT, AND DE MUSSET

The men who loved Cristina most during this part of her life were Heinrich Heine, Franz Liszt, and Alfred de Musset.

It was Lafayette who first introduced her to Heine, but although she did much to further his career, she did not return his love. The poet's letters to her have been preserved in the Belgiojoso family archives.

On 18 April 1834, he wrote:[1]

'In six weeks' time the French translation of my *Reisebilder* will appear. The first volume, which deals with Italy, has been printed, including the preface. Would you care to read the proofs of this volume? If you should, I will send them to you on condition that you do not show them to anybody else . . . Believe me, Madame, I have thought so much about you since the evening of the day before yesterday that I cannot wait to meet you again. Please name a day for this to happen . . . I am beginning to regain courage. I was a coward to flee from you half an hour before midnight. But now I can think of you without trembling. Only I would not yet dare to look you in the face. But I think that tomorrow or the day after tomorrow I shall have recovered my Teutonic sangfroid, and I shall be able to talk to you sensibly without being distracted by the glory of your hair. I have never seen anything so wonderful, so poetic, so fairy-like, as your black locks curling wildly against the transparent paleness of your face.

'And that face, you have stolen it from some painting of the fourth century, from some old fresco of the Lombardian school, perhaps from your Luini or even from the poems of Ariosto, or I do not know where. What I do know is that your face is ever in my mind like a riddle that I would like to solve. As to your heart,

47

which is no doubt very fine, I am little concerned. All women have hearts . . . But none have a face the equal of yours.

'Day and night I rack my brains trying to read what lies behind that face with its extraordinary eyes, its mysterious mouth, and all those features which do not seem to exist in reality but rather to be the imaginings of a dream, so that I fear all the time to find one morning that they do not exist.

'I beg you, Madame, not to vanish and to accept the assurances of the perfect respect and devotion with which I remain, your very humble and obedient, Heinrich Heine.'

Twelve days later, on 30 April, he was writing to her that things had changed.[2] 'I no longer admire only your beauty. I now worship everything that has to do with you . . . I don't care what this worship of you may cost me. Things in Denmark are not what they were, said Hamlet, who was the maddest of all men with the exception of your very humble servant.'

Next he was describing her as 'a beauty thirsting after truth'. When Heine found that Cristina was out of his reach, he started an affair with a vulgar and ugly glove saleswoman, whom he eventually married. The Princess, to try and prevent what everybody regarded as an unsuitable match, invited him to stay at her country retreat, La Jonchère. After first refusing, he accepted and spent the summer there. On 2 July 1835, he wrote to his publisher that he was living happily and peacefully in the home 'of the most beautiful, most noble and high-minded of women, but I am not in love with her. Now it seems my fate to fall in love with stupid, common women.'

On 30 October of the following year he wrote to Cristina: 'You have the most complete personality of anyone I have so far met in my life. Before I was introduced to you I imagined that women of your perfection of both body and mind only existed in fairy-tales or in poet's flights of fancy.'

When Cristina met Franz Liszt he was living with the blonde Countess Marie d'Agoult, who had left husband, home and five children for him, and who soon became very jealous of his association with the Princess. According to another Princess,

Mathilde Bonaparte, Marie had an interesting and noble face, but being tall and thin looked like the figure of Hunger.

Liszt undoubtedly owed much to Cristina, who organised recitals and introduced him to people whom she thought might further his career. He in return, always took her part when she was attacked. In May 1836, he wrote to Marie, who was staying with George Sand at Nohant: 'I have seen the Princess again. She is always charming towards me, does not compare me with other musicians, and scoffs at Thalberg's supporters. She has promised me several very useful letters of introduction.'

In January 1837, the celebrated contest took place between Liszt and Sigismund Thalberg, the favourite composer-pianist of the Austrian Emperor, who had gained first place in Parisian musical circles whilst the Pole was away living in Geneva with Marie. Heine had called him: 'The gentleman musician who actually has no need to play the piano in order to be received everywhere with pleasure.'

The world of music was divided as to which man was the finer pianist. Liszt's detractors claimed that he was too noisy, fidgety and theatrical. Cristina led those who supported him, and so sure was she of his superiority that she suggested the two men should take part in a musical duel in her salon, which was attended by all the celebrities then in Paris.

Thalberg was stiff and humourless with an unprepossessing string beard. He played first, taking for his test piece a Fantasy of his own on Rossini's 'Moses'. He was impressively correct and could not be faulted. Then Liszt pulled off his silver-white gloves and seated himself at the piano. He chose also a Fantasy of his own, based on Pacini's 'Niobe'. He waited for all scrapings of chairs, all nervous coughing, all rustling of silk and taffeta to cease, and when silence was absolute, he still waited a full minute so as to raise expectancy to its pitch. Then with practised elegance and with wrist leading, he raised his right hand before beginning to play. As his fingers danced over the keys, his sea-green eyes, flashing with hypnotic brilliance in the candlelight, rested on all the women present in turn. His willowy form would keep time with the music, now arching over the keyboard, now almost leaping backwards as he shook like a banner in battle his long fair hair. When he ended, the silence told him he had triumphed. It was followed by an explosion of applause that was the sweetest music of all to his ego. Then Cristina with grace and diplomacy gave her verdict: 'Thalberg is the best pianist in Paris, but there is only one Liszt in the world.'

The Princess's part in bringing about this success annoyed Marie d'Agoult. To avoid scenes with her over his friendship with the Italian, Liszt now disclosed only sufficient information concerning his relations with the other to escape being caught out. Consequently, although he saw a great deal of Cristina during the latter part of 1837, there is no mention of this in his correspondence with Marie.

Success was making him neglectful of keeping appointments. On one occasion when the Princess held a reception in his honour, to which she had invited Chopin, Meyerbeer, Herz and other famous musicians, he failed to arrive. François Mignet was scandalised and observed: 'There is great disorder in that young man's mind.'

But Cristina was indulgent and forgave him. Soon those who traded in gossip were retailing that Cristina had supplanted Marie d'Agoult in Liszt's affections. This exposed her to the Countess's vengeful nature. She never forgave the Princess, and her pen was always dipped in malice whenever she referred to her in the future. She called her *'La Comédienne'*.

Actually Liszt was still very much in love with Marie. The final break was not to come until some years later. But this did not prevent him from courting Cristina at the same time. From Como, on 15 December 1837, he wrote to her that as a general rule he preferred to receive no letters so as not to have the trouble of replying to them.

'But general rules do not apply to you, who from birth have been an exception to all rules, and who, whatever you do willingly or unwillingly, will die exceptionally. . . . Let it be agreed that you will write to me whenever you can. I will enjoy hearing from you, even if it be only to tell me that I am insupportable, detestable, etc.' He wrote this letter a month after Marie d'Agoult had given

HUMOROUS SKETCH OF PRINCE EMILIO *(centre rear)*
AT ARENENBERG IN 1833

VILLA TRIVULZIO AT LOCATE NEAR MILAN IN 1840

birth to their baby girl Cosima, who was to become Wagner's wife.

The same month Liszt commenced a series of concerts at Milan. Cristina had asked him to visit her dearest friend, Ernesta Bisi. The old drawing mistress wrote to her former pupil:

'Liszt has been here! Liszt has played! Liszt has written with this same pen with which I write to you and will send the letter from his home ... The piece from "Puritani" dedicated to you was played by him on my very poor piano, played with that virtuosity you know, and despite the inferiority of the instrument the effect was magical ... He wanted to please you and went out of his way to be friendly. I was moved by his noble features, his talent, and above all by the knowledge that you, my dear, my incomparable Cristina, had taken such trouble to give me so much pleasure. You, who are the delight of Paris, admired, idolised by all around you, have never forgotten me since I taught you as a girl ... Liszt read aloud the paragraph in your letter to him about me, and I was moved to tears. Imagine my confusion, knowing myself to be so very different from your description of me ...'

To this Cristina replied: 'If I had not loved Liszt before, I should now for having carried out my request so well. Isn't he extremely charming? Doesn't he play as no one else can in the world? I am pleased he showed you my letter. Now you know that I love you more than I can tell you ..."

On his way to give a series of recitals in Russia, after fourteen months of doing the same in Europe, Liszt in a long letter to Cristina confessed:

'You say, "Try and persuade yourself that writing to me will be a form of relaxation." It would not be difficult for me to persuade myself to believe many things about you which would astonish you. Shall I tell you? You are my ideal – you only do I worship (and I am not writing nonsense). But my devotion has not exactly made relations between us easy. My profession has made me a bird of passage. We have never been together for very long. Much more remains indefinite and unexpressed between us than we have been able to put into words. My life is full of obstacles, cares, and petty vexations ... You have helped and championed me when many people were hostile and unkind. I shall never forget that first year when I had the honour to make your acquaintance. Since then, if you will allow me to say it, you have been something very special in my life . . .

'In a fortnight I shall be in Berlin. Please be kind and write me a few lines, *Poste restante*. And above all, do not ask me any longer not to forget you. You know that I am devoted to you, heart and soul, and that I do not merely remember you, I worship you.

'I am at your feet, F.L.'

Once, before leaving to give a recital in London, Liszt asked her to do him a favour. After he left Paris, would she be so kind as to visit Marie who was far from well, and whom Cristina had not so far met. 'Be kind, Madame – open your heart to her – think of all she has suffered and what she is still suffering,' he told the Princess. 'Don't forget that it is someone who has suffered greatly whom I am entrusting to your care. Will you go?'

'Of course, I'll visit her if you wish it. But are you sure I'll be welcome?' Cristina replied. 'If my visit is unexpected, won't she look upon it as an impertinent intrusion rather than a friendly gesture?'

In her *Souvenirs* Cristina wrote: 'Liszt swept aside all my objections. He insisted on my promising to visit Nélida, as he called her, the very day he left for England. 'What am I going to say when I get there?' I asked myself. I regretted having given way to his request. I should have to be convincingly sympathetic and seem sincerely worried about her troubles. If I don't weep with her, she will think I have a hard heart. On the other hand, wouldn't her pride revolt at the very thought of being consoled by a stranger?'

When Cristina called on the Countess at 10 Rue Neuve des Mathurins she was received by a manservant in livery, and was shown into an elegantly furnished room, hung with velvet and satin. Lying on the floor lay a superb tiger-skin rug. Whilst awaiting Marie she looked around her, surprised to find so much tasteful luxury.

'But I thought to myself riches are no compensation for a wounded heart to a noble and passionate soul in the unusual and equivocal position in which she finds herself. She must at times envy the life of one of the humble peasants on her estate spent in a barely furnished cottage, living frugally but happily married to her husband, loved and respected . . .

'I was suddenly brought back to earth by the arrival of Nélida. She swept in with a light step and a gracious but slightly patronising manner. Her long black velvet dress, her black lace veil, artistically arranged over her fair hair in the manner of Mary Stuart or some princess of the Middle Ages, made her look like a painting by Van Dyck that had been slightly impaired by the hand of time . . .

'"How kind of you, Madame, to come to see me?" she cried. "I have so long heard people talking about you. How I've longed to make your acquaintance!"

'Nélida no doubt saw by the look on my face that her appearance was not that of the ailing woman I had expected to find.'

In the conversation that followed, Marie d'Agoult tried to upset her visitor by sarcastic references to Cristina's erudite *Un essai sur la formation du dogme catholique*, the publication of which was to startle Paris in 1842. 'And what are you busying yourself with now, Madame?' the Countess enquired. 'I am myself very diligently studying the love life of minerals.'

Cristina continues in her *Souvenirs* that fortunately this disagreeable conversation was interrupted by the arrival of other callers and she was able to leave. '"What a fool I was to visit her!" I said to myself when I was outside. "She is a person of real distinction. In other circumstances I might have appreciated her wit, her originality, and even been interested in what she had to say about the love life of minerals. But it isn't possible to enjoy the conversational charm of even the best of company when one feels oneself being pushed onto the slippery slopes of ridicule."'

Later, in her *Mémoires*, the Comtesse d'Agoult gave her own version of this visit. 'The Princess came to see me, but was unable to conceal her disappointment. She had been told that I was dying and that was why she had rushed to my bedside. She had come to prepare me for death, to convert me to the Faith. She behaved like a Sister of Charity or even a Mother Superior. Unfortunately for her I had only a cold. I received her standing. When she was satisfied that there was no likelihood of my dying, she lost interest and left.'

After Cristina's departure Marie wrote to Liszt:

'*La Comédienne* has just been to see me, and I am hastening to let you have my frank and candid impression of her. I found her raddled-looking, almost ugly. She was thin and puny, with no presence – not at all the great lady, and much less witty than I expected. She stayed an hour, and her conversation was dull and boring. She rolled her eyes in a very affected and irritating way. I felt she gave out an aura of insincerity and wickedness. I thought I behaved very naturally, and I was certainly far wittier than she was. At first she was rather reserved, then she became more and more talkative. Without being conceited, I am in every way superior to her. I have now a very low opinion of her. Did you know that she goes regularly to Holy Communion?'

But Liszt ignored Marie's spite when he replied, and continued writing to Cristina. In one letter he asks; 'Do you still intend to spend the winter in Milan? If you do, it will remove from me all hope of seeing you again. You ask: "What is that to you?" I don't know, I cannot tell – except to say that it matters very much. My worship of you remains unchanged . . . Be kind and indulgent towards your faithful worshipper as you have been in the past. Do him even the favour of putting him to the test (but not too rigorously if possible) and believe in his adoration and entire devotion.'

Balzac was one of the few men who was not attracted by Cristina. In a letter sent in 1838 to Madame Eva Hanska, with whom he was already in love, he claimed that the Princess had tried 'to become my intimate friend.' Later he informed Eva that Cristina had been 'fortunate enough to displease me' and that 'she affected the style of a vampire.' He had been to two of her Saturday salons and also once to dinner – 'but I shan't go again.'

Five years later, on 16 May 1843, there is this passage in a letter[3] of his to Eva: 'As for "La Belgiojoso", who during Liszt's last concert honoured him by sitting at his feet, she has now dropped him. She has just written four volumes on Catholic dogma, and that is her main interest at the moment. She has taken Liszt from the Comtesse d'Agoult, just as she has taken Lord Normanby from his wife, Mignet from Madame Aubernon and Musset from George Sand.'

But Cristina and Liszt must have become friendly again for in a letter[4] to Eva Hanska dated the 10 June 1844, he reports: 'I have just returned from the country home of Princess Cristina Belgiojoso. I saw Liszt. He behaves just as though he were the master of the house, and I am somewhat ashamed to tell you that the Hungarian is a real Bohemian who is always acting a part, either the comedian or the passionate lover . . . As for her, she has stopped allowing one to bring friends during all Liszt's recitals in her salon. Liszt does not know how to behave. He even gave orders in her presence to her coachman to take me back to the station.'

Another letter[5] dated 23 June 1844, reads: 'Liszt is living with the Princess Belgiojoso, and so openly that he returns there at half-past eleven each night and lets everybody know it. Cristina deserves no more respect.'

Some six weeks later, on 7 August, he tells Eva: 'You don't know the Princess like I do. She is, with regard to the Liszts and the Mignets and all her passing fancies, of the age of Louis XV. She is very imperious, with no regrets for the past, never allowing a man any rights and only loaning herself to him. She is a courtesan, a beautiful empress, but also horribly blue stocking.'

Then three weeks after this, he informs Eva that he lost some five thousand francs through the hasty way his *Splendeurs et Misères des Courtisanes* was published, but fortunately it was reprinted as a newspaper serial 'owing to the good offices of Cristina Trivulzio.'

In 1834, following a disastrous stay in Venice, the love affair between George Sand and Alfred de Musset had come to an end. Whilst she was seriously ill with dysentery, he had spent his nights with the local trollops, and then he in his turn had fallen ill. George called in a handsome blond doctor named Pagello, who diagnosed the trouble as *delirium tremens* and not only cured the poet but also became her lover, spending all his money on her till he had to pawn his clothes to buy her the coffee for which she had an insatiable thirst.

Alfred in a huff went off for a trip on the Rhine. He had for some time been a drinking companion of Prince Emilio, and as a result of this was introduced to Cristina and became a regular visitor to her salon. It was also in her country retreat at La Jonchère that he first met Caroline Jaubert, a friend of the Princess, who was to become an intimate friend of his, though not his mistress, and whom he was to call his godmother. She was not pretty, but very witty; a tiny woman with a child's hands, and feet so small that people used to beg a slipper from her to keep with other curios in their display cabinets.

Cristina listened sympathetically to his unhappy outpourings about how empty life seemed without George, and did her best to console him. As a result it was not long before he fell in love with her. Léon Séché in his life of the poet claims that he persuaded Cristina to dine with him in a private room in a modish Montmartre restaurant, the Cabaret du Divorce. It so happened that Prince Emilio was also dining there with his current mistress. When a waiter whispered in the Prince's ear that Alfred de Musset and a beautiful lady were in a nearby room, Emilio immediately went in search of Alfred to suggest that the four of them should join forces for the evening. Somehow or other Cristina managed to slip away without being identified by her erring husband.

The association between Princess and poet continued, but it increasingly annoyed him that for the first time in his life he had fallen in love with a woman who preferred to keep the affair devoid of sex. 'The penalty of vulgar amours,' she wrote to him, 'is the denial to those who indulge in them of ever experiencing the higher and nobler forms of love.' She went on to refer to the 'succès facile' he had enjoyed in the past, and to suggest that he should now rise above that sort of thing. He had been accustomed to flattery as a popular poet adored by society, and he resented this plain speaking. No one had resisted him until then.

When, owing to heavy drinking, he became capricious, bad-tempered and melancholy, Cristina preferred not to be in his company, seeing no reason to put up with his whims. Then Caroline Jaubert would act as peacemaker and persuade her to forgive him and see him again when he was sober.

One evening, whilst amusing himself drawing caricatures of various people, he told the Princess that everything could be caricatured, even the finest of Grecian statues. She challenged the truth of this, insisting that the regularity of their features made it impossible.

'To prove I'm right, I'll caricature you,' he returned.

'I defy you to,' she retorted.

Petulantly he set to work. What he drew exaggerated the size and distance apart of her eyes and gave her broad shoulders, thick arms, and an enormous bust. It was not a true caricature, and looked like the work of a spoiled child. Already aware that he had acted foolishly, he tried to make amends by writing beneath the drawing: *Pallida sed quamvis pallida, pulcra tamen.* She is pale and yet though pale, she is beautiful.

'It's not bad,' Cristina commented with dignity, but it was noticeable from the way she closed his sketch book that she was annoyed.

'You've burnt your boats,' Caroline Jaubert told Alfred when they left.

'Nevertheless, I was never more in love with her than when I drew that sketch,' he replied.

'So much the worse. You wounded her.'

For nearly a month Princess and poet saw nothing of each other. Then one afternoon when he went to take tea with Caroline, Musset found Cristina there. According to him, she at first ignored his presence, then took him aside before she left and heaped reproaches on his head. But it was obvious that she was not serious, and as it seemed to him that she wanted to become friends again, he went home and wrote a letter of apology in mock legal language, ending: 'To bear witness to the solemnity of these words, the undersigned has used a sheet of paper stamped to the value of ten sous.' Following this, the estrangement ended.

Alfred's friendship with Cristina had the effect of arousing the jealousy of François Mignet. There were several disagreements, but he, too, was never able to keep away from her for long. In a letter to Caroline, Cristina writes:

'Yes, the perpetual secretary, as Heine calls him, is back, but don't imagine that he has admitted he was in the wrong – not at all, for non-Christian philosophers such as he are always infallible. This is what happened. A nephew of his of whom he was very fond died, and I learnt he was extremely upset. So I sent him a letter of sympathy in which I regretted that he would not give me an opportunity of expressing my feelings to him in person. My gesture touched him and he came to thank me. I begged him to come again, which he did. But he is convinced that I am worthless and he thinks more of himself than ever. He is proud of the way he has behaved and ashamed of me, because he says I encourage my male admirers.

'How does this affect me? Well, when he enumerates the thousand faults which make me such a contemptible creature in his eyes, I become worried because I begin to wonder whether there is any truth in what he says. But once he has left, I regain my self-respect. I feel better and tell myself that he is quite wrong. I like to see him because friendship with me once born never dies, but I no longer trust his judgment.'

Arguments over de Musset continued. On a later occasion when on account of this Mignet had not visited Cristina for a particularly long time, their mutual friend, Adolphe Thiers, celebrated his own appointment as Louis-Philippe's First Minister in 1840 by trying to reconcile the couple, for he knew how lonely François had become since their ménage à deux had been broken through Adolphe's departure to marry a wealthy wife.

Fortunately the day Thiers called on Cristina she had just heard a sermon by an eloquent Abbé on the forgiveness of offences, so she told him that she was ready to make her peace with François, providing the event was celebrated by their attending a special Mass of thanksgiving together. Shortly afterwards they did this in the Madeleine.

Following that she refused to see Alfred de Musset for some time. But to show that she bore him no ill feeling, when he fell seriously ill later in 1840, she came to nurse him. He recorded that at first he refused to take the medicine she poured out, but that when she looked at him he could not resist her magnificent eyes, and meekly swallowed it.

One day when he was feeling very poorly he told her he thought he was about to die, and she made him smile by responding: 'You won't. No one ever dies in my presence.' On leaving, she promised to return next day, and he murmured: 'Then I shan't die to-morrow.'

Later he wrote her a confiding, frank letter about himself: 'I still love pleasures, I even love excess. That is my nature. But at present I have to do without it. As soon as something attracts me, I hurl myself recklessly after it. Satiety follows inevitably in its wake, then I feel a compulsion to do something else.'

Unlike the way he behaved towards other women, he was patient with the Princess. After she had left Paris for Italy in 1840, he wrote regretting not being able to hear her 'affectionate sermons.' She invited him to stay with her, suggesting that the climate and the food would be better for him, and that he would also find there stimulus for his poetic imagination. She offered him a large apartment in her villa, and the use of the family library with all its rare books. He could come and go as he pleased, and be chided by her in similar fashion to when he was in Paris and as often as he wished.

Her invitation delighted him. He kept mentioning it. When Paris palled on him, he now knew where he could go and be assured of a welcome. He replied that her offer would be some-thing to dream about, but he did not visit her. Instead he haunted the *Café de la Régence,* becoming 'absinthe-minded' as a wit put it.

It was some time before they corresponded again. Then on 29 January 1841, he wrote:

'I thank you with all my heart for the few words you added for me in your letter to Mme. Jaubert. Not only was I touched by your message, but it is the only thing which has given me pleasure for a long while. . . .

'I am missing you very much. It is a common human weakness for people to appreciate most the value of things when they have lost them. I have a wretched memory which only remembers happy events in my life. Now you are and always will be one of the very few people that I shall never forget.

'You have been kinder to me than I deserve. I know that when you visited me so regularly during my illness, it was not affection that brought you to me but your passion for helping the suffering ... The nobility of your character, your soothing and sympathetic manner, profoundly impressed me ... Several times since, I have wished to be ill in the hope of thus seeing you again.

'At the last ball held at the Tuileries the galleries seemed less long and the crowd less boring when you did me the honour of accepting my arm to escort you.

'Well, Princess, that is what I wanted to tell you, and what I beg you not to take for badly expressed compliments, for it is a fact that I have always felt embarrassed when talking to you, and I am still even when writing to you. As I may perhaps never see you again, I must let you know my true feelings. If you find my letter foolish, please burn it, but at least credit me with good intentions in writing it.

Devoted and respectful compliments,
    Alfred de Musset.'

From Locate on 11 February 1841, she replied: 'Your letter, which to be truthful I was expecting, reached me last night. It is I who ought to thank you for not having forgotten me, for to forget would be more excusable in you than in me. You are living in the midst of noise and bustle, whilst I am living in almost complete solitude ... You write that you may never see me again, and I hope that you are wrong. ... If you become ill again and if a change of air and surroundings might do you good, remember that in Italy you will find not only sunshine but also care and attention. I am living in a province where the air is ideal for chest complaints. If yours gives you trouble, don't forget the willing nurse who would care for you on the other side of the Alps. ...'

On 21 February 1841, he replied:
'If one did what one wanted to do in this world, Princess, I should reply to your letter with my own voice. ... If I were not chained here, I should be at this very hour on my way to you,

planning the masterpiece which I am continually being urged to write and which I shall never achieve in the agreeable mud of Paris. If only I could thank you in person for your excellent and charming letter, and sit for a while on a bench in your garden to see you pass by to visit your poor – or to receive from afar a friendly wave of your hand. I thank you for having conjured up for a moment an impossible dream.

'But let us return to reality . . . As you know, when I first saw you I fell instantly and deeply in love, the only time this has ever happened to me. Since you refused to take my love seriously, I have done my best to get over it, but without much success. As a result I have always felt embarrassed in your company, which I never am with other women. This was because the very sight of you has always revived the love I thought to have mastered.

'But you have continued to be indifferent and have even laughed a little at me. Perhaps I might have ended up by being very angry if you weren't kindness itself.'

He goes on to ask to be forgiven for writing in this way For these reasons he would not join her in Italy. It is interesting to note that Alfred de Musset read aloud both these last two letters of his to Paul, his brother, for criticism and editing before sending them.

Later that year in a letter[6] to Caroline Jaubert dated 9 October 1841, the poet wrote of Cristina: 'As for her whom I have now made up my mind never to see again, I can tell you frankly how I feel about her – I love her, I love her, and I love her immensely; and you, too. It is annoying, but I cannot help it.'

Corresponding again with Caroline, he expresses his conviction that there might have been between the Princess and himself 'an association which once we were accustomed to each other could have become very pleasant, even without our sleeping together but only under the same roof.'

In 1842 Cristina came back to Paris and he found that his passion for her had grown. He became more persistent than ever in his attempt to become her lover. In one letter he wrote that he had to go unexpectedly on business to Normandy and did not know when he would be seeing her again. 'I cannot put into words how sad that thought has made me. You will laugh, no doubt, and tell me with your customary calm that business must come first, and that we aren't in this world to amuse ourselves. But my life has been full of boredom for the last four years. Your return and the friendship you showed me, despite my moods and stupidities, are the only things which for ages have made me feel that I was alive. You know as well as I do that I love you. There is nothing tawdry about my love. It is full of respect, sincere, pure and idealistic. I have felt like this towards you for a very long time now. It kept me alive, and restored my morale ... Mock me if you wish, Princess, but don't take this letter for a declaration made by a pair of patent leather boots to a pair of glacé kid gloves ...'

But Cristina still could not bring herself to love him. During the hot summer of 1842 she invited him to stay in her country home at Versailles. He accepted, hoping that once installed in her house he would be able at last to wear down her defences, but she pleaded ill-health and kept most of the day in her room.

Louise Colet, the nymphomaniac writer, who won coveted French literary laurels by sleeping with influential men, chased Alfred de Musset for years, and succeeded in becoming his mistress in 1850 when they were both forty. But after six months he could not stand her any longer and ended the association. Whenever she called, his servant was instructed to say that he had just left for the country. She was known as 'la femme à scènes' because she always had violent rows with her lovers, one of whom wrote: 'I thought she was a dove but she turned out to be a mosquito.' Although she had lived with Alfred for only such a short period, two years after his death in 1857 she published a book about him, Lui, and in it she included a chapter in which she related what allegedly Alfred told her had happened during his Versailles visit to Cristina in 1842.

According to Louise, the poet was the Princess's only guest. After dinner on the day of his arrival, as it was a beautiful summer's evening, they went for a walk in the vast secluded park. 'The place lent itself to intimacy. She asked him to recite to her some love poems. This he did and then wanted to put their sentiments into action. But, fleet of foot like Virgil's shepherdess, she fled, pursued by the poet. Then his foot stumbled against a tree root. He twisted his ankle and fell with a cry of pain.

'Madame Belgiojoso turned back and helped Alfred to limp to a bench, where she made him sit down. Seeing him now dependent on her, she became more affectionate, more tender. The sharp pain in his foot made the poet unappreciative of his friend's caresses, so the lady ran to the house to summon help. Two servants went to the rescue with a large armchair, in which they carried him into his room and put him to bed. A doctor came to examine the leg and prescribed complete immobility for several days. The poet submitted obediently to this detention. Having nothing else to do, he fell seriously in love with his hostess. She attacked her helpless guest with all the weapons in a coquette's armoury. She was able to flirt and torment him with impunity.

'Circumstances favoured Madame de Belgiojoso's wiles. She had beside Musset two ardent admirers, but of quite different rank. The first was a cold and worthy politician, the scholarly Dr. Mignet. The second was an artist, a pianist, a pleasant, self-confident fellow. Both paid persistent court to the Princess. Confined to his bed by his unfortunate sprain, the poet would watch through his window his beloved and the diplomat walking in the grounds till they disappeared from view into unfrequented parts of the shrubbery, or he would hear her singing a duet in the salon with the pianist. All this roused his jealousy and frayed his nerves. "Ah, the coquette," he would murmur to himself, "how expert she is at digging her talons into a man's heart!"

'Should he make some jealous reproach when she came to offer him a cooling drink, she would reply with a smile: "But, my dear poet, I only associate with these men because I am interested in European affairs and want to improve my singing. You know I prefer you to all my other friends." And he, de Musset, on account of the good opinion he had of himself would believe what she said.

'One morning the Princess had her breakfast served by the poet's bedside. She went out of her way to excite him with provocative glances and allowed him to hold her hand. Then suddenly she rose and drew it away. "What, my darling," the sick man sighed, "you're not going to leave me?"

'"My music master must have arrived by now. I'm hoping to have a singing lesson." With these words she hurried away, laughing mischievously. She did not even take the trouble to close the door behind her. Left alone, the poet once more became a prey to jealousy. The burning, passionate notes that he heard vibrating in the neighbouring room enraged him. Unable to endure this mental torture any longer, he threw off his bed clothes, removed the bandage from his leg and hopped as fast as he could to the drawing-room door. He tore back the tapestry curtain and appeared like a spectre before the two singers.

'At that very moment the Princess was pressing her lips to the cheek of the pianist, who was gazing very tenderly at her as he repeated the love refrain of their duet. Madame de Belgiojoso started with fright on noticing de Musset, but she soon regained her composure and told him with a smile: "I knew you were there – I saw you – I wanted to test you!"

'"Well, Princess," Alfred returned in the same tone of voice as hers, "the test has been made. I have had enough of your hospitality. I'm bored here. All this music prevents me from sleeping. Perhaps this gentleman who seems to me to be very nearly the master of the house will ring for a servant, then I wish to be dressed and put into a carriage so that I can return to Paris."

'The pianist bit his lip, but he was obliged to obey a sick man, wearing only his nightshirt and whose sufferings caused him to collapse onto a sofa. The Princess did all she could to persuade him to stay, but without success. "Don't try and keep me – you love music too much for my liking!" he jeered. So he was dressed and put into a carriage. When he was about to be driven away, Madame de Belgiojoso called with a confident smile: "*Au revoir –* you'll come back to me!" This prediction was not fulfilled. Ten years passed before she saw him again.'

Although Louise Colet's account is obviously highly embroidered, it is certain that during his stay at Versailles the final break came. In a letter to Caroline Jaubert, dated 26 July 1842,

Alfred de Musset gives a different account from that of Louise. He complained that following his arrival Cristina gave him very little of her company. He lost a game of chess to her and they quarrelled. Then at lunch he became so angry that he scratched her with a fork he was brandishing. 'When she saw that she was making me miserable, she gave me that irresistible smile of hers, charming me with her dimples, which made me feel as if I had been beaten over the head with a stick.' Probably his wooing had became so importunate that Cristina decided to play a trick on him which she knew would end all between them.

Later de Musset was to write a further version[7] of what transpired. It is at variance with Louise Colet's in so far as it describes quite another episode as causing their final parting.

'The Princess had terrible eyes, like a sphinx, so large, so very large, that I lost myself in them and could not find my bearings again,' he complained. 'The two women who destroyed my life were George Sand and the Princess Belgiojoso. I never recovered from these two passions. One night I went to Cristina. I began by kneeling before her. I declared that I had yearned for her long enough. I shouted. I abused her. I compared her to Montespan, who was virtuous with Lauzun whom she loved, and who gave herself to the King whom she did not love, which is the lowest form of self abasement. But all Cristina did was to laugh and say: "Come with me!"

'She took me gently by the hand. I was almost frightened by my triumph. I allowed myself to be led with the illusions of a lover. But in her bedroom, instead of throwing herself into my arms, she threw me into the arms of a former mistress who did not want me any more than I wanted her, but who would not allow me to be happy with another woman.'

De Musset does not mention who the old mistress was, but Arsène Houssaye in his *Mémoires* claimed that it was George Sand.

This incident so infuriated the poet that he found balm for his offended ego by telling his friends that it was he who had tired of the Princess and not the other way round. Later he was to write: 'I was for a few weeks captive between her velvet paws, and I still retain the marks in my mind, but not in my heart, for the claws had only succeeded in scratching it superficially.'

Emile Henriot in his biography of de Musset sides with him and takes the view that as Cristina had encouraged his advances it was despicable of her not to have become his lover. He describes her as 'a greenish-hued Milanese, a hard-hearted coquette, with nasty savage claws'.

Alfred in his wrath now tried to destroy Cristina's reputation by writing his famous poem, *Sur Une Morte*. Unfortunately for him she retained all his letters, and his admiring references to her in so many of them make his denigratory verse picture of her sound like sour grapes.

Sur Une Morte, which appeared in the *Revue des Deux Mondes* for June 1842, ran:

> *Elle était belle, si la Nuit*
> *Qui dort dans la sombre chapelle*
> *Où Michel-Ange a fait son lit,*
> *Immobile, peut être belle.*

> *Elle était bonne, s'il suffit*
> *Qu'en passant la main s'ouvre et donne,*
> *Sans que Dieu n'ait rien vu, rien dit;*
> *Si l'or sans pitié fait l'aumône.*

> *Elle pensait, si le vain bruit*
> *D'une voix douce et cadencée*
> *Comme le ruisseau qui gémit,*
> *Peut faire croire à la pensée.*

> *Elle priait, si deux beaux yeux,*
> *Tantôt s'attachant à la terre,*
> *Tantôt se levant vers les cieux,*
> *Peuvent s'appeler la prière.*

> *Elle aurait souri, si la fleur*
> *Qui n'est point épanouie*
> *Pouvait s'ouvrir à la fraicheur*
> *Du vent qui passe et qui l'oublie.*

Elle aurait pleuré, si la main,
Sur son coeur froidement posée,
Eût jamais dans l'argile humain
Senti la céleste rosée.

Elle aurait aimé, si l'orgueil,
Pareil à la lampe inutile
Qu'on allume près d'un cercueil
N'eût veillé sur son coeur stérile.

Elle est morte, et n'a point vécu;
Elle faisait semblant de vivre.
De ses mains est tombé le livre
Dans lequel elle n'a rien lu.

(If the still shades of night slumbering in the sombre chapel where Michael Angelo had his couch could be called beautiful, then she was beautiful.

If gold given to the poor without pity entitles one to be called good, then she was good.

If a gentle, musical voice with no more thought behind it than a rustling brook suggests intelligence, then she was intelligent.

If prayer means no more than two beautiful eyes moving to and from the sky and the earth, then she could pray.

If the flower which had never opened its petals could do so when caressed by the fleeting, forgetful breeze, then she could have smiled.

If the cold hand on her heart could have been warmed by the dew of Heaven, she might have wept.

If pride like the useless lamp one lights near a coffin had not kept watch over her barren heart, she might have loved.

She is dead, and has never lived. She only seemed to be alive, and from her hands has fallen the book in which she has read nothing.)

As soon as the verses were published, de Musset wrote to Madame Jaubert asking her to let him know how Cristina had reacted. When she replied that the Princess had not read them, the poet was furious, not only disbelieving his informant but threatening worse. 'She hasn't read my verses? In that case I will write a novel to say even more, and if she doesn't read that, others will.'

Cristina's enemies, women who had failed to attract the men she had, were delighted with the poem, and when they heard that she claimed not to have read it, they called this a stupid pose. The actual truth was that during the first fortnight in October, Cristina could not read the verses because there was something wrong with her sight, and no one dared read them to her.

On 31 August she had written to Ernesta Bisi: 'Why did I not write to you? Because I am following a new treatment for my ills, suggested by Madame Récamier. This involves taking belladonna – but though I limit myself to small quantities, my eyes are suffering as I am very allergic to this drug. Later she wrote again: 'My eyes are useless to me. I am obliged to have everything read to me and to dictate all my letters . . .'

But the day finally came when she did read *Sur Une Morte*. De Musset had predicted that it would make her weep for days, and that she would flee from Paris, never to be seen there again. Neither of these things happened. Cristina made no comment and appeared unmoved. Meanwhile the poet had fallen ill with bronchitis. Caroline Jaubert had already told him she considered his verses a lapse of taste. On his sick bed he regretted having written them. When better, he wrote to his *marraine*: 'While I have lain as rigid as a rod under fourteen blankets, perspiring profusely and coughing loud enough to break the window panes, I brooded over my stupid verses and was truly sorry that I had ever thought of them . . . I swear that I do not love her any longer.' In this repentant mood he sent the Princess a note asking her forgiveness. Her reply he unfortunately destroyed, but one can speculate as to its contents from his reactions.

He wrote to Caroline Jaubert after receiving it:

'*Marraine*! Your godson has been humbled. Do you know what this poor fool has done? He wrote an impulsive, open-hearted letter of abject apology, and he was sent a reply. Oh, godmother, it was a reply that ought to be published, for it was boiling with pride and yet phrased with the most icy composure. It had the strength of two hundred horses or nearly. And do you know what this poor idiot did on receiving this immortal reply?

'He began by weeping for half an hour . . . Following this I found myself in such a flood of vexation that I swam in it. My room was truly an ocean of sorrow into which I dived again and again. Then after all this exercise I was in a monstrous rage – it is impossible to tell you against what, but I was very angry and it lasted for at least two hours. Thank God I did not smash anything.

'Then I began to feel tired and I started crying once more, but not very much – only to freshen myself up. Then I ate four eggs. I fried them in butter. Now I am feeling more tired than ever. I have suffered so much that I am exhausted, and that is why I am writing such nonsense. If you saw my face, you would die from laughing. My hair looks like a jungle; my left eye is starting out of its socket; my right eye (which is still running with tears) is half-closed and has several pouches beneath it; my nose is as red as a carrot; and my face is as long as a gingerbread mask that has been left out in the rain. Oh, Cupid, how you torment us!

'In future I will not correspond on any subject with Her Highness, not on any pretext whatever.'

But unfortunately for Alfred this was not the end of the matter. To make things worse, an Italian friend of Cristina's, Pier Sylvestro Leopardi, exiled for being involved with the *Carbonari*, challenged the poet to a duel, but so as not to involve her used some other pretext for doing so. The poet, rather than fight, sent his challenger a written apology for the mythical offence, which he need not have done as Cristina had in the meantime forbidden Leopardi to fight the duel.

But this was not the end of the matter. Soon after, Alfred encountered Prince Emilio at the theatre, and he confided to a friend that Cristina's husband had given him such hostile looks that, fearing he might be challenged to another duel which he could not avoid fighting, he hurriedly left and retired for a time into the country. Soon he was writing to Madame Jaubert: 'I've just come back from hunting and I can tell you that Horace was stupid when he said that sorrow accompanies the rider even on horseback. It disappears immediately one's mount breaks into a gallop. I write with a light heart, clear conscience, and hands that smell of the stable.'

Apart from her letter to de Musset, Cristina showed no sign of being affected by his attack. When an acquaintance dared to ask if she had read it, she replied: 'I should say the person he is writing about is Rachel.' Her visitor smiled and returned with malice; 'You must be right because I overheard her say to M. Buloz, the editor of the *Revue des Deux Mondes*: "So you have published those verses which M. de Musset dedicated to the Princess di Belgiojoso."'

The Princess and poet did not meet again for many years, but she soon forgave him for attacking her in print. In February 1849, after seeing his play, *Louison*, she wrote: 'I must let you know that in my opinion you have created a small masterpiece. Your *Louison* is splendid. It has grace, sincerity, delicacy and feeling. You have the thoughts and sentiments of a Shakespeare, and you express yourself like Marivaux. It is an unusual combination and the result is impressive. Perhaps you have forgotten that I exist. It does not matter; you have discovered a way of preserving your own existence in the memory of the most forgetful of persons. I thank you for the many moments of pleasure you have given me.'

CHAPTER 5

EXIT EMILIO

Cristina would have liked to have had her portrait painted by Eugène Delacroix. Caroline Jaubert in her *Souvenirs* wrote that though he admired the Italian's 'intelligent beauty' he had no desire to do this. 'The ample forms and the rich tints of Oriental women were what inspired him. Face to face with Cristina's marmorean pallor, her elongated body resembling that of a saint in a Gothic painting, her huge eyes with lids still as a statue's, he repeated: "Beautiful, very beautiful!" But he remained unmoved. "Only her smile," he said, "makes me feel she is a living woman."'

When the Princess invited Delacroix to dine with her at a country house she had rented at Port Marly, his natural reserve made him hesitate to accept, but she was so charmingly polite, leaving him to choose what day he would come, that he was obliged to accept. Towards six o'clock one evening, he entered her salon unannounced to find her arguing furiously with another guest, Nino Bixio, a man of letters and a politician.

After pausing to welcome the painter in a most friendly manner, she resumed the discussion which became increasingly heated. She maintained that her country was in every way superior to France, and refused to admit that there could be any exception to this rule. Bixio then retorted: 'But the French have the courage of their convictions. They won't ever disregard them to protect their pockets or not to offend their priests like the Italians do! That's why in this country they have long ago gained their liberty and are no longer living in a state of slavery as in Italy. The French are more frank and honest.'

To this Cristina replied: 'I cannot understand, Monsieur Bixio, how coming of Italian stock, you can make such a judgment!' He shrugged and with a laugh returned: 'I do not doubt that once roused Italians would fight hard for their freedom – but they would not do it in cold blood on principle.'

'On principle!' exclaimed the Princess in a passion. 'What do you mean by that? When would a Frenchman ever allow a principle to prevent him from eating his dinner!'

After this outburst, Caroline Jaubert wrote, a glacial silence prevailed. Then Delacroix rose quietly and went out into the garden through the open French windows. 'When dinner was ready, Cristina sent her servant, Pietro, to tell the absent guest. But after a few minutes, he came back and informed her that the gentleman had left. The rest of the explanation was in Milanese.'

No one enjoyed the meal that followed. 'More than anybody the Princess wished she had never spoken as she had. She was extremely upset at having offended a guest for she prided herself on observing her duties as a hostess. But it was not in her nature to admit she was wrong or express regret.'

Although Delacroix did not visit Cristina again, he never mentioned the incident or held it against her in any way. Mme. Jaubert states that soon after the ill-fated dinner party she met the painter at another salon where character reading through the study of handwriting was discussed. It was mentioned that both the Princess and George Sand had the same bold easily read way of forming their characters.

'Certainly there are intellectual similarities between the two ladies you have mentioned,' agreed the artist. 'Their foreheads are equally beautiful. But in the case of the Princess the lower half of the face is finer and more distinguished.' Then he added with a smile: 'And, damn it, who can resist the charm of her dimples?'

Elsewhere in her *Souvenirs* Caroline Jaubert wrote that in Cristina's estimation men fell into three categories: 'He loves me, he loved me, or he will love me.'

In 1838 a new Austrian Emperor was crowned in Milan, and he made an attempt to win over the *émigrés* by offering to pardon all who returned, and Prince Emilio di Belgiojoso, whose love of gaiety was stronger than his love of country, availed himself of the opportunity and was soon a frequent visitor to the salon of Prince Metternich in Milan.

Count Hübner, in *Une Année de ma vie* describes how one evening, with the composer, Rossini, at the piano, Don Emilio held them all enthralled with his singing. 'I have never heard a voice like yours!' enthused Princess Metternich. 'Then you will agree that it would have been a tragedy for all connoisseurs of music if your husband had had me shot!' jested the Prince. He had already taken pains to stress that though when in Paris he lived in his wife's house and frequented her salons, he had nothing to do with her plotting.

Meanwhile in France, Cristina was at the height of her social success. Constantly mentioned in the press, she was the most talked about woman in the capital. Celebrities crowded her receptions, and the public were now intensely interested in all she did. The American, Ticknor, wrote in his *Journal* that the person who attracted the most attention of the fifteen hundred guests present at the royal fêtes at the Tuileries was the Princess Belgiojoso.

On Emilio's return from Milan, his wife gave him the news that she was expecting their first child. This made him for a time more kindly towards her than he had ever been. The birth took place in Paris on 23 December 1838, of a daughter, Maria, who proved to be their only offspring.

The following year, Cristina spent from April till the autumn in England with her half-brother, Alberto, and her cousin, the Marchesa Litta Modignani. She rented Thickthorn House* in

* Ribton-Turner in his *Shakespeare's Land*, 1893, p. 107, referring to the road between Leamington and Kenilworth writes: 'The main road ... traverses Thickthorn Wood; it next passes on the right Thickthorn House, a modern Gothic mansion, built about 1830 on the site of a small farm house, and soon after reaches the suburb of Kenilworth termed Castle End'. Pevsner in his *Buildings of England: Warwickshire* has a reference on p. 326 under Kenilworth: 'Thickthorn Lodge, 1½ miles S.E., a castellated Tudor House of c. 1830. Elaborate Gate House.' Mr H. S. Tallamy, Librarian and Curator of Leamington Spa, informs me from local knowledge that Pevsner may have intended to describe Thickthorn House, and that the elaborate Gate House may refer to the lodge which was originally the lodge to Thickthorn House. Pigott's Warwickshire Directory for 1835 shows a Rev. John Wilson as residing at Thickthorn House. The next available Directory for 1841 contains no entry.

Warwickshire, and also visited Wales and the Isle of Wight, accompanied by her friend, Caroline Jaubert, who later was to write of this period of rest and quiet: 'Do you remember the hours we spent stretched out on the grass watching the clouds pass across the pale blue sky?'

In the October of the previous year, Prince Louis Napoleon had left Switzerland and his family home, Arenenberg, on the south shore of Lake Constance, where Prince Emilio had been a regular and welcome visitor on account of his voice which made leading composers like Rossini eager for him to sing their songs. The French Government had put pressure on the Swiss to expel the Bonaparte Pretender, and he had eventually departed to save them embarrassment. He found a refuge in England. It was fashionable to spend the winter in Leamington Spa, so he rented a house in its elegant Clarendon Square. Thickthorn House was only a few miles away and Cristina met him again at a banquet in the Spa.

This renewal of their friendship led to their attending a ball together, and then Louis Napoleon moved to London, where he took a year's lease of the Earl of Cardigan's mansion, 17 Carlton House Terrace. In the early autumn Cristina also came to the capital and once more they met at Lady Blessington's dinner parties in Gore House, Kensington. Louis took her to see the French plays that were performed every Monday at the St. James's Theatre, and also gave her a copy of his *Des Idées Napoléoniennes*, a defence of his uncle, which had just been published.

Whilst Cristina was in England, Emilio spent the time in Vienna. He wrote to d'Alton-Shée in May 1839:

'I arrived on 30 April after having spent several days in Venice, where the merchant who sells lotions for wounds gave me some excellent wine from Cyprus and introduced me to several pretty girls . . . I am very much enjoying my stay here. I have discovered a fine restaurant with French wines and many beautiful girls . . . I spend my time going from one wonderful party to another . . . I often go in the evening to Prince Metternich's place and sing. The most charming people throng there. . .

'Since coming here, necessity has forced me to chase wealthy society women, for I can't afford whores; and despite my great age (thirty-nine) I have had success. Nevertheless, they all want to be romantic and sentimental about it, which bores me. I much prefer our old regulars in Paris despite their drawbacks. It is so monotonous to be tied to one mistress, especially as I have been accustomed to keep three at the same time. One has followed me here, by the way. . . .'

Later, in another letter to the same friend dated 24 July, Emilio confides:

'I have here all possible amusements, swimming, good wine, good food, and a multitude of women. I am mostly in the company of blades from the embassies with similar tastes. I lead the same sort of life as I would in Paris just now. I often think of "J", for here it is easy to pick up very young and attractive girls as virginity is quite out of fashion. Regarding this, I have heard from Paris that Mlle. D. has sold hers for 60,000 francs! *Caramba!* . . .

'Please remind Mme. Merlin of the promise she made to send me some sherry as good as that which we drank so often at her place. She would be obliging me greatly if she would send me 200 bottles and as soon as possible, for I have promised Prince Metternich to let him have some . . . Now stop being lazy and do this at once, and keep reminding "La Merlina" till you are sure the wine is on its way, for she is very dilatory . . .

'Send me news of Paris, of the Jockey Club, of our friends, and particularly of Caccia, Merlina, Candia, Falcon of the Opera, of our gambling cronies – are they still solvent or are they broke?

'When I return, I'll tell you all about the meanness, pettiness, narrowmindedness and beastliness of my wife, for they deserve to be known. Nevertheless you are right in advising me not to break entirely with her on account of what people might say and the mud it might stir up, but when you know everything you will see that it is difficult for an aristocrat like myself to retain any respect for a woman who has conducted herself as she has. It's a pity I can't divorce her so as to be done with her. All I should have to do would be to become a Protestant.'

Like so many husbands of his time Prince Emilio believed that a gay life was for men only, that wives should be patient Griseldas, and that it was an affront to male *amour-propre* for wives even to pretend to have lovers, too.

In the late autumn Cristina travelled back from England to Paris, bringing with her as a nursery governess for Maria a Mrs. Parker, who was to remain with her for many years to come. Despite Emilio's neglect and dissolute life, she allowed him to continue living in the separate apartment in her house. When he was ill, he wanted no one near him save her. But when he was well, he was indifferent. However, in public life they were considered united, and until the end of 1842 all invitations for parties, concerts and balls were sent out in their joint names.

It was in his wife's salon that the Prince was to meet once more his old love, the Countess Guiccioli. But they were no longer interested in each other. She had married the old and immensely rich Marquis de Boissy, who was extremely proud of his wife's connections with Byron and even presented her to King Louis-Philippe as: 'The Marquise de Boissy, my wife, once for many years the mistress of Lord Byron.'

Both the de Boissys came to Cristina's salons, as did Lady Blessington, who, when the former Countess was absent, would entertain the company with her malicious recollections of the Byron-Guiccioli *ménage* in Genoa in the early twenties.

During 1840 and 1841 Emilio spent most of his time in Milan supervising the rebuilding of the historic Villa Pliniana on the Lake of Como. This had once been the home of the Roman philosopher Pliny, and was beautifully situated in a bay, formed by rocky promontories, covered with woods, at the base of which a cascade precipitated itself into the lake. The intermittent fountain mentioned in Pliny's Thirtieth Epistle, Book IV, flowed under three rude arches in the solid rock, supported on small pillars, and the gradations of its ebbing and flowing, which occurred once in three hours, were marked by lines.

'I flatter myself,' the Prince wrote to d'Alton-Shée on 6 January 1841, 'that I shall soon have a very fine and comfortable country house where we can swim and dive, enjoy short liaisons, and spend a few months each year recovering from the fatigues of the

'*Grrrand Monde*', with cigars in our mouths, our waistcoats un-
buttoned, singing, drinking, and sleeping like true philosophers.'

Whilst awaiting the completion of the work the Prince returned
to Paris, where he fell in love with the beautiful young wife of the
Duc de Plaisance. She was the daughter of one of Napoleon's
major-generals. It was not long before kind friends told Cristina
about it. The young Duchess tried hard to quarrel with her when
they met socially, but the Princess refused to be drawn into an
altercation until one day when they were seated opposite each
other at a dinner party.[1]

In the course of conversation Mme. Merlin's salon was discussed.
'There all that one admires most in cultured society is represented,'
Cristina remarked, 'the stage and music by Malibran and Rossini,
letters by Villemain, poetry by Alfred de Musset.'

'And beauty by Mlle. de Sainte Aldegonde, and wit by Mme.
de Balli,' the young Duchess interposed swiftly lest someone
should bestow those honours on the Princess.

'And you, Madame, what do you represent?' the Princess
asked with a wry smile.

The Duchess reddened at this and then replied ingenuously:
'*Mon dieu*, I don't know – virtue perhaps.'

'So you wear a mask?' retorted Cristina.

On 22 May 1843, Alfred de Musset wrote to his brother Paul,
who was travelling in Italy: 'I don't know whether you have heard
that Prince Emilio has eloped with the Duchesse de Plaisance.
They have been going around together for two years now to all
Paris's knowledge. The Duchesse it seems, quarrelled with her
husband. She arrived at the Prince's apartment with only a
handkerchief for luggage, and said to him: "Let's be off." And
though he was due to sing that night in a concert, he obeyed her
and they are reported to be making for Italy.'

The couple took up residence in the Villa Pliniana and remained
there for eight years, not once in all that time setting foot outside
the grounds. Then the Duchess gave way to pressure from her
relatives and left the Prince, but no further than a villa on the other
side of the lake. Go back to France she would not. This time
Emilio's heart did not mend. He informed d'Alton-Shée in a

letter dated the 27 June 1852, that his hair had turned almost white with the shock.

Commenting on the desertion, Alfred de Musset told Caroline Jaubert: 'The Prince has only himself to blame. When one has his temperament, one should not remain tied to the same woman for so many years. It is a case of the devil turning into a hermit.' This judgment proved correct, for from now on Emilio led an aimless, drifting existence until he died in the Palazzo di Belgiojoso, Milan in February 1858.

At the time of the elopment it was the family of the shameless Duchess which displayed for the world's benefit their sorrowing disapproval and went into full mourning. Cristina, older and more controlled, did not parade her hurt pride but maintained a digni-fied silence. She sold her house in the Rue d'Anjou to an American Mrs. Corbin, to try and rid herself of all thoughts of Emilio and bought another at 36 Rue de Courcelles, surrounded by trees and with a large garden, cut off from the rest of the world by a majestic wrought-iron gate. On the lawn grazed white goats that little Maria would chase. The life of the fashionable society hostess no longer appealed to her mother, and now seemed empty and futile.

Cristina had embarked on such a career with one purpose, to gain support for the Italian cause. But her mother's death and the final break up of her marriage made her decide to retire for a while from the social scene and try to puzzle out for herself the answers to the riddles of human existence.

There had been a revival of interest in religion in the 1830s largely owing to the influence of the Liberal element among the French clergy, led by Lacordaire, Lamennais, and the Abbé Coeur. The latter who had an exuberant nature and the en-thusiasm of an evangelist was famed for his sermons. Cavour, an agnostic, once wrote of him: 'The Abbé's ideas appealed to my intelligence and moved my heart. The day when they are sin-cerely and universally adopted by the Church I shall probably become a devout Catholic.' This was the Count's reaction after listening to Coeur lecturing at the Sorbonne.

Cristina, too, went to listen to him and was impressed. As a result they became very intimate. Soon scandalmongers were seeing more than met the eye in the Princess's new friendship. Marie d'Agoult immediately wrote to Liszt that Cristina had found herself 'a young, handsome, tonsured admirer'. Following her advice, the Abbé was being coached in secret by an actor from the Comédie Française in the art of gesture so as to make his sermons more dramatic. Marie adds: 'A priest is just what is missing to add to her collection of stonemasons, patriots and literary figures.' It is interesting to note that someone said of Marie herself about this time that she hid twenty feet of lava beneath six feet of snow.

Some of the Abbé's letters to the Princess are preserved in the family archives. In one he thanks her profusely for suggesting a subject for one of his sermons. In all he reveals himself to have fallen completely under her spell. For example, here is an extract from one dated 7 October 1838: 'Your letter filled me with admiration. More than ever I respect you, more than ever I am certain that you have a truly saintly nature. Why do you say that I know very little about you? I find an unusual grandeur in your outlook on life. You are both generous and high-minded. I have the satisfaction of not having made a single mistake about your character. I have studied you with the care one devotes to rare and precious things, with the zeal I would spend on trying to solve a divine mystery. Yes, Princess, you are a divine mystery. . . .'

From 1835 onwards Cristina had begun an intensive study of the history of the early church. Then in 1842, the year Emilio finally left her, her first literary work appeared. Everybody was astonished that this was not the romantic novel they might have expected but a theological work entitled *Un essai sur la formation du dogme catholique*. It was in two volumes with the promise of two further ones to come.

When the Princess's friends paged through the tomes, they became increasingly puzzled to find them packed with erudition. The general opinion was that it all seemed more like the work of a Benedictine monk than that of a woman of the world. Someone quipped that she was now qualified to become an abbess in a community of monks.

Collecting material for this monumental *Essai* had meant borrowing books from many sources. Among her papers is a note dated 27 June 1837, from the librarian of the *Bibliothèque Royale* of Paris which reads: 'I beg to remind you that on 7 November 1835, you borrowed two volumes of the History of the Church by Sozomen translated by Cousin. Will you please return them if no longer required.'

Sainte-Beuve, the critic, found the work 'serious, catholic in intent, written in a very simple and vigorous style; in fact, a very precious curiosity.'

But the *Revue des Deux Mondes* savagely attacked this attempt by a mere woman to enter the male preserve of philosophy. 'It consists of a series of biographies, of quotations from the writings of the Fathers of the Church and histories of early Christian times, with interpolated comments on the civil laws of the Teutons and the Lombards. So, instead of a book on the ideas behind the Christian religion, we have but an account of external events. Metaphysics and theology should have formed the foundations of this book. It is instead predominantly a collection of biographies. Christian dogma is not analysed in depth ... We hardly expect that an ecumenical council will be called to sit in judgment on Madame de Belgiojoso's conclusions, yet we doubt whether devout Catholics will be edified by her book. One finds neither the ardour of faith nor the questioning of intellect. Believers may be scandalised, but philosophers will not be satisfied. All the same, the book has merits. It is remarkable that a woman should have taken the trouble to read so many historical records. The style is elegant, and at times commendably precise.'

The critic objected very strongly to what he calls her superficial and prejudiced assessment of St. Augustine's character. She had written: 'St. Augustine is more curious than profound, more venerable than wise, more argumentative than convinced, more tireless than strong.'

The Princess's next literary work met with greater success, and it soon became generally accepted that she had genuine literary talent. This was the *Essai sur Vico,* a brilliantly lucid and aptly phrased assessment and translation of the Neapolitan historian and sociologist's work, *La Scienza Nuova*.

At this time some Parisian *bas bleus* had formed the idea of founding an Institute modelled on the Académie Française, but for women only. Both George Sand and Madame de Girardin wanted to become its president, and there ensued a furious struggle between their rival supporters who were equally divided. A compromise was reached by electing the Princess, in spite of the fact that she was a foreigner.

Cristina was actually very friendly with George Sand, but Madame de Girardin, on the other hand, was extremely angry at not being elected, and proceeded to take her revenge by ridiculing the Academy of Women in her book, *Le Vicomte de Launay*.

Meetings of the Academy were held in the Athenaeum in the Rue de Valois, but once the excitement of selecting a president had evaporated, the members of the Academy took less and less interest in its proceedings, until meetings were so thinly attended that the venture died an early death.

All the time Cristina was working in whatever way she could for the unification of Italy, and when another exile, Count Cesare Balbo, published his book in 1844 entitled *Le Speranzà d'Italia,* she was one of the first to appreciate the merits of its theme that before a successful revolution could take place, the people of the divided Italian states must be politically educated and made aware of the advantages of a united country. This appealed to her and suggested a way of bringing purpose into her existence. She decided to do all she could to achieve such an end, so she founded a paper, the *Gazzetta Italiana*, which was printed in Paris. In its columns she included not only reliable on-the-spot news from all the various Italian states, but also constructive, authoritative articles on social and economic problems. She aimed at presenting a picture of Italy as a whole, favouring no state or class, and trying to make the people of the peninsula interested in and willing to help one another. She kept urging landowners to care more for their peasants and employers for their workers. She wrote: 'Society as it is organised today is a striking protest against the justice of God, a protest, which it is urgent to end.'

Cristina now gave up her project of writing two further volumes on Catholic dogma. To her relief when she wrote to the Abbé Coeur telling him of her decision, he approved and replied: 'People are apt to resent perfection in others and to try to drag them down to their own level, so ignore all criticism of what you are doing. Do just what you feel is right. Be yourself. Only automatons keep in the same groove. I am quite willing for work on the "Dogma" to be suspended if you are no longer inspired by the project. As for your new interest in social reform, I can understand the attraction of devoting one's life to the public good, but you must be prepared for disappointments and a long, hard struggle.'

The Abbé was soon proved right in his warning for it became difficult to sell the *Gazzetta Italiana* in Italy, where sales were prohibited in Florence, Rome, Milan, and even Turin, on the grounds that what it advocated might lead to discontent and even to Communism. However, thanks to her friend, François Mignet, copies were smuggled into Italy by a French diplomatic courier. Then there was a clash of personalities between the brilliant but egotistical journalists contributing to it, and soon the Princess was left running the *Gazzetta* almost single-handed.[2] It was also above the heads of the average reader, who did not want to be educated but entertained. It proved impossible to sell enough copies to make it pay its way, so Cristina went to Milan in search of additional finance and invited the people there to buy shares in the venture. The Austrian Governor, Count Spaur, made no attempt to stop her, believing that if he did it would give her welcome publicity. That he was right in his psychology is proved by the fact that she succeeded in selling only thirty-eight shares.

Undismayed, she decided to put into being on her own estates what she recommended in the *Gazzetta*. So she left Milan and went to live at Locate, some twenty miles outside the city, and devoted herself entirely to improving the living conditions of those dependent on her.

What had begun as an impulsive gesture became almost a crusade with her when she entered the hovels of these near-serfs, and was appalled by what she saw. It became her mission not only

FRANZ LISZT IN 1837
by Henri Lehmann

DRAWING OF ALFRED DE MUSSET
by Princess Cristina

to better the lot of her peasants but also to persuade other Lombard landowners to do the same. Later she wrote them all a letter to this effect, suggesting that they should share their profits with the peasants.

She told them how she had given up the use of the largest drawing-room on the ground floor of her country house, as it was a sin against humanity for one solitary woman to own such a place when surrounded by so much squalor and human misery. This she had fitted out as a recreation centre holding up to three hundred peasants, where they could find rest, distraction and warmth any time they wished between daybreak and midnight. She had also given up to them her dining-room, where they were provided with bowls of soup at a nominal charge and which the needy could obtain gratis.

A workroom was set up where women were taught how to make gloves, and the money received from their sale was shared out amongst them. Meanwhile, in adjacent rooms and buildings their children were educated by teachers engaged by the Princess. The older ones were taught trades, according to their aptitudes, by qualified instructors.

She devoted several years to this work, spending from November until April in Locate and the rest of the time in Paris with her old friend, Augustin Thierry, the historian, who, now completely blind, was broken-hearted over the loss of his wife in June 1844. When dying, Julie Thierry, who had been very friendly with Cristina, asked her to look after Augustin. The Princess promised to do so, and had him installed in a comfortable well-furnished building in the garden of 36 Rue de Courcelles,[3] where attended by a valet and a secretary, the sightless historian tried to forget his sorrow through writing.

Cristina's regular letters to him when she was back at Locate give vivid pictures of her life there. For instance, she describes how on reaching Pavia at the end of November 1844, she found eight carriages full of her tenant farmers and employees waiting to accompany her home. On the way the peasants came out on their doorsteps, lamps in hand, to shout a welcome. Nearer Locate the villages were empty as everybody had gone there.

'I saw from afar a great brightness in the sky which I thought was the moon rising – it was Locate ablaze with light to welcome me.' On the outskirts the carriages had to proceed at a walking pace so as not to crush the people crowding the roadway. A kind of triumphal arch had been erected, and as she passed beneath it a military band appeared and accompanied her with music to her front door.

There she found all the children of the schools she had started the previous year, lined up in rows singing and reciting verses in her honour. This was followed by a firework display. Then they would not let her rest until she had walked round the village to admire the fairy lights that had been hung, so that there was not a dark corner anywhere.

'All the while the band followed me playing military marches. Nearly ten thousand people had assembled in my little village, of which the population is barely a fifth of that number. They crowded into my garden and my house, and there was no drunkenness, disorder or quarrels of any kind. That above all made me proud. The boys thanked me for educating them, and when they said that what I had sown would one day bear fine fruit, I felt they were sincere and not just making pretty speeches.

'Locate has changed. The children are clean and the young people polite. Now I am going to inspect all my schools. Then I shall busy myself with new plans, which perhaps the Lord will bless as He has my others.

'This is a confidential letter, my dear Thierry. I should not like people to suspect me of being vainglorious over these demonstrations. Instead I find cause for humility. I tell myself that among all those who welcomed me there can only be some whom I have really helped. If the gratitude of a few can spread to others, what possibilities does not that open out? I feel I have done only a millionth part of what I ought to do. I am responsible for all those souls who have shown their trust in me with so much feeling. God grant that I keep faithful to my intention of never ceasing to do all I can to better the lives of the people on my estates.'

That winter was the worst so far of the century in Locate. No one, wrote Cristina to Thierry, could remember so much snow.

The roads she described as being practically impassable, but despite this she went round the village planning new houses to replace the old.

'Sound, warm dwellings for all, a community centre with a hall for social functions, and a kitchen where food can be prepared and taken to the sick and the elderly are my present plans. I need all my powers of persuasion to make some of these poor people move from their hovels into houses, where the windows are paned with glass and which they must keep clean. There are some peasants who have moved away rather than sleep in a room with a ceiling, and others who have stripped their new houses of all the woodwork to sell or burn. But such setbacks don't dishearten me.

'These poor people regard me as a well-intentioned eccentric whom they cannot elude. They know that my estates here have belonged to my family since all eternity. I am a woman on my own, not old. I have visited foreign parts. I have seen much of the world and its inhabitants. I don't fear anybody or anything. I speak their language. I know all their names. I know their business better than they do themselves. Sometimes I cure their children and their wives when ill. They have discovered that once I decide on some form of action, nothing stops me. She must use witch-craft, some say behind my back.

'And when I ask these good people to do something which seems to them peculiar, they look at me with a smile and say: "We'll do what you wish, as we know you only want it for our own good."'

On 23 December 1844, she wrote to Thierry that the sun was shining, which was appropriate as it was her daughter's sixth birthday. Now she was preparing to write a history of Lombardy, and was seeking someone to help her with the research. Then on 7 January she was able to inform him that she had engaged as her assistant, 'a young man as studious as any professor and with a remarkable knowledge of charters, statutes, ancient manuscripts, etc. It is rare to find someone so young with such enthusiasm for research into the past ...

'There is only one disadvantage as far as I am concerned. He has a very handsome face. Still, I am approaching an age when such drawbacks should not affect me. A few more years and no one will suspect me any longer of gazing with pleasure at a good-looking man. But the contrary is true. The sight of the beautiful will always appeal to me, even if I reach a hundred. So things have turned out well, especially as my scholarly young man is as honest and unaffected as he is learned. Everybody congratulates me on having made such a find.'

Stelzi also proved useful in another way. As he was unknown, he did not attract the attention of the police when he travelled to and from Genoa, Florence, Rome, Bologna and Venice, collecting material for the Princess's projected history of Lombardy, and at the same time secretly arranging for the distribution of the *Gazzetta Italiana* after it had been smuggled in from France.

Whilst Gaetano Stelzi was busy with all this, Cristina occupied herself with the welfare of the peasantry. In view of her past, the Austrian police in Milan regarded her activities with suspicion, but owing to her popularity, Count Spaur decided not to take any action against her.

She wrote to Thierry describing the opening of the heated public rest-room two days previously, and how she had had to turn away many for lack of space. She would build a larger one next year. She believed they were more grateful for the rest-room than for the schools.

'My people have taken a great step forward. Now that they have themselves frequented my house and have seen how the dwellings of people richer than themselves are furnished, they are beginning to acquire a taste for the beautiful, the comfortable and the convenient.

'You can have no idea of the life I am leading here and the company that I have around me. Farmers, craftsmen, workmen, peasants are freely admitted to my home. Nothing is more democratic. And yet they are more courteous and respectful to me than those who thronged my salon in Paris.'

She had also started up four more classes, one for singing. 'All those in charge of schools and workshops meet me in the evenings to discuss their plans. Maria makes use of their company to organise games, in which I sometimes take part. Then when she has gone to bed, I smoke my narghile and go back in the library, where I work on my book for an hour or two.'

She intended completely to rebuild her village and give everybody a new house. 'The cleansing of the Augean stables was one of the labours of Hercules, and I have several hundred stables to cleanse.'

Accompanied by Gaetano Stelzi, Cristina left Locate on 3 April 1845, for her yearly visit to Paris, which she reached on the 1 May. Thierry had obtained permission for her assistant to inspect all documents bearing on the history of Lombardy that were in the French Royal Archives. She had bought land in the Rue du Montparnasse where were being built two houses side by side, destined for the use of the blind historian and herself. He was already interested in the furnishing of his future home. She encouraged this, discussing where his furniture would go, visiting shops and bringing back samples of curtain material for him to feel whilst she described their pattern and colour. She read aloud to him, took him for carriage drives and held parties, to which she was careful to invite people with whom he would enjoy conversing.

As autumn neared, she prepared to return to Locate. When she saw how miserable Thierry became at the prospect of their being separated, she suggested that he might accompany her, but his health prevented his accepting.

On 16 November she left Paris, pausing *en route* to visit Louis Napoleon who was imprisoned in the fortress of Ham, following his unsuccessful attempt to overthrow Louis-Philippe. It upset her to see the lively and gay young man she had known twenty years previously in Rome looking so ill and listless. Describing her reunion with him on the 18 November, she wrote in her *Souvenirs dans l'exil*:

'On entering the courtyard, I noticed a little bent man standing in a doorway watching me. Regulations did not permit him to move any nearer. I did not at first recognise M. Louis Bonaparte. When I reached him, he took my hand and kissed it, then led me into his room where we had a long talk. He was riddled with rheumatism. The room was small, miserably furnished, and its walls were di coloured through dampness.

'The first thing I said to him was: "How can you stay here quietly without trying to escape?" He replied that it would have been very easy for him to have done this a hundred times. All the soldiers and N.C.O.s in the garrison had suggested it to him, but he preferred to remain on French soil than be in perpetual exile which flight would bring about. Here, at least, he was in France – breathed French air – and stood on French soil.

'"May I point out that a prison is nobody's fatherland?" I interrupted. 'How can you love a country you left a few days after you were born and which you have only seen through the barred windows of a prison?"

'He then abandoned his patriotic pose and pointed out the obligations he owed to his companions in misfortune. It would be cowardly to run away whilst they were still imprisoned for serving his cause. . . . He assured me that Italy was his second fatherland. His brother had already died fighting for it. "If I ever get back what should be mine, what wrongs I shall then put right!" he told me. Here he fell into a deep reverie as if he was trying to make up his mind how he would start. I should have liked to know of what wrongs he was speaking and what methods he proposed to employ to redress them. I almost asked but curbed my curiosity not wishing to upset him.'

She left him and continued on her way to Locate where blue skies and sunshine awaited her though it was the end of November. The schools and the community centre were thriving and many new houses had been built in her absence. Then three weeks later, bad news came from Paris. She had left the *Gazzetta* in charge of a man named Falconi, together with a sum of money sufficient to keep it going for a while. But Falconi spent what she had given him to settle his own debts, and the paper ceased publication.

Her disappointment over this, together with the wear and tear from the journey and the never ending flood of visitors who kept calling since her return, caused her to become seriously ill. In a letter dated 28 December to Augustin Thierry she wrote that she had been cured by an excellent doctor named Maspero. From this time onwards he became Cristina's personal physician and remained with her until she went to Syria. She added details about the progress Maria was making with her education, that she could translate into four languages, and had her own spirited little horse.

Now the future of Cristina's scholars was concerning her. When they left school, nearly all became weavers. She felt other careers should be open to them. She thought of starting up a printing works, where she could have any future journals printed at much less cost than elsewhere. She discussed the matter with people in the trade and they became very interested. Two editors from Milan visited her and promised to let her print their papers if she went ahead with the project.

It seems that a small printing works was started up. This enabled the Princess to launch a new journal called *Ausonio*, after the Latin poet. It was a high quality periodical, modelled on the *Revue des Deux Mondes*, and first appeared in March 1846.

Cristina and Gaetano now undertook the management, composition, publication and administration of the *Ausonio* entirely on their own. She had already discovered from his work on the *Gazzetta* how capable he was. Tireless and conscientious, he became indispensable to her. He alone was worth a whole staff, supervising the typography, selecting the print, correcting the proofs, editing copy, attending to the correspondence.

Gaetano was unfortunately consumptive, which roused her compassion. She began to worry increasingly about him. Once when he was travelling to Florence, she wrote: 'Your letter was a great relief to me when I learnt that wretched night spent in the diligence, which upset me so much, did you no harm. Remember, dear friend, that you are necessary to me, and that your health always preoccupies me.'

CHAPTER 6

ITALY IN FERMENT

Two months after the birth of Cristina's new journal in 1846 Pius IX was elected pope. As a cardinal he had shown himself to have Liberal leanings, and the democrats of Italy waited hopefully to see how he would act. But although he swiftly embarked on a policy of sweeping reforms, the more he granted the more the populace wanted, and soon they were taking the initiative. Although he did not officially authorise freedom of the press, a rapidly increasing number of political papers started being published. It all gave a tremendous impetus to the Liberal movement throughout Italy.

There was only one possible candidate for the throne of a united country and that was Charles Albert, ruler of Piedmont. In the very month, April 1831, when Cristina had first arrived in Paris its autocratic King had died, to be succeeded by the tall, romantically good-looking Charles Albert, who ten years earlier had become the heir presumptive following the death of the three nearest to the throne. His mother had been a revolutionary Princess from Saxony who dressed as a Jacobin and had him educated in Geneva where a professor tried to inculcate him with the ideas of Jean-Jacques Rousseau.

In 1821, at Metternich's instigation, King Charles Felix persuaded his new heir to sign a secret document promising to keep unchanged the kind of government he found in Piedmont at his accession. Much of his subsequent behaviour can be explained by this.

Although his 'Young Italy' party had been formed with a republic as its goal, Mazzini was sufficiently impressed by the Liberal past of the new ruler as to send him an open letter inviting him to become the leader of the Nationalists, and to declare war on Austria and the petty foreign potentates who ruled over so much of Italy.

But Charles Albert was not so foolhardy as to oblige Mazzini. He had suffered too much for his rebellious youth, and instead of tempering his character, this had made him evasive and equivocal. Desirous of greatness in a vacillating sort of way, he lacked the determination and authority to be the creator of a new nation. He lived, he once said, in daily danger of being murdered, either by the dagger of the extreme left or by the poisoned chocolate of the extreme right. Consequently he followed an indeterminate policy, so that he came to be called King Wobbler.

Meanwhile Count Camillo di Cavour was putting into being in Piedmont some of the social improvements Cristina had suggested in the columns of her papers. Originally an officer in the engineers he had resigned his commission so as to devote all his time to agriculture. He turned his estates at Leri into a model farm where he introduced new methods and never tired of experiment in rotation of crops, sub-soil drainage, and livestock breeding. He replaced men with machinery for polishing rice and made sugar from beet.

When in 1845 the prominent Liberal Massimo d'Azeglio returned to Turin after visiting the chief Liberals in the rest of Italy, he was invited to see Charles Albert in his palace. After listening to what the other had to tell him, the King declared, looking him full in the eyes: 'The time is not yet come, but you can inform those gentlemen that if the occasion presents itself, my life, the lives of my sons, my sword, my treasury, my army, shall all be spent for the Italian cause.'

The following year an opportunity arose for the King to show practical proof of his apparent change of heart. The Canton of Tessin, which had bought salt from Austrian-ruled Venice, was allowed by the King in 1843 to import it through Piedmont from Marseilles or Geneva without incurring any duty. This meant that Austria suffered a loss of revenue, so Metternich sent a strongly-worded protest to Charles Albert, claiming that his action was contrary to the terms of treaties between both countries. But as the King surprisingly refused to be intimidated, the Austrians in reprisal doubled the duties on wines entering their territories from Piedmont. Even then Charles Albert was not cowed, and insisted that what he had done did not break any agreement. It was Austria which had committed a hostile act by increasing the wine duty.

This brave defiance of the greater power by their king was applauded by the people of Turin. When a timid Minister, during a Council of State, suggested that it was dangerous to make an enemy of Austria, Charles Albert answered: 'If Piedmont loses Austria, she will gain Italy, and then Italy will be able to govern herself.'

But the King's mood of defiance did not last very long. It was his custom every Thursday morning at ten o'clock to show himself to his people by appearing on the balcony of his palace. A huge demonstration by the Liberals was planned for one such Thursday. When the King heard that they intended to shout for war with Austria, the cautious side of his character won the day and he did not come out onto the balcony.

In September 1846, a scientific congress was held in Genoa. A hundred years previously the rebellion that had driven the Austrians from the city had taken place. Politics soon replaced science as the main subject under discussion, and on the actual anniversary itself the crowds celebrating everywhere shouted anti-Austrian slogans.

Cristina felt that the time was approaching when Italians might once again attempt to rid themselves of foreign domination. Displaying remarkable political foresight, she also judged that Louis-Philippe's days as King in France were numbered, and that a revolution was imminent which must lead to his being succeeded by the Bonaparte leader who had once been a member of the *Carbonari* and had taken their oath never to rest until Italy was united.

In a war of independence, victory would be more certain if the insurrectionists had the support of a major power against Austria. Louis Napoleon had corresponded with Cristina following her visit to him in the fortress of Ham. In a letter dated 9 March 1846, he had written: 'Whatever some men might say it needs courage to remain six years between four walls. If there were here eyes like yours to warm this icy atmosphere, it might be more tolerable.' On 26 May 1846, the Bonaparte pretender decided that events in France were moving in his favour and that he would be best placed to take advantage of them if he were free. So he escaped and went to England.

Believing that he would soon be in power in France, the Princess made plans to visit him and wrote telling of her intention. He replied on 20 June from the Brunswick Hotel, Jermyn Street: 'I thank you for the note you have sent me. Believe me that free or captive I regard your friendship as always dear to me. . . . As soon as you arrive here, let me know, for in London it is difficult to trace a person when one does not know where they are staying. . . . It will make me truly happy to see you again. . . . Adieu, Madame, and receive the assurance of my sentiments of respectful and tender friendship.'

Cristina travelled to England attended by Doctor Maspero, and had a long and emotional interview with the Prince. Not only Italy but France, too, was discussed. The nephew of the great Napoleon realised that her long stay in Paris and intimacy with prominent personalities in all political camps gave her assessment of the French political climate authority and value. He liked Cristina and was stirred by her enthusiasm. When the time came for her to leave, he took her hand and promised: 'When I am in power in France, then I will help Italy.'

In mid-October 1846, she was reunited with Augustin Thierry, who incidentally had given her a letter of introduction to Disraeli, who had seen her in London, but the results are unrecorded. Very soon she returned to Locate, where she fell ill again with a form of typhoid which lasted for nearly three weeks. After that time she recovered with a rapidity that surprised everybody. She attributed this to the medical skill of Maspero and Gaetano Stelzi's attentions. The latter was ill himself and his coughing alarmed her. Once she had recovered she insisted on sending him for the rest of the winter to the warmer climate of southern Italy. She

93

herself went to Venice for a month, where her health appeared to benefit from the change.

The new houses in the Rue du Montparnasse were now completed, so in the spring she and Thierry moved into their adjacent residences. She once more started holding a salon, which was soon crowded with Italian exiles. There all manner of schemes were discussed for the future of Italy.

When autumn came she decided she ought to take a more militant part in the liberation movement. She considered that she had done all she possibly could for Augustin. He was happy in the fine house she had had built for him and immersed in the writing of history. For her the moment had come to try and make history, so she set out on a tour of Italy, with the intention of using her charms to excite people everywhere to rebellion.

Things were rapidly reaching flash point. In September inflammatory speeches were made during an agrarian congress at Casale in Piedemont. Before it ended Count di Castagneto, an intimate friend of Charles Albert, delighted the astonished delegates by reading a letter from the King that had just reached him. 'If ever God allows us to proclaim a War of Independence, it is I alone who will take command of the army . . . It will be a blessed day when we can raise the cry of national independence.'

In Genoa the populace clamoured for the King to order mobilisation. October 2 was his birthday, and the evening before crowds demonstrated by torchlight, cheering him. Speeches were made, calling on him to celebrate the occasion by following the Pope's lead and allowing his subjects similar rights and liberties. Then, to the shocked stupefaction of the multitude, *carabinieri* suddenly arrived and arrested the speakers.

What had prompted the King to behave in this way, the disheartened reform-seekers asked one another. Was he after all a double-dealer? Did that account for his having a pro-Austrian Foreign Minister and a pro-Liberal War Minister?

The explanation, that Charles Albert was incapable of making up his own mind and could be swayed by the adviser with the most glib tongue, was accepted as the most likely one, when an astute diplomat, Lord Minto, came to Turin on a secret mission

94

from the English Government and persuaded him to dismiss his reactionary Ministers. This was followed on 30 October by the announcement of free elections and improvements in the administration of justice.

When in the middle of November Cristina reached Genoa, she found the population in a state of great jubilation at the prospect of at last enjoying some measure of democracy. Their happiness spread to her, and perhaps that was why the illness which had struck her down each winter in Locate did not recur. Not for years had she felt so well.

Next she visited Florence, which was a centre of all shades of Italian revolutionary opinion. There were the moderates who merely planned a Confederation of Italian States, retaining their old rulers and hoping they would become more democratic in time, whilst the radicals under Mazzini on the other hand wanted to replace the old order by an Italian republic.

In Florence Cristina, Maria and Stelzi all enjoyed good health. The climate was such, she wrote to Thierry, as to 'even bring the very stones to life.' She had met and spoken to people on both sides and had reached the conclusion that the radical party was the better. 'If the moderates were to have their way, there is no future for Italy. It will remain broken up in feeble factions.' They were out of touch with the new ideas that were abroad in the world.

She arrived in Rome at Christmas to find herself receiving a welcome such as might be accorded some popular visiting royalty. But her pride and pleasure at this was clouded by Gaetano Stelzi's falling ill again.

In Vienna Metternich blamed the new Pope for what was happening in the peninsula. Repeated representations were made by the Austrian Ambassador to the Holy See, pointing out to the Pontiff the perils of his policy of reform, but Pius took no heed. Under the terms of a treaty of 1815 Austrians had garrisoned the citadel of Ferrara in the Papal States. In August 1847, as an expression of Austrian disapproval, these soldiers, fully armed, occupied the whole town.

This roused the populace to fury. Men seized arms and banded themselves together as civic guards. University students rioted. The Pope with difficulty tried to quieten the agitators.

Rome was still in a ferment when Cristina reached it. On 30 December she wrote to Thierry:

'My reception everywhere has resembled that given to Daniel O'Connell when touring Ireland. In every town I have found the civic fathers waiting to welcome me. Nothing has been spared to make my visits memorable. In Florence I was asked to address a public meeting that had been arranged in my honour. I was astonished to be greeted with such a storm of cheering that I had to put my hands to my ears. I was led to a seat high up, all on its own and overhung with tricoloured flags. Speeches were made, to which I had to reply. What an ordeal – one woman on her own and six hundred men listening intently to every word I uttered. One's own voice in such circumstances sounds the most important in the world. Here in Rome there is rivalry between the various parties as to which one will entertain me first. The Radicals have informed me that a mass torchlight procession of their supporters, headed by their leaders, will march past my window one evening. The Moderates, who represent the middle classes, are holding a banquet in my honour next Sunday. There will be many speeches and I fear I will be expected to reply.

'Le Cercle Romain, which has not admitted any woman till now, has sent two of its members to call on me with an invitation to become the first woman to enter their precincts. The papers are full of articles praising me, and all Rome is knocking at my door. I must admit that this gives great satisfaction to someone like me who loves her country and who has so often been the object of mean and stupid slanders. I tell myself today what I have always believed – that in an age of publicity like ours the truth in the end always emerges triumphant.

'I have borne all this travelling very well, but I have just had an attack of neuralgia, which is not surprising. Never has a woman found herself in a similar position to mine; and the emotions which I feel when facing the public are enough to frighten anybody. What is the emotion of an actress compared with mine? Mlle Rachel assumes for her audience the character of Camille or of

Phèdre, but in my case it is my own personality that I display before them.

'I have not the time to write to you in detail about the political climate here. I shall do that some other time and will limit myself today to saying that things are not going smoothly. The animosity between the various parties is intense, and it seems to me that most of them are either cowards or madmen. I have come across only one or two men with any intelligence although I have met quite a number.'

One detects in all this a certain vanity. The adulation of the masses undoubtedly delighted Cristina. She enjoyed being in the limelight. She always received a gratifying ovation when she told her audiences that the Italians of that day must not forget that their ancestors were Romans. This was proved by the way the people had behaved at Brescia, she claimed. There the Austrian military commander had shouted contemptuously in a café: 'In Vienna a man's head is worth five florins. In Milan it isn't worth fivepence.' The Italians who had heard this insult had killed him and had thrown his head into the gutter, crying: 'Here it is worth nothing at all!'

At the beginning of 1848 in the Papal States, in Tuscany and Piedmont, the leaven of liberalism was working in earnest at last. Reform followed reform and a Customs Union was planned. Meanwhile in Naples, Lombardy, Venetia, Modena and Parma the old order clung to power and refused to yield an inch.

Trouble first erupted in Sicily, when the people of Palermo rose and drove out their Bourbon King's troops. Soon Naples itself was in revolt, and Ferdinand II was forced to agree to far-reaching constitutional reforms. A general amnesty permitted the return of exiles, and Cristina went there to see what she could do to help the new democratic régime.

She found Naples almost in a state of complete carnival. Everybody seemed to be out in the streets at night with torches in their hands, giving the impression that the town was about to be set on fire. The reactionary King appeared to have changed his tune completely, and spent most of every evening bare-headed on his balcony waving to the crowds. 'He looked as pleased as a child who had received the first prize for good conduct. The other night at the theatre I saw him leaping about at the back of his box like a merry bear.'

On 13 February 1848, a crowd of Neapolitans called to tell her that Charles Albert, too, had granted the Piedmontese a Constitution, so that eleven million Italians were now enjoying democracy. In Rome the common people and the middle classes had given her the greatest welcome, whilst the aristocracy stood aloof. In Naples all classes welcomed her. When she attended a banquet to celebrate the new Constitution, everybody seemed to rush at her as she arrived, seizing her hands and kissing them. Toast after toast was drunk to her, and when she spoke they applauded every sentence.

Next evening, when she was alone in her drawing-room and about to retire, suddenly there was a tremendous uproar in the courtyard outside as it was invaded by *lazzaroni* carrying torches and flags. Several small vehicles were among them, covered with human pyramids. 'Don Michele, who was regarded as the leader of the working class of Naples, was perched on top of one of these pyramids, and when I came out onto the balcony he addressed me, saying that the workers had not at first approved of their King's new Constitution, but that now it had been explained to them they did. This was followed by compliments to me. I spoke to the people, asking them to have confidence in the new democratic régime, but most of what I said was drowned by applause. I know so many people here now that my drawing-room is crowded all the day long, and each new arrival asks for permission to bring his friends.'

With so much enthusiasm about, she decided to publish the *Ausonio* in Naples in future and to bring out both a daily paper, the *Nazionale* which appeared on March the 1st, and a twice weekly popular journal. Now there was freedom of the press she thought such papers would thrive.

Metternich in Vienna was not particularly worried by the success of the popular uprising in Naples. He gave strict instructions to the eighty-one year-old veteran Marshal Radetzky that no concessions of any kinds were to be allowed in Lombardy-

Venetia. An order was issued that should Cristina set foot in any Austrian territory, she was to be arrested and taken to Milan.

Meanwhile, the course of events in her native Lombardy were causing her increasing concern. In 1847 when the Austrian born Archbishop of Milan died, the Pope had pleased its people by appointing a member of an ancient Lombard family to the See. This proved the occasion for wild scenes of rejoicing. When after three days these began to get out of hand, Marshal Radetzky, the Austrian Commander-in-Chief, ordered his troops ruthlessly to re-establish order. 'Three days of blood will give us three years of peace,' he told his associates. He longed for a rebellion on a large scale so that he could exterminate the trouble makers.

To show their indignation at the repressive measures taken, the men of Milan agreed amongst themselves to stop smoking from New Year's Day, 1848. The Austrian government had a tobacco monopoly, and this move was designed to hit back at the régime through its pocket. This enraged Radetzky. His officers and soldiers were issued with free supplies of cigars and instructed to blow the smoke into the faces of the townspeople they met in the streets. Disturbances broke out when this was done. They reached their peak on the evening of 3 January when drunken soldiers insulting the citizens they encountered caused a riot, and mounted troops brutally quelled it by attacking with lances all in their path and galloping over and trampling the fallen, thus killing some fifty-nine persons. Other cities – Brescia, Verona, Bergamo – had followed Milan's example and there, too, were ugly scenes.

On 27 February news reached Cristina in Naples of the revolution in Paris, and she wrote on the 7 March to Thierry that the fall of Louis-Philippe's government delighted her. She suggested that until things became settled in Paris he should join her in Naples. If he did not want to do that and her presence could help him in any way, she would return to Paris until 'the tempest had abated.'

Thierry replied that he would remain where he was. He approved of most of the members of the Provisional Government under Lamartine, but he had misgivings about the future. She wrote back urging him to change his mind. In Italy, with an income of ten thousand francs, he could live like a prince. She would take a villa at Portici by the sea, surrounded by orange groves, palm trees and aloes, where the very air 'seems impregnated with intelligence and is sympathetic and invigorating.' She would return to Paris, arrange everything, and bring him back with her.

But events changed such plans. As this letter reached Paris, Hungary revolted, and in Vienna Metternich was overthrown. On 18 March the people of Milan, heartened by all this, rose themselves. They had no weapons except a few hundred fowling pieces, whilst the Austrian forces numbered at least fifteen thousand disciplined soldiers. There were six squadrons of cavalry and over sixty pieces of artillery to support them. No impartial observer could have predicted that five days later the Milanese would have turned all Austrians out of their city. The citizens seemed suddenly endowed with superhuman power. They barricaded the streets with their furniture, tables, chests of drawers, precious pianos, even their own beds, not to mention carriages, scenery from the theatre, benches and pulpits from churches, and on top of all this they placed paving stones which they had torn up. They ransacked all the armourers' shops for arms.

In a clever and successful attempt to unnerve their oppressors, they rang the bells from the towers of the city's seventy churches without ceasing. When night fell, a furious storm broke, adding its cannonades to the clanging of the iron tongues. From the roofs the men hurled down huge stones on the heads of the enemy, whilst from the windows of the narrow streets the women poured pails and saucepans of boiling water and oil. From loopholes in every barricade sharp-shooters fired into the lines of their assailants. At close quarters bayonets were used or musket buttends as clubs. The dead bodies of those who had attempted to storm the defences served to reinforce them. Students, peasants, nobles and beggars, old men and women, stood in the drenching rain eager to face death for freedom.

For five days the fighting lasted. Radetzky's superstitious Croats, demoralised by the tumult of the bells, committed unspeakable atrocities. The owners of the great palaces threw open

their doors, so that all could enter there for food and rest. Palla-
vicino, in his *Memorie*, wrote: 'The people of Milan for five days
behaved to each other as if they were angels.'

When the loathed head of the secret police, Count Bolza, was
dragged out of his hiding place by the insurrectionists, their
leader, Cattaneo, told them: 'If you shoot him, you will be
meting out justice, but if you spare him, you will be proving that
you are his superior.' And the patriots, moved by these words, let
the man go free.

The humanity shown by the Milanese has been vouched for by
Count Hübner, Metternich's representative. When the mob
stormed the Royal Palace, its terror-stricken occupants thought
they would be torn to pieces, but instead they were unmolested.
'Nothing was pillaged. Our soldiers stationed at the windows and
on the near-by cathedral roof had during the past two days shot
many insurgents. But when they had the chance to take their
revenge, none of them (although they were nearly all common
people) hurt the inmates or damaged their property.'[1]

Slowly but surely the people of Milan drove the soldiery out
of every street. From the highest spire of the Cathedral flew the
Italian tricolour. Radetzky asked for an armistice, but the Provisional Government that had been set up by the victorious
citizens did not trust him and insisted on unconditional evacuation.

Volunteers from Monza, Como and Bergamo were now
storming the gates from without, and the Austrians were in
danger of being caught in a trap. By the morning of the 22nd the
latter held only the Castle and the walls. The Milanese now attacked
the gates from within, and towards evening, led by the young
hero, Manara, they captured the Porta Tosa, thereby admitting
the volunteers. As a final act of despair, the Austrians in their last
rallying point, the Castle, bombarded the town during the night
before withdrawing under the cover of darkness.

The revolution spread throughout Lombardy, whilst in Venice
patriots overthrew their Austrian rulers and proclaimed a republic
with Daniele Manin as President. From Milan the 'White Coats'
retreated eastward and concentrated in the strategic area known
as the 'Quadrilateral'. Its sides were each about thirty miles long

and it lay between Lombardy and hostile Venetia. In the west facing Milan, the River Mincio formed a natural defence, stretching between the fortified towns of Mantua and Peschiera, whilst the swampy Po Valley shielded it on the south between Mantua and Legnano. From the latter on the east to Verona, the River Adige, its waters overflowing from the rains of winter, provided another easily held barrier against attack. In the north the lower slopes of the Alps, with the passes still blocked by snow, made the fourth side of the 'Quadrilateral'.

The triumph of the Milanese fired the whole of Italy. The Austrian garrison withdrew from Parma and its new Bourbon Duke was forced to grant a Constitution, whilst the Duke of Modena fled with the Austrians. In Florence its Duke declared war on Austria, and their embassy was sacked.

Once the news of the 'Five Days' rising reached Turin, crowds assembled before the royal palace demanding war with Austria. University students formed themselves into companies of *bersaglieri*, and on 22 March made for the frontier, cheered by huge crowds. Then late next day came the news that the Austrians had left Milan. The Provisional Government in that city sent a messenger begging Charles Albert to invade Lombardy with his army.

Camillo Cavour wrote a strongly-worded article in the *Risorgimento*: 'The decisive hour has arrived. In view of what has occurred in Lombardy and Vienna itself, further hesitation is impossible. We Piedmontese are known to have phlegmatic temperaments, to be ruled by reason rather than sentiments: today both reason and sentiment agree there is only one policy for us to pursue, and that is war – war immediately and without delay.'

Meanwhile the King and his Ministers debated the matter, and the crowds waiting outside the Royal Palace grew denser. Then, at midnight, the balcony of the armoury was flooded with light as the window curtains were drawn back and the tall form of Charles Albert appeared. Immediately the multitude fell silent. Then, raising the tricolour scarf the city of Milan had sent him, he waved it as a token that he had joined their cause.

Two days later he issued a proclamation to the Peoples of Lombardy and Venetia offering the help 'that brother expects from brother and friend from friend' and on the 25th declared war on Austria. But secretly, with unpardonable duplicity, his Minister, Pareto, sent a message to Austria that the King had intervened only to avoid a Republic being proclaimed in Lombardy and Piedmont.

While Charles Albert was making up his mind, Radetzky was retreating along the roads of Lombardy. His column was fifteen miles long. It was open country, and had he then been harassed by guerrillas and his retreat delayed until the Piedmontese army appeared, and if the latter had then manoeuvred to get between him and Verona, the Austrians would have been decimated. But the Milanese had been exhausted by their fighting. The Provisional Government was more concerned in keeping the troops they could rely on in the city, lest the more republican elements start seizing property.

When the revolution erupted in Milan, Cristina was in Naples. Stimulated by the news, she decided to go to Milan as soon as possible and chartered a steamer to take her to Genoa. She let it be known that she would give free transport to 'any men of spirit' who would care to accompany her. She could not formally invite them to do so because King 'Bomba' of Naples was at peace with Austria, and it would have been an unfriendly act to allow an armed expedition to set out from his territory.

She was to write later:[2]

'For forty-eight hours before I sailed my house was besieged by would-be volunteers, Over ten thousand Neapolitans were prepared to accompany me, but there was only room aboard for two hundred passengers. I agreed to take that number. Their enthusiasm impressed and stirred me. Some came from the most prominent families in Naples and were stealing away from home without the knowledge of their parents.

'The others, office and shop employees, were exchanging without regret the routine existence that gave them their daily bread for the excitement of camp life. A number of officers in the Neapolitan army risked being regarded as deserters to join me.

Husbands left their wives and families, and one young man, whose long awaited marriage was due to take place on the morrow, took a tearful farewell of his bride-to-be, finding the love of country the greatest love of all.

'Our ship was easily identifiable from all the others in the port on account of the weapons piled high on its decks. The volunteers were already on board to greet me. As we waited for the steamer to sail, disappointed men kept calling from the skiffs round us, begging me to find room for "just one more!" But the ship was packed and it was impossible for safety's sake to give way to their pleas. Then as we moved out to sea, from the skiffs and from the shore one hundred thousand frustrated patriots shouted as if with one voice: "We shall follow you!" The weather was propitious and the sea like a lake. Providence, it seemed, was smiling on this enterprise.'

Those on board invited Cristina to become their commander. She agreed, then proceeded to appoint her officers and had commissions prepared, which she signed. These began: 'We, Princess Cristina di Belgiojoso, hereby name and appoint . . .'

'Our voyage was swift,' she recorded. 'At Genoa we had a wonderful welcome, but nothing to compare with that we received from the people of Milan. My little army and the soldiers of Piedmont were the first Italians to reach Lombardy to take part in the war of liberation. It changed the aspect of the conflict, making it an Italian war rather than a local affair between Austria and her rebellious Lombard subjects backed by Piedmont. Four legions of Neapolitan volunteers followed in quick succession.'

On 7 April 1848, Cristina wrote[3] to Thierry to say that she had arrived at her home in Locate two days previously, and had entered Milan the day before by the Roman Gate to cries of 'Viva Cristina! Viva Italia!'

'I was met by a representative of the General Staff and one from the National Guard. I got out of my carriage and, escorted by these gentlemen and followed by my volunteers, I approached the toll-gate. There I was greeted by a member of the Provisional Government, who made a speech of welcome, to which I replied.

Then we continued on our way, followed and preceded by members of the National Guard from all districts of the city, and greeted by cheering from the whole population.

'When we reached the Palace where the Provisional Government was installed, its members came out to meet me in the courtyard and led me in. The crowds shouted for me to appear on the balcony, which I did twice, to the wildest cheering. Never have I witnessed such enthusiasm in Milan.'

The Austrian Count Hübner, in his *Une année de ma vie,* wrote that on the 6 April 1848, he arrived in Milan in the afternoon and found the town in a state of jubilation. 'They weren't celebrating, as I feared, some victory over the Marshal, but the solemn arrival of Princess Belgiojoso at the head of one hundred and eighty young Neapolitans. All carriages had to halt to let them pass, and I was able to view at my ease the heroine of the day whom I had in the past often met in the drawing rooms of Paris. Ten years had elapsed since I had last seen her and they had left their mark, but she was still very beautiful. Followed by her *giovinetti napoletani,* she carried unfurled a large, red, white and green flag. From every crowded window and balcony came cheers and the waving of handkerchiefs, and the air rang with cheering from the crowds. When they reached the square of San Fedele before the Marino Palace, she was officially received by Count Casati, who delivered an extremely eloquent speech.'

But while the Milanese themselves gained heart from the arrival of the Princess's volunteers, the Provisional Government itself was far from enthusiastic, despite Count Casati's public welcome. When later she told him that she expected a hundred thousand men in all, he exclaimed: 'God protect us!'

She wrote: 'I judged it useless to prolong the discussion. All the same, it was volunteers from Naples who joined the defenders of Treviso and Vicenza, and today the walls of Venice are being protected by men who to defend them have left the beautiful shores of Sorrento or the wild gorges of Calabria.'

Count Hübner, who was being held as a hostage by the Milanese, tells a different story from that of Cristina. 'Two days later these would-be heroes, after having been lavishly entertained at the city's cost, were packed into the train at the station of Porta Tosa and taken away to the front line. As I write, three weeks later, twenty or so unkempt and bearded young fellows in tattered uniforms could be seen begging in the streets. They are all who remain of the gay gallants from Naples. They never came to grips with their enemy, but committed such excesses robbing and raping women that the infuriated peasants set about them and slaughtered them. And so dismally ended their Republican expedition, begun with such high hopes. The Princess will no doubt soon get over the fiasco and find some other way of amusing herself: the citizens of Milan have had four days in which to relieve themselves of their patriotic fervour and enjoy a free spectacle. Everybody indeed should be satisfied, except the unlucky youths from Naples.'

Thus ran the Count's cynical commentary on the affair. The Provisional Government had been secretly dismayed by the arrival of the Neapolitan volunteers, because they were all Republicans, and the Government, pledged to support King Charles Albert, did not want to offend him.

CHAPTER 7

MILAN BETRAYED

Aware that she might be suspected of having become a Republican, Cristina decided to make her position clear by writing a letter to Charles Albert. This, dated 13 April, read: 1948

'Sire – May your Majesty excuse the frank language of someone unaccustomed to Court etiquette. You know how ceaselessly I have called for your intervention in Lombardy. It is unfortunate that you hesitated to take any action till the Milanese had achieved unaided what they regarded as the most hazardous part of the present operations. This delay imperils the victory which would have been certain had your Majesty crossed the Ticino a day or two before the rising in Milan.

'My views remain unaltered. I fervently desire that Lombardy and Piedmont be united, and I also represent progressive and influential people in Naples who want to negotiate a union between the party there and that in Lombardy, which has for its goal a country united under your kingship. The fate of Italy depends on what the Lombards themselves now decide. If it is to unite with Piedmont, then within two years the whole country might be one under the House of Savoy. But should we proclaim ourselves a Republic, and Genoa follow our example, then Piedmont itself will become militarily of no account. Italy remaining divided into countless States will sink back into medieval chaos. Your Majesty will understand that my personal wish is for the first of these two alternatives to come about.

'This morning I was urged by the emissary of a powerful and friendly disposed country to assume the leadership of the pro-Piedmont party. In reply I raised the following objections, which your Majesty could dispel. In Milan there are two rival factions.

Those supporting union with Piedmont consist almost entirely of the aristocracy, who a year ago were pro-Austrian and who have changed their politics through fear of losing their possessions. They are hated by the common people, and all they do alienates both them and those with progressive views.

'The Republican party is drawn from the middle and lower classes and the young. My sympathies lie with neither party, but I prefer those belonging to the Republican side. If your Majesty were to support me, I should like to form a centre party, composed of the middle class and pledged to unite Lombardy with Piedmont. It would have nothing to do with the narrow, selfish aims of the aristocrats. But before I take any such steps I should like your Majesty's assurances that if such a union took place, Lombardy would retain its own institutions and laws. If your Majesty were to do this, then you would find supporting you the most enlightened and distinguished people in Lombardy.

'I implore your Majesty not to rely on the present Royalist party, for the reactionaries in control of this will soon be swept away by the people.

'I have not yet replied one way or the other to the representative of that foreign Government which has approached me, because before attempting to form such a party as is in mind I want to be certain that the proposition is a practical one, and that depends on your Majesty's reply. This I now await. I lay at your feet the homage of my respectful devotion.'

Cristina never disclosed the name of the major friendly power whose representative had approached her, but in view of her many links with France it was probably a French diplomat.

The King himself did not reply to her letter, but she received a message through an intermediary, thanking her for it and saying that he was not offended by its tone.

On 21 April his secretary, Count Castagneto, sent a copy of the Princess's letter to the Chevalier Farina, the King's representative in Milan. 'The King asks me to impress on you the importance of not mentioning the Princess's proposals to anybody. See her and give her my personal salutations, and say that regarding her letter it would be necessary to know much more and what exact conditions she had in mind. Tell her that the King relies on her more than anybody else in Milan.'

The Princess replied that she considered the capital of the new State should be transferred from Turin to Milan, as the former was badly placed.

It is likely that there was further correspondence between her and the King or the Count, for on the 15 June Castagneto wrote to Farina that should he see the Princess he was to impress upon her that 'a simple declaration of fusion, with a mixed Ministry which shall immediately assume the direction of affairs, is the only possible solution.'

The value of the Princess's letter as far as Charles Albert was concerned was that it brought home to him the need of appeasing both sides in Milan. Mazzini had arrived there shortly after Cristina, and had received a tumultuous welcome from adherents of all parties, who hoped in this way to gain his support. The leader of 'Young Italy' now realised that Lombardy could only hope to be independent if protected by Piedmont. Reluctantly he withdrew opposition to the political union of the two countries. When Charles Albert learned this, he offered him the premiership of a Government 'constructed on democratic lines.'

The Princess had started holding a salon in Milan, and was busy putting over her ideas through her persuasive personality and her pen. Not only did she contribute articles to the French press, write and distribute political pamphlets, but she started and edited two new journals, *Il Crociato* (The Crusader) and *La Croce di Savoia* (The Cross of Savoy). In all this work she was ably seconded by Gaetano Stelzi.

In her columns she stressed the fact that what was needed above all else was a trained army capable of freeing them from the Austrians. Such an army only existed in Piedmont, which made it essential that the two countries should be united, and as the Piedmontese were ruled by a King and as the vast majority of them supported a monarchical form of government, Lombardy could only hope for union with Piedmont through abandoning republican leanings. To her delight she found more and more people supporting these views until it was clear that they were in the majority.

Later that year, in the *Revue des Deux Mondes*[1] in Paris, she was with discernment and brilliance to describe the Italian Revolution of 1848, and to put forward her opinions as to why it had failed. 'I will try to relate simply and accurately the facts as I know them from first-hand knowledge, but leave to others to explain those of which I have only second-hand information.'

She pointed out that during the previous thirty-six years of domination, the Austrians had carefully kept all natives of Lombardy out of the administration, so nobody had any experience of such work. Regarding the new Provisional Government, she stressed that they were not elected but men who had gone to the Marino Palace after the Austrians left, to share out offices and power amongst themselves. Some were Royalists who wanted union with Piedmont, and others were Republicans. As they could not agree, chaos had been the result.

Lombardy under the Austrians had been ruled by Police Commissioners with almost dictatorial powers, who were completely unscrupulous in the methods they employed to spy on the populace. She thought that the new Chief of Police's first act should have been to remove these men from office, but not one of them was dismissed. She suspected him of being a secret supporter of the Austrians, and was later proved to be right.

Within nine days, she tells us, there was no money left in the city's treasury. Attempts to raise loans at high rates of interest failed, so appeals for voluntary gifts were made, and four million raised, mostly in small sums from the poor. As this was inadequate for the Government's needs, they ordered the land tax to be paid a year in advance, and taxed all loans, making the borrowers pay, which had a ruinous effect on business. This, too, proving insufficient, all private persons' silver and the jewels on the images in the churches were confiscated. But even then the Government ran into debt.

People, she writes, began asking how Lombardy, which had maintained up till then an Austrian army, eighty thousand men strong, and which had also sent forty million lire a year to Vienna, could not manage now that these burdens had been removed. The reason, she explains, was that the Austrian army had been partly replaced by the army of Piedmont, to the cost of which the Provisional Government had agreed to contribute over three million a month.

On taking charge the Government had, without considering the consequences, abolished income tax and the state lottery, as well as cutting the duty on salt. These measures, which would have been praiseworthy whilst there was peace, were foolish in time of war.

Cristina claimed that the lack of control exercised by the Provisional Government over its underlings hastened bankruptcy. When the Austrians left, many Milanese had just taken over the jobs they fancied. Later, friends of noble families were given the most lucrative positions. A good many civil servants formerly employed by the Austrians remained at their posts, pretending they were patriots but secretly counting on the return of the Austrians, and doing all they could to this end whilst they lined their pockets at the expense of the Government, or rather, their fellow citizens.

A Ministry of War had been set up, but the official responsible for buying the army's supplies was a former business man who, she alleges, had been involved in four fraudulent bankruptcies. The Lombard army and its volunteers consequently lacked shoes, uniforms and overcoats, not to mention munitions. Rumours had spread round Milan that he and members of the Government were stealing the money that should have been used for these purposes. But the Provisional Government had refused to hold an enquiry.

When the Austrians had left, the entire population had clamoured for arms, which they were promised by the authorities. But despite, this, the National Guard received hardly any, and later, a week before the capitulation of Milan, when the people assembled before the Marina Palace refused to disperse unless they were given arms, they were told that this was impossible owing to lack of weapons in the city. Nevertheless, a week later the people discovered six thousand two hundred rifles hidden in a Government building.

Soon after reaching Milan, the Princess had begun to have doubts about the strategy employed by the Piedmontese and the way the services of the volunteers were being utilised. The King, it was true, at the head of some fifty thousand trained troops was marching against the fortified places still occupied by the enemy. 'Nevertheless, any knowledgeable person must have become concerned over the course of the war. Assisted by his staff of Piedmontese noblemen, appointed for reasons of rank rather than of merit, Charles Albert was busy evolving plans of campaign that might have been effective in the days of Frederick the Great, but which had become useless since Napoleon had revolutionised the art of war.'

The troops of Piedmont had moved sluggishly towards Mantua and Verona, preparing for long sieges of these towns. They were courageous, but inferior in training and equipment to the Austrians. The King, who wore a hair shirt, relied on inspiration through prayer and the prophecies of a visionary nun. He made his troops march late to battle rather than miss Mass. All military operations were suspended on Sundays, Holy Days and major Saints' Days.

The members of the local councils had not been replaced and were mostly in the pay of the Austrians, so that supplies intended for the Piedmontese were often diverted to the enemy. At the same time, not a move of the Italian army escaped the notice of Radetzky's spies. As a result, the soldiers from Piedmont began to distrust the Lombards.

According to the Princess, the war took on another character on the frontier defended by the disdained volunteers from Naples. She praised them, claiming that thanks to their valiant efforts the only places through which the Austrians could force a way were the defiles of the Tyrolean Alps.

Ever since returning from Naples at the beginning of April 1848, Gaetano Stelzi had been deteriorating rapidly in health. It gave the Princess, who had grown very fond of him, increasing concern.

On 15 June she wrote to Thierry[2]:

'Yesterday towards four o'clock in the afternoon his coughing became almost incessant, and I noticed with alarm that all colour had drained from his lips. The attack lasted for nearly two hours, during which I gave him his various medicines. After this he became calmer and his breathing more normal. Seeing him better and feeling myself exhausted, I told him I was going early to bed and that the doctor and Mrs Parker would spend the night in his room. He was to ask them to call me if he felt worse.

'But when I lay down I could not sleep. Three times I rose to enquire how he was and received reassuring replies. At last I closed my eyes and was about to fall asleep when I heard someone calling me. I jumped out of bed as the doctor hurried into the room looking very upset. "He's dying – he's dying!" he cried. In a few seconds I was at Gaetano's side. He died without regaining consciousness.

'Why had he to be taken from me? God alone knows. I did not realise till then how much I loved him, that his life had became so intimately linked with mine, and that he was so necessary to me.'

She decided to have Stelzi's body taken for burial at Locate, and applied for the necessary permit from the municipal authorities. This was granted, on the usual conditions that the corpse should be placed in a leaden coffin enclosed in an outer wooden one, that it should be moved at night accompanied by the appropriate officials to the cemetery of Locate, where it was to be immediately interred.

The parish register of Locate contains a belated entry made the following year: 'Gaetano Stelzi, aged twenty-seven, doctor of law, died 16 June 1848, at 1 a.m. and was buried the 19 June in this cemetery. Cause of death – tuberculosis.'

But Cristina wanted to keep his body in a better final resting-place. In a letter to Augustin Thierry she disclosed: 'I have had him brought to a tomb in the precincts of my house, so that Mrs Parker and I might have the sad satisfaction of surrounding him with flowers and of maintaining the place more like a room than a sepulchre.'

It would seem that whilst awaiting the building of a permanent vault, the Princess had arranged for Gaetano's body to be surreptitiously transported from the mortuary chamber of the

Locate cemetery into some outer room of her large villa. The vault's construction would have taken time, as all able-bodied men were under arms.

The course of events in any case prevented Cristina from proceeding further with whatever plans she may have had regarding Stelzi's final resting-place. She had suggested to the Provisional Government that a plebiscite should be held in Milan, asking citizens to vote as to what form of government they wanted, and whether such a change should be made then or after the war. Her suggestion was adopted.

The people were told Milan was facing bankruptcy. They could not afford to raise and equip an army. The alternative – immediate union with Piedmont under Charles Albert – would mean the end of financial worries, for Piedmont was prosperous and wealthy, and its administrators and civil servants were experienced and would soon put the finances of Lombardy right. The forces of Piedmont would then defend Lombardy, and Lombard soldiers brought into the strength of Piedmontese regiments would be trained and led by capable officers.

The result of this plebiscite was overwhelmingly in favour of union with Piedmont, and some members of the Provisional Government at once visited Charles Albert. But he appeared none too eager to gain the allegiance of Lombardy, and said that it would be for his Parliament in Turin to make the final decision. The latter, however, were not at all enthusiastic over the proposed union. The Piedmontese Royalists, believing that the Republicans were very powerful in Lombardy, feared that once its representatives joined the Parliament in Turin they might agitate for the deposal of Charles Albert and the proclamation of a republic. There were others who also feared that such a union would lead in time to the seat of government being transferred from Turin to Milan.

To quell such qualms, the delegates from the Provisional Government promised to accept the monarchical form of government and that the capital of the new State should be Turin for all time. The Union was agreed and the Provisional Government was replaced by a Royal Commission on 20 July 1848.

MEDALLION OF PRINCESS CRISTINA STRUCK IN MAY 1835

GAETANO STELZI, CRISTINA'S SECRETARY
drawn by Ernesta Bisi in 1845

On the 26th of the same month news came to Milan of an important victory by Charles Albert and the taking of Verona. But this was followed almost immediately by a serious defeat. 'We reassured ourselves with the thought that one defeat is not disastrous provided effective counter-measures are taken,' wrote Cristina. 'But soon it was announced that the Piedmontese army had given up its strategically well-placed positions in Rivoli, Valeggio, Volta and Somma-Campagna to concentrate in Goito. The enemy it seemed, had crossed the Mincio without any opposition.'

From then onwards every day brought further bad news. Abandoning Goito, the Piedmontese army retired to Cremona. A day later they had fallen back to Pizzighettone. Next day the retreat had reached Lodi, whilst the King's headquarters were at Codogno, a large market-town five miles away. It was only when they entered Lodi that the troops of Piedmont halted, whilst Lord Abercromby went as an intermediary to the General commanding the Austrians to ask for two months' armistice in the names of England and France.

Cristina wrote:

'I was then living at Locate in the country, some ten kilometres from Milan on the road to Padua and in the direction of Lodi. Since the situation had become so grave, I went every day into the town, for I regarded it as important that those of the nobility whose devotion to the nationalist cause was known should, by their presence in Milan, show their disapproval of those of their class who, dreading the return of the Austrians, had already fled abroad. When I heard the Piedmontese were in Lodi, I went there to learn at first hand the position.

'That day, 2 August, was calm. Charles Albert, people said, owing to lack of supplies had been unable to defend a line based on the Mincio. These had been sent instead to the Austrians through the treachery of certain civil servants. He had been forced therefore to withdraw to the Adda . . .

'Despite the gravity of the situation, when I left Milan to go to Lodi, the city was calm. In the country, on the contrary, I became sadly aware of all the symptoms of despair and terror. For a radius of twelve to sixteen kilometres south from Milan all the villages were deserted, and the main road was congested with whole families who dragged after them provisions and cherished belongings. The old people and the children followed as best they could. The infirm were carried by the young and the strong.

'From time to time something near panic broke out in this tearful procession. If the distant noise of wheels, the tramp of horses, the slightest suspect sound were heard, then everywhere shouts would arise: "The Austrians are coming!" The order kept by these long columns of fugitives would be broken, as cries and sobs escaped from every mouth. The most timid would flee across the fields. The brave or those resigned to their fate would sit on the edge of the road and, judging all effort useless, would commend themselves to God.

'Distressed and not knowing what advice to give the unfortunate peasants who pressed round me, I did my best to try and rally them. I told them the object of my journey, and a large number agreed to await my return before continuing on their way.

'I found the town of Lodi full of troops. The soldiers seemed weary but not downhearted. They spoke only of the future and never of the past, which is always a good sign. Their talk revolved round the war, the forthcoming rout of the Austrians, and the protection whch God could hardly refuse them. I admired the martial expressions on these gaunt faces. I listened with emotions to the soldiers' songs which came from those blistered lips as optimistically as if the campaign were just beginning. Something told me that Italy could not perish so long as she relied on such men.

'Charles Albert being still at Codogno, I had asked to see either the King or an aide. One of these, whose name I had better not mention, soon came to find me. I told him about the state of near-panic which prevailed in the countryside, and the misgivings in Milan as to the King's intentions. This officer gave me a moving account of the army's sufferings and how at times they had had no rations at all. He seemed to doubt the desire with which I credited the people of Milan to defend their town, but when I questioned him as to the King's intentions he suddenly became strangely reserved, but assured me that these had already been communicated to certain members of the former Provisional Government. I replied that I was not asking to learn any secret, but only to be given some idea of what the people of Lombardy might expect.

'I stressed the danger arising from keeping the population of Milan in a state of uncertainty. I demanded a message of reassurance from the King to the Milanese that he would defend them. The officer still hesitated. At last he said that the route chosen by the King should be sufficient guarantee of his intention to defend Milan at all costs. Then he added: "But I must stress that I am not speaking in the King's name. He has not authorised me to do so."'

Try as she might Cristina could not get the aide to commit himself any further, except to say that Lord Abercromby was in the Austrian camp and that conceivably he would obtain an armistice. 'Without that, the destiny of Milan will be decided in Milan,' he told Cristina.

'I went back the same way as I came and I tried to calm the people I met, assuring them that they had nothing to fear from the Austrian advance so long as they did not see the Piedmontese troops making towards Milan. If that were to happen, they should follow them and take refuge in the city.

'The evening of the same day, the 2 August, I myself went to Milan. I was awoken early the next morning and given the news that the King and his army, forty-five thousand strong, had arrived during the night and were encamped outside the Roman Gate. This meant that Lord Abercromby's mission had failed, and that the war would continue without a pause.

'But the presence of the Piedmontese maintained the morale of the Milanese. "So the King really means to defend us. . . . He isn't abandoning us. . . . May God reward him." Such was the gist of the conversation everywhere. People waited for an official announcement that the King had entered the city itself, but by evening none had been made, and misgivings multiplied. . . .

'To learn for myself what the poor thought, I walked round the slums asking how they felt about the war. I was pleased to find them confident of victory and determined to defend the town, to see it in ruins rather than yield . . .

'It was clear to me that misunderstanding was growing between the King and the people. The latter were being told that the King did not want to continue the war, whilst he was being told that the citizens of Milan did not want to fight. I realised that immediate steps were necessary to put the King on his guard against this false report, and I decided to take the matter into my own hands.

'Charles Albert was staying in a small inn just outside Milan. I went there that same evening, and explained the purpose of my visit to his secretary. After listening to me, the Count admitted that several people had told the King the Milanese did not want to fight, and that the time was rapidly approaching when he must know if this were true. The King, he insisted, would defend Milan to the last extremity. It was impossible to doubt this, since Charles Albert had refused to withdraw into Piedmont and had preferred to come to Milan. When I left, I asked the Count to congratulate the King on his commendable intentions and to stress that the future of Italy depended on his fulfilling them.'[3]

The Committee of Public Safety had spent the whole of that day having food and munitions brought into the town. Cristina watched the peasants from the villages around Milan arriving to work on the strengthening of the fortifications. It saddened her to see all the trees that had lined a magnificent promenade being felled and converted into stockades. She watched the three city gates opening on the roads the enemy was expected to take being walled up for greater security, and the long convoys of supplies entering through the others.

'On 4 August a review of the National Guard was ordered for 6 a.m. The King, invited to appear, refused under the pretext, somewhat frivolous to my mind, of a promise he had made to himself not to enter Milan till he had expelled the Austrians to beyond the Alps. His place was taken by General Olivieri. I attended the ceremony, and the sad forebodings that had worried me the previous day were dispelled by the spectacle I witnessed. Only those who know the parade ground in Milan can form any idea of the scene. When I emerged from the sombre alleys of the Piazza-Castello, three sides of the immense square were lined by the National Guard of Milan and the Piedmontese troops stationed in the city. There were twice as many of the former as there were of the latter. Thirty-three flags represented the various districts in Milan. Also present were National Guards from neighbouring towns and battalions of peasants. Thirty-three pieces of artillery followed by their wagons reassured me as to the resources on which the city could depend, even if the support of Piedmont were withdrawn.

'All those who took part in this review were full of confidence. There were there that day no fewer than thirty thousand National Guards under arms, and several Captains confided to me that barely a third of their companies had been able to attend the parade. Milan therefore had for its defence nearly fifty thousand National Guards, backed by resolute citizens. Whilst the troops marched past in silence cannon started to boom, but no one took any notice. From 8 a.m. till noon the noise came nearer and nearer, and at last shells started to fall into the city.'

Cristina says that the unexpectedly early arrival of the Austrians took people by surprise. That morning they had been told that the enemy were several miles away from Milan, at a short distance from the Piedmontese artillery-park at Noverasco. The King and the main body of his army were encamped outside the Roman Gate nearest to Noverasco. Had the Austrians managed to advance as far as the Roman Gate without encountering any Piedmontese forces and without the Milanese being warned of the enemy's approach? As impossible as this might seem, one had to admit that it was what in fact had happened.

Cristina went immediately towards the Roman Gate. She watched the men who had been working on the barricades near the walls rushing to take cover from the shells falling amongst them. She then hurried to the Committee of Public Safety and told them that she thought a grave emergency had arisen. They would not believe her, saying that the Piedmontese army outside the walls would engage the Austrians and repulse them. Meanwhile, to the sound of the church bells ringing the alarm, the National Guard had marched out of the city to meet the Austrians.

'Once more paving stones were dug up and barricades rose as if by magic. Mines were laid in strategic places. Milan became a heap of stones and projectiles, a forest of small citadels, forts and redoubts, enough to daunt the most seasoned soldiers.

'At dusk the National Guard returned. They had forced the Austrians to retreat some three miles, had captured five cannon and two hundred prisoners. This initial success excited and encouraged the population. We expected the Austrians to attack again in force at dawn. That night the National Guard manned the walls and the civilians the barricades. The King had at last decided to enter Milan to escape being captured by an unexpected attack, and he went to stay in the Greppi Palace in the Corsia del Giardino in the very centre of the city.' Later it was learned that a great part of his army had withdrawn from their positions outside the walls and had followed him into the town.

The morning of the 5th came, and time passed without a sound of cannon or gunfire from without. People began to speculate as to what this meant. Some thought the Austrians would launch their attack at midday. Then a rumour spread to the effect that the King had capitulated. The Milanese at first refused to believe this, and two men caught in the Market Place spreading these rumours were seized by the crowd, taken to be Austrian spies trying to demoralise the people, and lynched.

But soon the rumour became too widespread to be ignored. It was learned that at about four o'clock on the previous afternoon one of the Royal Commissioners had announced to a member of the Committee of Public Safety that he had sent two of his generals to Radetzky, but it was not said on what errand.

Then on the morning of the 5th, the King sent for the municipal council, saying that he wished to explain to them the reasons which had induced him to propose terms to the Austrian Marshal for the safety of the city.

Dismayed by this extraordinary news, the councillors asked that the three members of the Committee of Public Safety and

Generals Zucchi and Giorgio Clerici, the two commanders of the National Guard, and their staff might also be present.

Cristina writes: 'This was agreed, but instead of being admitted to the King's presence they were received by several of his generals, led by Olivieri, Salasco and Bava. The former declared that the King had come to Milan with the firm intention of defending the city, but that circumstances had made it impossible for him to realise his desire. The unfortunate outcome of the fighting of the day before had seen the loss of one battery. Most of the army's ammunition, together with a large park of artillery, had also been intercepted; and there was, consequently, only enough ammunition left for one day. They knew too well that there was not sufficient food to feed both the army and the citizens, apart from a deficiency of money, and for these reasons the King had determined, on the previous day, to propose terms to Radetzky that would save the city from utter destruction, since all further attempts at resistance would be useless.'

The terms proposed to Radetzky were the following: that the King and his troops should retire beyond the River Ticino, that free pardons be granted to all who had fought against the Austrians, and permission given to any citizens who wished to leave the city to do so.

To these proposals Radetzky replied that he would allow the army of Piedmont to retire across the frontier, that he would spare the city, that as far as he was concerned he would act equitably, that he demanded military occupation of the Porta Romana, and that he gave permission to any citizens to leave Milan with the King's troops until six in the afternoon of that day.

The capitulation was referred to by the Generals Bava and Olivieri as an accomplished fact, and that since the King's conditions had been granted, there was nothing more to be said.

General Zucchi of the National Guards admitted that Milan could not defend itself without the assistance of the army, but objected that insufficient time was being allowed to citizens wishing to leave, and that the King should be asked to insist that Radetzky grant an extension.

The lawyer Restello, speaking on behalf of the Committee of Public Safety, declined any responsibility for the terms the King had chosen to make. The allegations regarding food and money were untrue. There was no want of provisions, there being at that time flour for eight days, and corn and cattle for a fortnight more. Neither was there a shortage of money, as the treasury then contained upwards of a hundred thousand lire, and on that very day and the next the first moiety of four millions of a forced loan imposed upon Milan fell due. While he could not deny that the army might possibly be short of ammunition, he could assure them that there was within the city a plentiful supply. So much for the reasons given for the capitulation. He called the agreement with the Austrians ignominious, and said that even should the Piedmontese army retire beyond the Ticino and leave the city unprotected, it ought to defend itself, and that were the city to fall, at least it would then have saved its honour which, by the capitulation, was shamefully compromised.

Cristina wrote: 'All present agreed as to the unshaken determination of the citizens to resist, a fact which was recognised even by the Piedmontese Generals themselves. It was asked why the Lombard army had not been included in the capitulation. General Bava gave it as his personal opinion that the Lombard soldiers would be allowed to follow the Piedmontese army with the citizens, but that this was only his interpretation of the agreement, and he could not guarantee it. Thus the King left it entirely to Radetzky's personal interpretation of the terms of capitulation, whether or not thirty thousand soldiers belonging to the Lombard troops should be shot as rebels!'

Cristina continues that she was unable adequately to describe the consternation and despondency with which the people of Milan learned the news. Men wept. Women ran distractedly about the streets, screaming with terror. She herself saw an old man struck with apoplexy and falling onto the pavement, which pooled with his blood. 'I saw scenes which even when in a feverish nightmare I had never imagined. Then indignation replaced despair. People swore they would stop the King from leaving, that they would force him to denounce the capitulation.

On all sides was heard the cry: "Better die than see the Austrians again!"'

The enraged citizens surrounded the Greppi Palace. The mounted *carabinieri* guarding it judged it wise to retire. The King's carriage and those of his suite were overturned and used to barricade all the doors of the palace. Some added logs and tried to set them on fire. Others smashed windows and tried to climb inside, howling for the blood of 'Citizen Charles Albert' and demanding that his son, the Duke of Genoa, be handed over to them as a hostage. Fusillade after fusillade of bullets raked the windows of all upper rooms where the King might be.

Signors Litta and Anelli, the only two members of the former Provisional Government still in Milan, issued a proclamation protesting against the capitulation, and delivered a copy to the King. He appeared shaken by the tremendous reaction aroused in the populace, and went out with the deputation onto a balcony and declared that, seeing the citizens were so resolved to defend themselves, he, and his sons also, would shed the last drop of their blood in the defence of the city. The mob shouted back: 'Then tear up the capitulation!' And more shots were fired at the King.

Overcome by this response, and after a moment's hesitation, he took out of his pocket a document, held it up for all to see, and tore it in two.

Immediately the rest of Milan heard the news there was wild jubilation, and all went ahead improving the city's defences. The Austrians, who had been due to enter the city at 6 p.m. on the 5th, did not appear.

And the King, to lend credence to his proclaimed determination to resist, ordered all tall houses by the walls near the Roman Gate to be blown up, so as not to leave standing any buildings from the roofs of which the inner city could be shelled. Property to the value of eighteen million Austrian lire was thus destroyed. The Milanese became convinced that the King now really intended to defend their city. Consequently, the menacing crowds round the Greppi Palace melted away.

And then when night came, one of Charles Albert's aides slipped through a window into an alley, and making his way to where two crack regiments were stationed, brought them back to the Palace. Midnight had just struck when, protected by these men and disguised as one of them, the King mounted on a horse escaped. The news of this desertion stunned the Milanese. The situation was a desperate one, and there was no one left on whom they could vent their anger. The Royal Commissioners had followed the King. The Committee of Public Safety was already on its way to Lugano. All the Piedmontese army, including the Lombard battalions attached to it, had also left, concealing the sound of their departure by muffling their feet. Both the Lombard and Piedmontese artillery had gone, taking with them all the munitions that had been assembled in the city, and the four million lire that had been raised from private persons and the churches.

The people went from house to house looking for their leaders, from palace to palace searching for munitions. They could not bring themselves to comprehend the extent of their misfortune until an envoy from the Austrian army came to announce that General d'Aspre and his troops would enter the town at midday, that all men between the ages of eighteen and forty would be immediately enrolled in the Croat regiments and sent away for army service beyond the mountains away from their native land, and that those who preferred exile to such a fate would have until eight in the morning to leave the town.

This alternative, Cristina writes, was accepted with joy by many. More than a third of the entire population went in mass to the gate furthest away from that through which the hated Austrians were due to enter. She saw long columns of emigrants of every age, of both sexes, from all walks of life, carrying possessions, or their children, or a sick relative that they feared to leave to the mercy of the victor. Some horses and carts following these bands of disconsolate fugitives carried the weakest and the most infirm.

Cristina wrote: 'The sky was red over Milan, and columns of black smoke reached up to the very clouds. What caused this smoke? Did it still come from the houses that Charles Albert with his tongue in his cheek had ordered to be burned to help Milan's defence? Or were the Austrians already beginning to execute their vengeance? Or had some desperate citizens decided to leave the enemy only smouldering plunder? Many palaces were half consumed by fire, whilst the army headquarters, the Customs House and the military hospital were completely gutted. How it was caused remains a mystery.'

Thus the Austrians came back as conquerors to the city from which they had fled in haste four months earlier. Twenty-five thousand soldiers had taken without a blow being struck a town defended by forty-five thousand regulars outside it, and by more than forty thousand National Guards within. The capitulation agreement having been torn up by Charles Albert, General d'Aspre felt justified in ordering the city to be sacked.

The convicts of Porta Nuova were set free. They joined forces with the soldiers to enter deserted houses and rob them of any valuables. After the houses they visited the churches and museums.

Decrees confiscating the property and money of those who had rebelled against the Austrians proved hard to put into being through lack of Tribunals and officials to operate them, so the Austrians resorted to a system of imposed levies which exhausted the funds of all the banks.

CHAPTER 8

CRISTINA IN THE WARDS

On 8 August Cristina wrote[1] to Augustin Thierry that both she and Maria, who had been with her throughout the trouble, were safe and well. They had left Milan when its capitulation was arranged and were on their way to Grenoble, where she hoped to see the French General Oudinot and urge him to cross the frontier with his army. 'If I fail, I shall go quickly to Paris, with the intention of calling on all the Ministers and the members of both Houses. I shall agitate in the very streets, demanding that France send its soldiers to free my people.'

By the middle of the month she was back in her new house in the Rue du Montparnasse indefatigably trying to persuade the new French Government to declare war on Austria. But they were too busy putting their own house in order, following the overthrow of Louis-Philippe, to embark on any adventures. Besides, at the opening of hostilities, Charles Albert had told them that he did not want any military aid, and had moreover asked them to withdraw their forces to some distance from the Alpine frontiers so that no false impression could be given in the rest of Italy that the Piedmontese were acting as puppets of a foreign power.

Cristina's old enemy, Count Rodolphe Apponyi, the attaché at the Austrian Embassy, was also back in Paris after a visit to Vienna. He wrote in his memoirs:[2] 'It was I who brought the refusal of my government to allow France and England to mediate in our Italian affairs.' The British Ambassador, Lord Normanby, was an intimate friend of the Princess – at one time the gossips pretended that he was her lover. Apponyi continues: 'Lord Normanby is furious because he thought we would accept the humiliating proposal of perfidious Albion. Never has any country at any time behaved so badly towards us. At the beginning of our difficulties in Italy when we asked for nothing better than to submit to the arbitration of England and solicited her services to avoid the sad necessity of war, she refused all intervention and to the contrary did all she could to sow discord. Today when we have shed the blood of our finest sons, when we have gloriously reconquered what belongs to us by right, she wants us not only to give up Milan but even an important fortress like Mantua. Lord Normanby does not limit himself to fury against us, he does all he can to bring France into the war. . . .'

The Count then mentions the bad news for him that: 'La Belgiojoso has returned to Paris. She is crazier and more of a firebrand than ever. She escaped from Milan and came here to become the despair of Cavaignac and his Ministers. She never ceases to bring them all sorts of news more or less false to excite them into intervention. The day she arrived she appeared like a phantom in Cavaignac's office, her thinning hair hidden by a flowing black veil, and wearing a black dress all open in front and cut low in the back – no sleeves, only shoulder straps. She raised her eyes to Heaven and her arms, too, then she started to declaim and gesticulate. 'Milan is in flames!' she cried. 'Charles Albert has broken his oaths! I left the unhappy city in flames – they soared into the sky demanding divine vengeance on a miserable King!'

'"But, madam," said Cavaignac, when at last she allowed him to speak, "Milan has not been burnt down. The flames only exist in your imagination."

'"But, sir, I have seen them!" she screamed. "They massacred women and children. All was burnt to the ground – all has perished! Vengeance! Vengeance! Pity Italy! Save her – save my tortured country! You promised – you must!" And she went round calling on all the Ministers and repeating the same thing.'

That Cristina's accusations, exaggerated by Apponyi, were based on truth has since been supported by the writings of responsible Austrian officers admitting that Croat soldiers committed atrocities in Milan, mutilating and burning prisoners and burying hostages alive in quicklime.

As a result of these activities the Princess found herself the target of Austrian counter-propaganda. In a pamphlet printed in Vienna that year both in German and Italian, she is called 'a bloodthirsty murderess' and accused of killing nine Austrians. It was distributed in Vienna and in Italy.

Some French journalists suggested that the main cause for the collapse of the insurrection was the unreliable character of the Italians themselves. This infuriated Cristina. She wrote in the Paris *National* of 19 August: 'Events in Italy have been reported up till now in an inaccurate and often contradictory way. Grave accusations have been made against a people which recently attempted to free itself by its own efforts . . . As an eye-witness of what happened, I can affirm that if there were any traitors and dupes in Italy, the common people themselves were in no way involved in the shameful intrigues that led to defeat.'

At a fancy dress ball held by Armand Marrast, President of the new *Assemblée Constituante*, the Princess made a tremendous impression when she arrived dressed in a tricoloured costume personifying Italy, the Vicomte de Beaumont-Vassy tells us in his memoirs. A few days later she sent letters to all members of the *Assemblée* which read:

'Public opinion and your Government have not been sufficiently informed about the affairs of Lombardy. The principal events of the revolution and the war, their background, and all the factors involved have been presented in a very prejudiced way. It rests with those who witnessed these events or took part in them to provide the necessary correctives.

'The undersigned believe it to be their duty to announce that they are preparing to that end a concise and informed account of what actually occurred, and trusting in the fairness of your Assembly, they hope you will postpone making any pronouncements till you have been able to read this.

'In the meantime they are even prepared to answer verbally any questions the Deputies might like to ask on the subject.'

The first of the four signatories to this was that of Cristina.

She wrote in her *Souvenirs dans l'exil*:

'When M. Louis Bonaparte saw his chances of being elected

French President grow greater each day, he left London and came to Paris. On arriving in the capital he politely returned the visit that I had paid him. For my country it was then the supreme moment when hovering between liberty and slavery, honour and shame, life and death, France was called upon to decide her fate. On receiving Prince Louis, I brought the conversation at once to bear on the subject which concerned me most of all. "If you succeed, as everybody appears to predict," I said to him, "what will you do for my country? Do you remember how strongly you attacked Louis-Phillipe for his failure to give support to the risings of the people demanding independence, which broke out in Italy in 1831?"

'"How can you doubt it?" exclaimed the great Napoleon's nephew. "Your country's security and freedom will be one of my first objectives." Then he added with feeling: "You will be pleased with me!"'

Cristina's hopes rose after the visit. She had an additional reason for optimism. She knew that he had brought with him to Paris his English mistress, a one time actress who had mysteriously become very rich while "resting" and was now financing the ambitious Bonaparte's election campaign with her fortune. Most of the English were pro-Italian and Miss Howard was said to be so inclined.

The Princess wrote in the last of her remarkably perceptive series of articles which appeared in the *Revue des Deux Mondes*[3] :

'If a terrible disaster has ended the War of Italian Independence it is not, I must stress, lack of courage in the people that is to blame. It was caused by certain men whose actions it is easier to describe than to understand. It is difficult to discover the correct answers to the questions one asks. Whilst refraining from attempting to do this, I must mention the justifications advanced for the conduct of the accused by their most faithful friends.

'I should like to place myself at a distance, to cast off all political passion and become completely neutral. It must be recognised first of all that the faults of the Provisional Government seriously handicapped those who succeeded them. The legacy of disorderly and ruinous administration inherited by General Olivieri and his fellow Royal Commissioners could only be a burden for them.

'As for the accusations brought against King Charles Albert, however uneasy about the future he may have been owing to the prevalence of Republican tendencies among the Lombards, is it likely that he would have been so base as to betray them?

'If the King of Piedmont did not dismiss and replace his inefficient Generals, if he did not follow a more energetic plan of campaign, it is his weak and irresolute character that one must blame; and, in the last instance, when he capitulated, it was because the intentions of the Milanese had not been presented to him in their true colours. It was because he did not believe the people were disposed to fight. It is above all because he had little confidence in the success of his own efforts, and that he feared for Milan the wrath of a victor entering at the head of an unbridled soldiery a city taken by assault.

'What will lift the veil which envelops those events? Who will finally decide the innocence or the guilt of the principal actors in these sad scenes? I believe for my part that it would be ill advised to decide yet, as we do not know enough about the affair. Moreover, the interested parties are still on the stage, the last act of the drama has still to be performed, and we do not know the end. We have better things to do than to accuse or defend. The only defendants that one cannot leave under the weight of suspicion are the people; for if the people are considered unworthy of liberty, they cannot hope to gain it. As long as the war lasts, all other causes than that of a united Italian nation must take second place.

'It is most important that we take advantage of this prudent truce to redouble our efforts for unity. Do not let us utter words which arouse political discord among those whose goal this is. Let us hold out a hand to each other and reserve our hate and our energy for the enemy. The Austrians are back in Lombardy. Charles Albert, has he not still an army to oppose them? Could he not tomorrow yet win a victory? Then the past will be forgotten and forgiven him for liberating Italy.

'Piedmont, we must remember, is preparing to take up arms

again. The Lombard volunteers led by Garibaldi await with impatience the moment when they can begin again their guerrilla warfare. Venice has proclaimed itself for the second time a Republic, and alone she defends the standard of Italian independence. Those are the forces which well directed can suffice to efface the memory of our recent disaster, quite apart from the help we may yet obtain from France. Let us then hope that the honour of Italy will at last obtain reparation. Let us hope that fatal differences will no longer impede so many fine efforts, and that our independence, once secured, will never again be put in jeopardy.'

In a letter to Liszt, Cristina reiterates this belief of hers that the ordinary people of Italy could not be blamed for what had happened. 'I cannot speak highly enough of them. They were staunch and steadfast, honest, courageous, qualities that one might have hardly expected them to have after being so long slaves of the Austrians. We succumbed, it is true, but we shall have our revenge and we shall have learnt our lesson.'

She wrote to a French journalist soon after: 'It is time that the people were no longer held responsible for the faults of those who govern them.'

On 15 January 1849, in another letter to Liszt she wrote: 'I know that you don't take politics seriously, and yet what merits our attention more than the rights of the people? We are, it is true, here today and gone tomorrow and it is foolish to become attached to personal possessions that we must leave behind us; but if what we achieve and gain in life is for the benefit of others, then our striving and acquiring is worthwhile. It is personal pleasures which are not worth the trouble we take to obtain them.'

That winter was an anxious one for Cristina. In Piedmont the armistice continued. The troops remained under arms, and the cost of this was a severe drain on that country's economy. The soldiers themselves were poorly paid and wretchedly accommodated.

Meanwhile there was trouble in the Papal States. Though Pope Pius IX had sent troops to support Charles Albert's army, he had never officially declared war on Austria. A close friend of Cristina, Mamiani, had formed a Government. But he proved too much to the left, even for a liberally-minded Pope. His successor, Rossi, pursued a policy that pleased neither side, and he was assassinated on the very day he went to open parliament and announce his programme. Rossi was anti-Jesuit, and they were blamed for the crime. A mob stormed the Pope's residence, demanding complete democracy. Pius refused to surrender to threats. The Swiss Guards unwisely tried to make the crowds disperse by firing their rifles. The common soldiers in the Pope's army then joined the rioters and swept into the Quirinal Palace. To save his life, Pius gave way to their demands but, fearing that mob rule would now usurp the function of government, he fled during the night to seek refuge with King 'Bomba' of Naples.

Louis Napoleon had now been elected President, and the Princess believed that once his own position was secure, he would do something to honour the promises he had made to her. But the French people were already tired of strife and revolution. They longed for stability, peace and order. The elections for the Legislative Assembly, which replaced the *Constituante*, saw the moderates in the majority. At their head was Adolphe Thiers, who sixteen years earlier had been in love with Cristina. They were still very friendly.

The water-carrier Ciceruacchio had taken charge of the Government in Rome, and was showing commendable skill in holding in rein the victorious and unruly revolutionaries. Mazzini, who was in Tuscany, hesitated before taking advantage of the Roman rising. Then when, on 18 February, the Pope invited the Catholic powers to restore him to power and was promised forces by Spain and Austria, Mazzini decided to join the revolutionaries in Rome. On 5 March he set out southwards, about the same time as Garibaldi. When the leader of 'Young Italy' arrived, he, Saffi and Armellini were elected Triumvirs by the new Assembly. A Republic was proclaimed, but he soon became the real ruler of the city.

On 30 March 1849, the armistice between Austria and Piedmont expired. Stung by the reproaches which had been levelled at him, Charles Albert asked for nothing better than to take the field again. Despite advice as to the foolhardiness of it all, he marched

his army to the village of La Cava, near where the Po joins the
Ticino. Marshal Radetzky advanced to meet him. Through errors
of judgment, treachery and misfortune, the Piedmontese encountered disaster. After a setback at La Cava came the shattering
defeat of Novara, and the abdication of the demoralised King in
favour of his eldest son, Victor Emmanuel, who then made peace
with Austria. The war cost Piedmont 250 million lire.

Shortly before the three days' war began, Cristina had travelled
to Turin to offer her services. She was actually only twenty miles
away from the scene of battle when she came across the remnants
of the Piedmontese army in flight. There was nothing she could
now do, so she left for Rome with little Maria to find out for
herself what was happening there. She found the city preparing
for a siege and expecting to be attacked from the south by the
Neapolitans, supported by the Spaniards, and from the north by
the Austrians.

Like a chameleon, Cristina was always appearing in a new guise.
She was asked by the Constituent Assembly in Rome to take over
the organisation and direction of the military hospitals. She
appealed to all Italian women to help, thus creating the first
voluntary corps of military nurses four years before Florence
Nightingale did the same thing in the Crimea. Twelve hospitals
were fully organised within forty-eight hours, and they were
ready to receive the wounded by 30 April. Despite lack of
adequate help she managed to achieve almost the impossible,
thanks to her resourcefulness and determination. She was ably
assisted by the American Margaret Fuller and the Swiss Julia
Modena. A committee was formed to raise funds, on which the
American sculptor, William Story, served.[4]

The Princess had no illusions about her wartime voluntary
nurses. Later she wrote in her *Souvenirs dans l'exil*:

'After having selected my staff, I had constantly to play the role
of a strict duenna, armed with spectacles, going on my rounds of
the wards with a stick in my hand to put a sudden end to conversations which might become too intimate. These girls and
women from the streets of Rome had no morals and in peacetime
led disorderly selfish lives, but now redeeming qualities in their

characters became apparent. No longer did they think of themselves or their personal well-being. I have seen the most depraved, the most corrupt among them keeping watch at a dying man's bedside, never leaving him either to eat or to sleep for three or four days and nights. I have seen them undertaking the most unpleasant and distressing tasks, remaining for whole hours bending over malodorous and gangrenous wounds, putting up with the moods and curses of the doomed men, and doing it all without showing disgust or impatience. I saw them at the end, remaining composed and unafraid, whilst cannon-balls and bullets passed and whistled overhead, oblivious of everything except the needs of the human wreckage from the battlefields.

'In nearly all the women I engaged to work in the hospital, I have seen this contrast between what they were and what they became. All changed in the same way. Once pity entered their hearts, it drove away at least temporarily all the vices which up till then had possessed them. It makes my own heart bleed to see women capable of such nobility and self-sacrifice forced to lead lives no better than beasts through lack of education and equality of opportunity.'

In her journal Cristina also wrote:

'Whilst I was going from one hospital to another my carriage was held up by crowds of people swarming in the roadway. I opened the window to find out what was happening, and saw that a convoy of carts and other vehicles filled the whole street into which we had just turned. Into these from the windows of all the houses people were throwing down mattresses, bolsters, coverlets, shirts, sheets and linen of all kinds. Above the noise rose cries of "Long live the Republic! Long live the defenders of Rome!" . . .

'Such enthusiasm proved contagious. Nobody wanted to give less than his neighbour. All were busy feverishly stripping their houses for the benefit of the wounded. The well-to-do gave money, the poor their best clothes and even crusts of bread.

'Whilst I was sitting in my office in the Pilgrims' Hospital, a gaunt and haggard man dressed in rags arrived and asked if he could have a word with me in private. Then he produced from underneath his arm a worn shirt made out of coarse cloth and said:

"I possess nothing – not even the money to buy bread tomorrow. I have only two shirts – one will do me for the time being. Give this one to a wounded man." I could quote many other examples of people behaving in this altruistic way, and it was whilst such things were happening in Rome that rumour-mongers without its walls were saying and writing that the people of Rome were being terrorised into submission by a handful of revolutionary Republicans.'

To Cristina's astonishment and anger it soon became clear that Louis Napoleon, despite his promises to help Italy to become united, was having second thoughts in the matter now that he was in power. His secret ambition was to become Emperor, and the men in Rome were Republicans. He needed the support of the clergy, and to obtain this he would have to aid the Pope. All the professional politicians, whose backing he needed, believed in the old French policy that a united Italy would be a danger to France.

In the Paris press doubts were being openly expressed. The *Moniteur*, for example, stated: 'France cannot suffer herself to be enfeebled by the rise of a neighbouring power from which she derives no advantage.'

In pursuance of this new policy, the French Government sent General Oudinot and fourteen frigates of trained soldiers with secret orders to occupy Rome and restore Papal rule. On 26 April they entered the harbour of Civita Vecchia, disembarked and took possession of the port.

Soon after on the same day two steamers arrived packed with six hundred men of the Lombard *Bersaglieri*, who had refused to lay down their arms after Novara. Among them were youths who had left Milan to serve in the Piedmontese army when the Austrians had returned. They were led by Luciano Manara, the hero of the "Five Days."

The French General refused to allow them to disembark. When Manara asked why, Oudinot replied: 'What have Lombards to do with Roman affairs?' To which the other retorted: 'And what have gentlemen from Paris to do with them?'⁵

Such treatment so angered the *bersaglieri* that they would have swum ashore had not the steamers been able to move on to Anzio, where they were able to land. Meanwhile Garibaldi and his men had ridden into Rome. The officers only as yet wore red shirts, but all had black ostrich plumes in their Calabrian caps. Crowds cheered, trumpets blared, and shots were fired into the air. Two days later, after a tiring march across the scorching Campagna, Manara's contingent joined them. They, too, received a tumultuous welcome from the Romans as they came through the Porta San Giovanni.

When it became clear that General Oudinot intended to destroy the Republic and restore the Pope, Mazzini, supported by the whole Assembly, called on the people to prepare for battle by arming themselves and erecting barricades. Posters proclaiming 'La Repubblica è in Pericolo,' were stuck on walls throughout the city.

The French General commented contemptuously: 'Italians don't fight – they run.' Then, on the morning of 30 April, he sent his troops along the direct road to Rome with orders to storm the Porta Pertussa, only to find that it had been walled up. They then tried to break through the Porta Angelica, but being repulsed, went on to the Porta Cavalleggieri, near the Vatican.

From high up on the terrace of the Villa Corsini on the Janiculum, outside the city walls, Garibaldi watched the fighting through a telescope, and decided to attack the enemy in the flank with the fifteen hundred strong Students' Corps, but they proved no match for Oudinot's regulars. Then Garibaldi at the head of his Roman Legion charged the French, and soon they were in full retreat, leaving hundreds of dead and wounded behind them. Rome celebrated the victory with wild jubilation.

Margaret Fuller wrote in a letter to Ralph Waldo Emerson: 'It was a terrible battle from dawn till the last light of day. I could see all its progress from my balcony. The Italians fought like lions. It is a truly heroic spirit that animates them. Many, especially among the Lombards, are the flower of the Italian youth.'

The French repulsed, Garibaldi and his men, together with Manara's Lombards, left under cover of darkness to deal with the

Neapolitan troops of King 'Bomba', who were marching on Rome from the South. When the news reached the Pilgrims' Hospital many of the seventy wounded men there tried to struggle out of bed, and the anxious nurses had to ask Cristina to calm them and persuade them to stay.

It was a strange new employment for her, but she had a clear head and a ready wit and they made up for her lack of experience. She now had the American, Margaret Fuller, to help her at the other main hospital. On 30 April she wrote to Margaret confirming the appointment on behalf of the Committee for the Care of the Wounded. 'You are named *Regulatrice* of the Hospital of the Fate Bene Fratello. Go there at twelve, if the alarm bell has not rung before. When you arrive, give the women your orders and see that you have a sufficient number of them on duty, both day and night, to cope with all emergencies.'

Mrs Story, wife of the American sculptor, wrote in her diary that thanks to Cristina and Margaret all the work in the hospitals was skilfully divided, so that there was no confusion or hurry. 'From the chaotic conditions in which these places had been left by those who had previously had charge of them, they brought them to a state of perfect regularity and discipline.'

William Story describes in his journal[6] how he and his wife called on Cristina on 2 May to contribute two hundred and twenty-five dollars to the hospital fund. 'She had grown much older and was negligently dressed. She was sitting surrounded by men and women, giving orders calmly and clearly and showing sound judgment and common sense in all her arrangements. She has laid down strict rules and has brought discipline into the establishment; for three days and two nights she has been without sleep and even now refuses to rest. Then we went to Spillman's for an ice-cream to cool her parched throat, and while we were there, there came screaming and hooting from a crowd, which dragged along two Cardinals' carriages magnificently painted and gilded. These with pickaxes and clubs they broke entirely to pieces and set fire to, crying out: "This is the blood of the poor." Returning to the hospital, we carried our ice to the Princess and she divided it between her little daughter and herself. Then we went over the wards – but how horrible is this reverse side of war! . . .'

Writing on 6 May, Story pays yet another tribute to Cristina. 'I went this evening to the Pilgrims' Hospital to take what the Americans have subscribed for those wounded in the late battle. Everything was in complete order – clean floors and beds, good ventilation, attendants gentle, and without confusion. These the hospital owes to the Princess, who has a genius for ordering and systematising. She said that nothing was more pleasant to her than to attend to the sick; it was, indeed, a sort of passion, for she added that in the sick-room one is sure of doing good. All efforts of charity may fail in their end – money given may be squandered or do injury, but the relief of physical pain is a thing definite and certain.'

After leaving Cristina they went to the Vatican gardens and walked along the walls to survey the scene of the late battle. 'We saw the monks under the black flag looking for those who had fallen in the ditches or among the hedges. The French had retreated without an attempt to bury their dead, and in one instance a living wounded man was found with the bodies of two dead soldiers lying across him.'

On the 10th came news of the rout of King 'Bomba's' Neapolitans by Garibaldi. The danger from the south was thus averted. Fearing that the French were planning another attack, Mazzini then recalled Garibaldi. But on 15 May there was a diplomatic surprise when Ferdinand de Lesseps arrived in Rome as the official envoy of Napoleon III to the Triumvirate. He told Mazzini that he had been entrusted with the authority to negotiate with the infant Republic and come to some friendly agreement with it. But, completely without Lesseps's knowledge, his Government was planning revenge for the defeat of 30 April and sending reinforcements by sea to Oudinot.

Although Lesseps came as a plenipotentiary, when he reached agreement with the Triumvirs on the basis for a treaty, Oudinot refused to ratify it, saying he had surpassed his powers. Lesseps then went back to Paris for further instructions.

At the beginning of June, Mazzini's intelligence brought him the disturbing news that Oudinot's forces now numbered nearly thirty thousand, and that six batteries of artillery and several siege trains manned by expert sappers and engineers had been landed.

The night of 2 June was dark and almost moonless. The successful defence of the city hinged on the Villas Corsini and Pamfili, high up on the Janiculum west of the San Pancrazio Gate. These were held by only four hundred Garibaldini. Suddenly, in the early hours, those in Rome heard the sound of gunfire coming from the direction of the Villas.

Garibaldi did not succeed in mustering his troops until five o'clock that morning, and by then the Pamfili and the Corsini were in French hands. The loss of the latter was extremely serious, for from these heights the whole of Rome lay exposed. After the bloodiest of fighting, a counter-attack led by Garibaldi succeeded in recapturing it.

As the Pilgrims' Hospital was some distance from the fighting, the Church of San Pietro in Montorio was used as a temporary hospital. The scene there would have unnerved most women. The French threw rockets into the city. One burst in the courtyard before Cristina, but she remained unafraid, supervising the nursing and dressing wounds herself. Then when dusk fell on the following evening it was learned that the French had recaptured the Corsini, and that Oudinot now had Rome at the mercy of his artillery.

Every day saw more and more wounded for Cristina and her helpers to care for. Churches on the Tiber were transformed into hospitals, so that the defenders on the walls could be treated as soon as possible.

Cristina took little sleep. She seemed to regard it as her personal duty to sit through the night by the most desperately ill patient, and she kept awake during her long vigils by reading the novels of Charles Dickens, which had been sent her by Vieusseux of Florence. 'When I begin to read anything of his,' she wrote to this bookseller, 'I become so interested that I read each book ten times over ... Although I am so exhausted that only my will power keeps me going, though I know I am in great danger, I feel nevertheless in good health and contented because I am not witnessing events that will make me ashamed of being an Italian, but instead very, very proud. We may be conquered, but we shall have saved our honour.' She ends in the Roman fashion: 'Greeting and brotherhood – "*Salute et fratellanza.*"'

Later, when living in Asia Minor, she was to write to Caroline Jaubert:

'I have been unable to sleep but it is not insomnia. When my eyes become heavy and I lose consciousness of the reality which surrounds me, a procession of both happy and sad phantoms file past my bed. They do not address me with bitter reproaches or terrifying threats – far from that, they smile at me. They remind me of what they suffered, and of the courage which I tried to give them to help them cross the grim frontier of life and death.

'Does the forgetting of the present which brings back such a past deserve the name of sleep? . . . I can never forget those days and nights during the bombardment of Rome when I remained of my own choice near the wounded. It was hard for me then to fall asleep. I kept thinking of those whose feeble voices had wished me good-night, and who I knew would not be able to wish me good-morning. I have lost count of the number of hands which then pressed mine for the last time . . .'

For eighteen days the siege lasted, then on 21 June the French in a night attack captured two bastions on Pope Urban's walls. Mazzini ordered Garibaldi to recapture these strategically vital positions at all costs, but the other refused to sacrifice his men in what he regarded as suicidal tactics. The Triumvir then roused the mob with his oratory and prepared to lead them against the French, but Garibaldi's legion barred their way.

The heavy guns thundered incessantly, pounding at each other in deadly duel, but those of the French were the more powerful and gradually knocked out the defenders' batteries. Half the houses in the Trastevere quarter were battered into ruins. The Pilgrims' Hospital was so damaged that Cristina had the wounded moved to the Quirinal, and she personally directed their transport through the debris-strewn streets.

As the military position deteriorated, so too did the relations between Mazzini and Garibaldi. The former wanted to defend

Rome stone by stone, even if the whole city were laid waste. Garibaldi more sensibly pressed for an attack on the French lines of communication, and if that failed, he favoured a withdrawal into the mountains so as to preserve their forces intact.

June 29 was the feast of St. Peter and St. Paul. The Romans tried to maintain their morale by celebrating it as if in peacetime with a display of fireworks. At nightfall torrential rain soaked the participants. It was then that the French launched their most murderous attack.

By dawn it became clear that the end was in sight. The Lombards and the Garibaldini fought until they had no cartridges and no powder, until they had stripped the corpses of all the ammunition they could find. Garibaldi, aware that defeat was certain, addressed the Constituent Assembly from the tribune. An eyewitness has described him as being covered with dirt and blood, his clothes pierced by shot and bayonet-thrusts, his sword so bent that it would go only half-way into its scabbard. Further resistance was futile, he said. He asked all fighting men who would to leave Rome with him that night and become guerrillas in the Apennines. 'I offer neither pay, nor shelter, nor food. I offer hunger, thirst, weariness, battle and death.' Despite Mazzini's opposition, the Assembly voted to end the defence of the city.

In the Lateran they gathered at dusk on 2 July, four thousand Red Shirts, *Bersaglieri*, students, and former Papal Dragoons. The Princess left her post for a brief while to see them set out, followed later by Mazzini and his supporters. Then back she returned to await the entry of the French army. This took place next day. Meanwhile she wrote to both the American and British Consuls, asking if she could place the wounded under their protection. The American agreed.[7] There were still 781 casualties in the Quirinal.

One of the first acts of the victors was to turn Cristina and her women out of the hospitals, to dismiss all the Italian surgeons, and transfer all the patients who were not actually dying to the Termini Prison. The official excuse for this was economy. The Princess wrote an indignant letter which was printed in the *Concordia* of Turin. In it she described what had been done as cruel and brutal, and stressed that no one on the staff had been paid. She added that the dying left behind were put in charge of fanatical Capuchin monks, who would give them neither food nor water nor any attention until they confessed as a mortal sin having rebelled against the Pope.

This was certainly the finest period in Cristina's life. Gone was the *poseuse*, the *femme politique* in the large plumed hat. As one who was with her all the time in the Pilgrims' Hospital has written: 'The wounded and the dying blessed her. No trained nurse could have done more than she did. She possessed, too, all the qualities that a hospital matron ought to possess. She would not hesitate to call on the Triumvirs to obtain arrears of pay for sick soldiers, or demand the instant provision of essential medical supplies.'

She herself tended Goffredo Mamelli, the poet, whose *Fratelli d'Italia* became the *Marseillaise* of the Italian Revolution. He died listening to her softly singing to him his words for the revolutionary chant.

But though the toll of young lives was heavy, some lived on to continue the struggle. Cristina nursed back to health Nino Bixio – a national hero later under Garibaldi, during the conquest of Sicily and Naples.

She remained in Rome until the end of July. Except for Venice, the whole of Italy was once more in thralldom. Marshal Radetzky, to punish the Lombard nobility who had rebelled against Austria, fined them enormous sums. In Cristina's case the amount was 800,000 lire.

Then the secret police, whilst searching her villa at Locate for incriminating documents, discovered the embalmed body of Gaetano Stelzi. According to the records, he had been buried in the local churchyard on 19 June the previous year. When the grave was reopened, his coffin was found to contain a heavy log.

Soon rumours were in circulation, which the Austrians encouraged as it was such a tempting opportunity to discredit someone who had given them so much trouble. It was alleged that Mrs Parker had helped the Princess to do the embalming in the kitchen, that they had then clothed the body in full evening dress, and that it had been found hidden in a wardrobe in her bedroom. All this, scandalmongers said, indicated that she had been in love with Gaetano, and could not bear to be parted from him by death.

The discovery caused a sensation both in Milan and Paris, and when the news came that she had left Rome with Maria and Mrs Parker on 3 August 1849, to embark on the *Mentor* for the Orient, it was claimed that she had done so to avoid arrest.

CHAPTER 9

CRISTINA FINDS HER EDEN

Cristina was near despair. Everything to which she had devoted the best years of her life had failed to bear fruit. She felt a compelling need to go to some country where she had never been before and begin a new life.

The *Mentor* was crowded with refugees from Rome, many of them Lombards like herself. She had a Count for her footman, she wrote later, and a Captain of Artillery as her *valet de chambre*.

From Malta she went to Athens, where she stayed in a villa with a superb view of the Aegean, but in her state of mind it failed to move her. On 27 November she confided to Caroline Jaubert:

'I am becoming old. It isn't noticeable physically, but I am experiencing that mental change which comes through age. But this change is infinitely more pleasant than I imagined it would be. It consists principally of this – that I live much more in the past than in the future. Now contemplating the future has become more disturbing than before, whilst thinking about the past when it does not cause remorse calms and reassures one's spirit. All the same, thoughts which formerly frightened me have now lost their terror and have even gained a certain charm. . . . I am resigned to the inevitable hour and will say when it arrives: "Welcome! How much I have dreaded the coming of this time. How wrong was I to believe that a natural process could be entirely bad. . . . I cannot imagine what interest we can take in living when other eyes no longer regard us with love."'

Bad news reached her from Augustin Thierry, telling of the death from cholera of Madame Récamier and of a decline in his own condition. The semi-paralysis of his limbs which had remained static for a number of years was starting to worsen again. This further disheartened Cristina. Her gloom made her regard the much-vaunted wonders of Greece with disenchantment. When she visited the plain of Marathon and tears came to the eyes of her companions as the guide described the heroism of Themistocles, she recorded: 'All I felt was how hot it was.'

She wrote letters to Caroline giving her detailed impressions of the country, which were published with her permission in the *National*. In these she was extremely critical of all the Greeks she had met, and stated that she could not bring herself to believe that they were the descendants of the god-like men sculpted in marble everywhere she went. She also told Caroline: 'We have here nearly seventeen hundred Italian refugees literally dying from hunger, for whom I am trying to do what I can. I cannot get them settled here. Perhaps the Turkish Government will be more Christian.'

When copies of the *National* reached Athens, the people were furious, and she was treated with such hostility that she left for Constantinople. She was very impressed by the view from the sea as the ship approached the shore, but was disappointed with the town, finding it ugly. However, she received such a friendly reception from the Turks that she rented a very pleasant house on reasonable terms. She wrote[1] to Augustin Thierry that in the bazaars one could buy the most beautiful things at trifling cost. She was delighted to discover that the Sultan Abdul-Medjid was benevolently disposed towards all political exiles from the West, and was encouraging them to settle in his country. She visited a colony of Polish refugees, and was so impressed by their successful farming of the land that she became fired with the idea of starting a similar settlement for Italians.

Meanwhile, back in Paris, Augustin Thierry was missing Cristina more and more. In a letter sent her in May 1850,[2] he writes: 'Fifteen months have passed since you left the houses you had built here and the beautiful garden which we were to share each summer. But these plans have come to nothing, like so many others. Please write and assure me that you will one day return, even though there may be a risk of your not keeping that promise.

Patience is the daughter of hope . . . Tell me what you are doing. Write about the future. Give me all the details you can, so that I can imagine I am with you. That in my blindness is for me the greatest of pleasures.'

In July she replied at length. She had been thinking of settling near Constantinople when a Turk 'with great influence in Government circles' had visited her. 'Princess, I believe you are about to ask the Grand Vizier for a lease of land to farm near this city. I have something far better to suggest. For exactly the same amount of money as such a lease would cost, you can purchase in Asia Minor a small kingdom of your very own. The price – six thou-ands Turkish piastres, or twelve hundred French francs! And it would belong to your descendants for ever!'

Cristina had expressed interest, and the man had taken her to see this new Eden, which was half-way between Angora and Scutari on the eastern shore of the Bosphorus, and some five days' journey from either place.

She wrote to Augustin: 'If I were to describe to you what I saw you would call me a visionary. Nevertheless, it really does exist and nothing can explain the complete neglect of such a paradise, unless it be the indolence of the Moslems and the sparse-ness of the population. My compatriots await the signal from me to emigrate and settle in this little kingdom. The difficulty is how to choose the right people from a distance. If light-headed young enthusiasts, easily discouraged, were to join me, they might leave after a few months. But if I succeed in attracting a dozen hard-working reliable families, the success of the venture will be assured. I may not make much profit to begin with, but Maria in some years' time will find herself in possession of a fine estate.'[3]

The Princess went on to say that she was going to Stamboul immediately to sign the deed of purchase. She would take posses-sion in a month or two, and then await the arrival of those exiles willing to work hard cultivating the land. Lest this should depress Augustin and make him think he would never see her again, she reiterates that the only thing preventing her paying him a visit is that France has for President 'the man half an idiot and half a

CRISTINA AND HER NEAPOLITAN VOLUNTEERS
ON BOARD THE *Virgilio*

BUILDING A BARRICADE, MILAN 1848

scoundrel who stabbed the patriots of Rome in the back.' Never-theless, she hoped that when Louis Napoleon's term of office expired in 1852 he would not be re-elected. 'As soon as justice is meted out, I shall leave everything, however much I may become attached to my new home, to come and stay for at least a while near you. Don't worry about the distance – that is nothing to me. It wouldn't give me more trouble to leave tomorrow for Mar-seilles than it does you to go to the Institute. So don't have any doubts on that account. I never take root anywhere, and once I can return to France without a heavy heart I shall rejoin you.'

On 15 November she wrote to Thierry from Ciaq-Maq-Oglou that for over a month she had been living in a valley far from civilisation and enjoying perfect peace of mind. To reach it coming from the west, one had to travel for several hours across bare mountainous slopes covered with the ruins of an ancient town. Then one descended a ravine and travelled for a time by the side of a river which flowed in a northerly direction. Suddenly, after this had swept round a hillside, the scenery changed. Now a range of well-wooded hills separated the mountains from the plain. At the foot of these, vast meadows sloped gently down to the river banks, whilst others penetrated into the mountains, forming fertile valleys. Springs gushed forth all along the way.

Cristina claimed that hers was the most attractive of these valleys. Right in the middle of it, where the shrubs and trees ended and the alluvial tracts of flat land by the river banks began, stood the cabin where she first lived.

On her arrival it had been uninhabited for years and frequented only by birds and beasts. Fortunately she had brought with her from Constantinople two Italians; one, a carpenter, was, as she puts it, the very man to have for companion if shipwrecked on a desert island. The place was soon cleaned, and she lived in it with Maria and Mrs Parker as best they could whilst waiting for the carpenter to fit it with doors and windows. One room had been completely finished and furnished, but the rest of the house, including the recess where they slept, was still 'in direct com-munication with the valley.' The mildness of the climate and the healthy air prevented this inconvenience causing them any harm.

They were all enjoying excellent health, and Maria was delighted with her new surroundings.

Pastori, the lawyer in charge of her affairs in Milan, had spent a fortnight with them and had brought packed in strong cases from Italy curtains, chairs and beds. Thanks to this unexpected windfall she had been able to furnish her room in European fashion, which had aroused tremendous interest. The Turks had all been coming from miles away to admire these wonders, and as a result her stock had risen considerably.

The delay in the transfer of money to her had held back work in the fields and she would be obliged to do her sowing in the winter, which fortunately was not very severe in her valley. She had animals enough to support her household; a cow buffalo provided them with excellent milk, whilst chickens and turkeys were there to be eaten when meat was in short supply. Two pairs of buffaloes sufficed for the time being to do the ploughing and carry timber. Four horses were available for bringing provisions and for transport. She had quite a number of people on her hands at the time and had to accommodate between eight and ten masons, who had come to erect her stables and outbuildings and to add an extension to the existing house.

Once everything was finished she hoped to devote at least part of each day to study and writing again. She asked Augustin to send her the best text book he could find on mineralogy.

There was much shaking of heads in Paris when the Princess's old friends learned what she was doing. They thought it the height of foolhardiness for a woman alone, and a Christian, to live miles from civilisation and surrounded by Moslems. She must be mad, commented François Mignet. But trouble when it arose came from Paris. Owing to shortage of money, Cristina on leaving Rome had written to her friend, Caroline Jaubert, asking her to try and sell for publication the lengthy letters she had sent her during the siege.

Caroline, whom de Musset called his 'godmother', was the eldest sister of the dandy companion of Prince Emilio, Edmond d'Alton-Shée. A kindly, popular woman, she was married to an important judge. She took the letters to Léopold Duras, editor of the *National*. Not originally intended to be seen in print and penned under conditions of severe strain at odd moments snatched from the running of the hospitals, they had provided an outlet for Cristina's feelings and were trenchantly critical of what annoyed her. Owing to the busy life she had led, there had been no time available to keep a journal, so this correspondence provided the only record of that eventful period of her life. Possibly she had forgotten exactly what she had written, or relied on Caroline Jaubert and any editor's discretion to omit anything that might cause her harm.

But Duras thought only of the interests of his paper. He realised that published in full they would create a sensation and increase the *National's* circulation. He was right, for a storm of angry protests broke out when Italians read such passages as the following, which appeared in his issue of 9 September, 1850. 'In Rome the people lack even the thinnest veneer of civilisation. It is as if they had just emerged from the primeval forests of America. They obey only their instincts. So you can understand what the women's morals are like.'

The Italian press quoted what had been published in Paris, and the Princess was violently attacked. When the news eventually reached her she sent the *Concordia* of Turin an explanation, which they printed. She claimed that the offending passages had been taken out of their context, and that the wording too had been altered. She had not criticised the Romans but the old Papal Government, which through failing to educate and better the common people had left them in a such a sorry state.*

But Cristina's attempt to vindicate herself only made matters worse. Duras retaliated by offering to show the original letters to anyone to prove that not a word had been changed or omitted,

* An English traveller, Thomas I. Ireland, in his journal describing a tour of Italy in the 1840s confirms the judgment of Cristina regarding Rome: 'The population, 150,000, includes 50,000 foreigners who fill the majority of the trades, even the ground is tilled by them, and idleness and depravity distinguish the degenerate race of the modern Romans. The windows are filled with women, lolling out in listless sloth from morning till night. . . . The women in the quarters of Monti and Trastevere, carry knives and often use the long pins stuck in their hair as offensive weapons.'

and Caroline Jaubert sent the Princess an indignant letter which the latter, when writing to Augustin Thierry, described as containing expressions 'which I did not think were still used in the nineteenth century.' It had made her ill for several days. However, she did not want to continue the controversy and she asked Augustin to act as a peacemaker between them, which he did, and soon the two women were friends again and writing regularly to each other. Caroline began sending her parcels of newspapers.

In one of them the Princess read of the death of Madame Josephine Grassini, the former opera singer, from La Scala, Milan, who had been for a short while one of Napoleon's mistresses, and of whom, according to Greville, Wellington, too, had been very fond. Cristina wrote back:

'She was a fine woman and adorably ingenuous ... People with a warped sense of humour used to bait her with insincere compliments, and thus induce her to sing long after her voice had disappeared. It was only necessary to ask her for the song which the Emperor liked best for her to grapple hoarsely and rustily with the cavatina from *Romeo*. What a tragedy for a once superb contralto to come to this. She looked upon her imperial conquest as her pass-key to immortality, and never failed to introduce the subject at the most unsuitable moments.

'One day in my salon some intellectuals were discussing Fontenelle's *Dialogue des Morts* ... Whilst this was taking place Mme. Grassini arrived and sat silently listening. Heaven knows what she understood of the conversation! Later we changed the subject and started speculating on what famous persons of modern times would say to each other if they met in the Elysian fields.

'"What do you think Napoleon and Louis XVIII would have to say to each other?" someone asked ...

'"I can tell you that!" cried Madame Grassini before anyone else could speak. "I knew the Emperor intimately, and I am sure the first thing he would have to say to Louis XVIII would be: 'So there you are, you fat pig. It was you who ordered the Government to stop the pension I had arranged to be paid to that poor Grassini who loved me so dearly.'"

Meanwhile Cristina's new venture at Ciaq-Maq-Oglou was

prospering. The wheat harvest had been a good one, and she had become very popular with the inhabitants of the surrounding district. She had learned a great deal about medicine and the art of healing in Rome. Here there was no doctor, and through her having given a few peasants successful remedies, she was now regarded as the physician for the whole province. 'From five in the morning till six in the evening hardly an hour goes by without my being brought the sick or the dying. I am quite startled myself at some of the cures I have achieved. Among other cases, there was a woman brought to me paralysed for six months on her right side and who can now move both her arms and legs, thanks to my massaging her and giving her belladonna and sal ammoniac to take. As a result, the people believe that I am capable of curing everything. An old woman of eighty, riddled with leprosy, called on me the other day and begged me to give her some healing medicine. Not knowing what to do, I told her to wait till spring and then to bathe in the sea, whereupon she went away smiling happily and calling on Allah to bless me.'[4]

It was not only with the peasantry that the Princess was popular. She had become very friendly in Constantinople with one of the Sultan's chief Ministers, Ali Pasha, and he wrote to the Governor of the province in which she now lived instructing him to exempt her from taxation for three years. The Governor replied that not for three or even six years could he attempt to make her pay any taxes, because the whole population would oppose it.

The Princess's popularity certainly did not arise through her handing out baksheesh. Owing to the difficulties of communication and the lethargy of bankers, she did not receive any money for over three months after her arrival. She lived entirely on credit. 'I bought animals and agricultural implements, wheat and barley – I had all the buildings completed entirely on credit. There were on several occasions somewhat lively arguments between my dragoman and my suppliers, but if I appeared and told the latter: "My friends, you have good reason to be dissatisfied, but I can't pay you, since my money hasn't arrived. So you must either remove everything you have sold me or be very patient and wait. That's all I have to say." Then they would reply: "We'll wait, Pearl of the West. Don't worry yourself on account of us. Your money will arrive and we shall be paid." That's how they behaved towards me, and that is why I shall never forget those poor Turks and their patience.'

Everything went well for Cristina at first. A Turkish friend of hers who was a skilled agriculturalist visited her, and discovered that it would be very easy to change the course of her river so as to irrigate all her land. This solved many problems and enabled her to look forward to early success. Apart from the excellent climate, what appealed most of all to Cristina about her valley was its tranquillity. 'A tranquillity which had become necessary to me,' she wrote to Thierry. 'I hope to regain here the strength to return later to the world and its torments; but my morale is so very low that I am easily upset. I spend any leisure this retirement gives me working. I have started painting again. I am preparing for publication the private and official correspondence of the Governments of Piedmont, Rome and Tuscany during the years 1848 and 1849. And when I want to really relax, I amuse myself writing a novel and two one-act plays . . .

'Maria is the happiest child in the world. She has appointed herself my poultry-keeper. Chickens, turkeys, geese and ducks acknowledge her as their sovereign, and when she appears in the yard a chorus of delighted gobblings, cluckings and quackings greet her, of which she is very proud.'

In a letter[5] dated 27 March 1851, Thierry acknowledged receipt of Cristina's painting of Maria in peasant costume, attended by her cow, her donkey and her poultry. He found it charming, but it would have pleased him better if he had known it to have been painted nearer Paris, say in a cottage outside London or a chalet by Lausanne. 'I am glad you are so well, but who would look after you if you were ill? That is what everybody asks me. Here there has never been so much illness. All my visitors can talk about is influenza, pleurisy and pneumonia.'

In April, Cristina went to perform her Easter duties in the ancient town of Saffran-Bolo, where there was a Greek Orthodox Church. To her surprise her fame as a doctor had reached even here, and the hotel where she was staying was besieged by the sick and the crippled wanting to consult her. When she went out a procession of them followed her, and even invaded the houses of the people on whom she was calling.

Commenting on Thierry's wish in his previous letter that she were living near London or Lausanne, she points out it would be impossible for her to do so in similar style to that which she enjoyed in her valley at anything like the same cost.

'Since arriving seven months ago I have bought several rice fields, have rented a mill for twelve hundred piastres a year (nearly three hundred francs), have also bought a saw-mill, four pairs of buffaloes, six cows, two donkeys, five horses (of which two would cost in Paris more than a hundred *louis d'or*), two hundred Angora goats, paid the wages of the workmen who have built my stables, outbuildings and part of my house (please note that two of these men were Europeans and I had to pay their travelling expenses here), paid for the daily keep of some thirty souls, have stinted myself nothing and have stinted nobody else, led the life of a banker, lending to one, giving to another, buying without bargaining, living in fact as if I had the resources of M. de Rothschild, all this have I done and have not spent more than ten thousand francs.

'Tell me in what country in Europe could I do the same? And remember that this year I had to buy everything – wheat, barley, hay, straw, butter, cheese, meat, etc. And bear in mind that from next September I will be able to obtain all this from my own farm.

'But you won't be convinced. I can hear you replying: "No, you certainly would not be able to lead in Europe and so economically the life you are leading there, but you could live differently without spending so much." And how should I live, may I ask?

'As I lived in Paris during the winter of '48 to '49? Working twelve hours a day, having to alter what I write to suit the whims or not offend the prejudices of an uncouth fool of an editor like M. Buloz or a pomaded one like M. de Mars, to earn a few hundred francs a month? Walking kilometres everywhere because I cannot afford to hire a hackney, mending and patching my dresses to save buying new ones, refusing myself even flowers because I should have to buy them ...

'No, everything would upset me in Europe. I should lead a life of physical and material privations – and what should I receive in return? Only mental torture . . . Here I enjoy calm, freedom from all passions, a pleasant and easy life, genuine friendship from everyone. I have put on weight and have never been so well. My neuralgia, my palpitations, my shortness of breath, my fevers, all have vanished as if by enchantment.

'I remember that when I was living in Paris I once attended the meetings of Pierre Leroux, the philosopher, who believed in reincarnation and how the Countess Marliani claimed to have been in past lives Semiramis and Queen Elizabeth, whilst Madame George Sand was credited with having been both Sappho and the Blessed Virgin. I have no such lofty pretensions, and I content myself with the claim that in a former existence I was a wandering gypsy, and that is why the vastness and silence of uninhabited places, the fatigues of travel, resting in a tent, and all else associated with such a life give me so much pleasure. I feel as I wander through these lands a strange excitement. It really seems to me as though I have been here before.'[6]

The Princess was convinced that once Louis Napoleon's term of office expired he would not be re-elected President, and she planned therefore to visit Augustin Thierry in Paris once this had happened in 1852, but when instead Louis was returned to power with an overwhelming majority, the news came as a tremendous blow to her. She wrote to Caroline Jaubert that to try and dispel her despondency she had suddenly decided to go on an extensive tour of Asia Minor. She engaged to take charge of her estate during her absence a man from Alsace, whom she felt she could trust and whom she believed to be an experienced agriculturist.

CHAPTER 10

JOURNEY TO JERUSALEM

She set out in early January accompanied by Maria, a cousin from Milan, the Marquis Antinori, Mrs Parker and a few servants. Her original plan was to travel via Angora, Caesarea, Aintab, Aleppo and Damascus to Jerusalem, arriving there in time for Easter. But in fact her travels were prolonged and she was away eleven months. She kept a daily account of all that she saw and experienced, which later appeared as a series of articles in the *Revue des Deux Mondes* and was eventually published in book form.[1]

The Princess told her readers that the Syria and Palestine she visited bore but little resemblance to the lands she had previously read about in books. She began by claiming that of all the virtues held in honour by Christian society, hospitality was the only one which Mussulmans believed themselves bound to practise:

'Enter his house and beg him to quit it, leave him to wait in the extremes of heat and cold at his own gateway, exhaust his store of wine and brandy, break his crockery, ride his horses and return them foundered – do as one pleases and he will not utter a single reproach; you are a *mouzafir*, a guest . . .

'Your host overwhelms you with kindness during your sojourn at his house, but if on your departure you do not reward him twenty times the value of all that he has given you, he will wait until you quit his roof, until you have, consequently, resigned your sacred title of *mouzafir* – and then he will pelt you with stones.'

An exception to this rule, she states, was the old Mufti of Tcherkess. Like most of the better houses of the country, his consisted of a main building reserved for women and children, and an additional one containing both summer and winter apartments, with two rooms for the servants attached to them. The former had a fountain in its centre, next to which would be placed divans for sitting or reclining. The latter was a warm room with a fireplace, thick carpets, and also divans.

The Mufti, aged ninety, had many wives, the eldest being only thirty, whilst his children ranged from a six-months old baby to a sexagenarian. 'He professes a creditable repugnance to the clamour, disorder and uncleanliness of the harem. He visits it during the day, as he goes to his stable to see and admire his horses; but he lives and sleeps, according to the season, in either one or the other of his two saloons. The brave man comprehended that if long habit could not accustom him to the inconvenience of the harem, so much the worse would it be for me, newly arrived from that land of enchantment and refinement which they call here "Frankistan."'

Accordingly, he offered the Princess his own apartment, the winter saloon, which she gladly accepted, whilst he retreated to his summer saloon. 'Although it was the middle of January and everywhere was covered with snow, he preferred his chilly fountain, damp pavement and blasts of cold air to the warm but impure atmosphere of the harem.'

Cristina claimed to be the first writer to describe the harem as it really was, and not like others who had falsely made it out to be a luxurious abode of love and beauty. 'What a mistaken idea! Imagine blackened and cracked walls, wooden ceilings split in various places, covered with dust and cobwebs, torn and greasy sofas, ragged curtains, and everywhere traces of spilled oil and candle grease.'

When she entered her first harem, it almost sickened her.

'The mistresses of the place, however, did not notice it. Their persons are in keeping with this. Mirrors being scarce, they pile on clothes and tinsel haphazardly, producing a bizarre effect, of which they have no conception . . . Nothing can be more slovenly than their hair, the very great ladies who had lived in the capital alone possessing combs. As to the paint, which they apply immoderately, both in variety of colour and in quantity, its distribution can only be regulated by mutual consultation, owing to the lack of mirrors, so, as all the women living under one roof are rivals, they willingly encourage the most grotesque decoration of their respective faces. They apply vermilion to the lips, red to the cheeks, nose, forehead and chin, white wherever a vacant spot occurs, and blue around the eyes and under the nose.

'What is yet more strange is their manner of constructing eyebrows. They have doubtless been told that to be beautiful the eyebrow should form a great arch, and from this they conclude that the arch must be the more beautiful according to the width of its span, never inquiring if the place assigned to it had not been irrevocably fixed by nature. Believing this, they allot all the space between the two temples to eyebrows, and paint thereon two immense bows, the root of the nose and the temples on either side serving as piers for their support. Some eccentric young beauties who prefer straight lines to crooked ones, trace one single ray direct across the brow, but these instances are rare.'

She continued that every woman's face being such a complicated work of art, they left it as it was for as long as they could, only retouching it occasionally.

'There is not one, daubed as they are with orange colours, even to hands and feet, who does not dread the application of water as an injury to beauty.

'The crowd of infants and servants, especially negresses, who people the harem, and the footing of equality upon which mistresses and domestics live, are likewise aggravating causes of the general filth. I will not speak of children, for everybody knows the manners and customs of these little creatures; but let us imagine what would become of our elegant furniture in Europe, should our cooks and chambermaids rest at will on the couches and sofas of our saloons . . . Smoking, eating, drinking and flogging rebellious young ones are about the sole daily occupations of these mortal houris of faithful Mussulmans.'

What was utterly lacking in these apartments, Cristina claims, was air, but no occupant ever complained about that. 'Naturally sensitive to cold, and without the resource of creating heat by exercise, they remain squatted on the ground before the fire for

hours, wholly ignorant that the fumes of the coal they use sometimes suffocate them.'

She paints a vivid picture of the Mufti. Though ninety, he
looked no older than sixty. His tall figure was slightly bent, but
'the inclination seems to proceed rather from an air of condescen-
sion than from feebleness.' His regular features, clear and transparent skin, blue eyes and white waving beard falling to his
girdle, his noble brow, surmounted by a white or green turban
'enwreathed in large folds as formerly worn, present an appropriate model for the painter of a Jacob or an Abraham.'

At first she felt that he was a saintly man. The passages of his
house were constantly thronged; devotees of every age and condition flocked to kiss the hem of his garment 'to ask counsel and
prayer and to request charitable aid, all departing gratified and
singing the praises of their benefactor. He appeared to be proof
against human weaknesses, and was attentive and fatherly in every
sense of the word to his children.'

But she began to have misgivings as the result of a conversation
with him and one of his confidants. She asked what happened to
the children once they grew up, and learned that the girls were
all married or given away as soon as they reached their tenth or
twelfth year. The boys, not being so precocious, required support
until their fourteenth year. Then they were found work and he
saw no more of them.

The town of Tckerkess, once the ancient Antoniopolis, she
described as consisting of houses of wood and mud falling to
ruin, scattered here and there as if by chance, the intermediate
spaces remaining as receptacles for every description of dirt, with
half-savage dogs, jackals and birds of prey acting as scavengers.
'Such is a faithful picture of Tckerkess, and of every other town
of Asia Minor.'

Two days' march separated it from Angora, which she reached
in February 1852, after a hazardous journey over mountains
covered with snow, and where she stayed with its Mufti who was
blind, caused, it was said, by cataract. Cristina states that her
reputation for medical skill had become so well-known in Asia
Minor that he asked her to treat him. She could find no signs of

cataract. 'I prescribed accordingly a simple treatment, which he submitted to without hesitation, and which at the end of a few days brought him some relief. This was sufficient to excite in the old man's breast a warm friendship for me; he sent his coadjutors to enquire about me every morning, and to place himself and themselves at my disposal for any excursion and for all investigations that I desired to make.'

In return he sent her eight miracle-performing dervishes. At first she watched their spectacle sceptically, anticipating a scene of gross imposture. She was horrified when, as the climax to feverish dancing, one of the dervishes buried the blade of a dagger in his cheek, its point projecting from the interior of the mouth.

'The blood soon streaming from the two openings of the wound, I could not restrain myself from making a sign to the old man to have this horrible scene brought to an end.

'"Would the lady like to examine it closer?" he said. Making a sign to the performer to approach, he made me notice that the dagger's point had thoroughly pierced the flesh, and was not satisfied until he had forced me to touch the point with my finger.

'"Are you convinced that this man's wound is real?" he finally asked me. "I have no doubt of it," I replied hurriedly.

'"Enough, my son," he resumed, addressing the dervish, who during the examination remained with his mouth open, filled with blood, and the steel still resting in the cheek, "go and heal thyself."

'The dervish bowed, withdrew the dagger and, approaching one of his brethren, knelt before him and presented his cheek to him, which the latter washed outside and inside with his own saliva. The operation lasted only a few seconds, but when the man arose and turned towards us, all traces of the wound had disappeared.'

Another dervish gave the same display, wounding himself in the arm, which was dressed and healed in the same manner. 'A third frightened me. He was armed with a large two-edged scimitar, which he held with both hands by its two extremities and then applied the concave side of the blade to his belly, causing it to penetrate by a see-saw movement. A line of purple colour immediately appeared on the brown and lustrous skin. I entreated the old man to desist and not to carry his experiments further. He smiled and assured me that I had seen nothing as yet, that this was only the prologue; that his children would cut their limbs with impunity, and if necessary, their heads, without the slightest inconvenience to them.' But Cristina had seen enough.

She continues: 'It was in vain that I recalled the tricks of our ablest European conjurers; my memory furnished nothing comparable to what I had just witnessed. I had to do here with ignorant and simple men; their feats were of the greatest simplicity and left but little room for artifice ... I have faithfully described a scene which, for my own part, I am unable to explain.'

From Angora, travelling on horseback seven or eight hours a day, exposed to storms and sleet with no protection but her furs or a tent as a place of last resort, she eventually reached the Turcomans. At Kircheis the lodging place was a good one.

'A wood fire, lighted in the chimney, compensated for everything, it being, moreover, a source of infinite satisfaction after having to use for so many days the Turcomans' usual fuel. In the provinces where trees have vanished, they burn the dried excrement of animals. This fuel is good enough for furnishing heat . . . there being no bad odour or disagreeable exhalations from it.

'But when one comes to ponder over the idea of food prepared on such coals, it produces a sensation of nausea. I lived in continual dread of being offered a narghile lighted by this material, and being compelled to inhale the smoke from that. I burnt my tentpoles and mutilated my travelling furniture rather than submit to inhale the smoke from such fecal matter.'

After leaving Angora the country had become more and more sombre, and people more unfriendly. The same state of affairs persisted between Kircheis and Caesarea. They travelled for days through mud and snow. In the miserable villages where they passed their nights they saw only discontented faces, sometimes threatening ones, and they were greeted with nothing but insults. Generally speaking, their escorting guard was useless, and occasionally more of a liability, because to the mutinous population it represented the authority under which they chafed.

At Caesarea, thanks to the English consul, they were comfortably housed with a wealthy Armenian merchant, and were impressed by the richness and taste of the embroidery on the women's colourful dresses, by their hair arranged in from twelve to fifteen braids of equal length, descending as low as possible. Gold coins, sewn to a small black riband and afterwards attached to the braids half-way between the neck and the lower part of the hips, formed a brilliant segment of a circle and contrasted brightly with their dark hair. A profusion of such coins decked the front of the fez a woman wore, falling over her brow and hanging from her ears, and also covering the neck, bosom and arms, as if with a coat of mail.

'Various specimens of jewellery find room amid these coins. Diamond flowers sparkle around the fez, or in the braid that encircles the forehead, while clasps of precious stones, necklaces and strings of pearls fasten the corsage below the breasts, or pass underneath the chin, stretching from ear to ear. The daughters of wealthy parents are magnificently adorned, for, in the shape of jewellery, they bear their marriage portions about them, and this sometimes amounts to very considerable sums.'

She next visited a Greek settlement. Here she was very impressed when she inspected a school run by one priest, who, to her astonishment, managed to teach and effectively control seventy girls and one hundred and fifty boys all on his own.

They then crossed the Taurus mountains, which took them five days. 'I will not narrate the incidents of those five days. Why dwell on the ever-recurring adventures which bad roads and worse quarters constantly afford to travellers in certain parts of the Orient?'

In Adana Cristina called on the Pasha in his audience hall, one side of which was furnished with an ottoman or divan stretching along its entire length. This was simply a platform of boards nailed together, and was considered as an elevation of the floor and not as a piece of furniture. They seated themselves there on their heels. Cristina goes on to mention how she had in her house in Ciaq-Maq-Oglou some rush-bottomed chairs, sent to her from Milan. In the early days of her residence in Turkey she was imprudent enough to offer one to a very corpulent bey, who had come to pay his respects to her.

'You may imagine my fright when I saw him raise his robe, in order to execute a very difficult movement, and place his big foot on my delicate chair! The poor bey, on hearing a very significant snap, was quite astonished. He accordingly withdrew his foot and seated himself on the floor. Since that time it is an established belief in this region that the Franks are incomparably lighter than the Turks, since they are in the habit of seating themselves on furniture which the weight of a Turk dislocates.'

When the Pasha of Adana learned that Cristina planned to travel to Jerusalem by land, he advised her not to do so as between Adana and Alexandretta she would be obliged to cross part of the Djaour-Daghda, which he described as the graveyard of travellers. 'But why can you not go by sea?' In reply the Princess asked if she would be able to find a steamer at Tarsus to transport her to Jaffa. The Pasha turned to his entourage, all of whom shook their heads. After discussing the matter with them in Arabic, he ended by confessing that the coming and going of steamers at Tarsus was very erratic, and that she might have to wait for as long as three months for one.

He then suggested that she should embark on a sailing vessel, but his advisers opposed this, stating that the wind in the gulf blew from every quarter of the universe. 'They furnished such a list of terrible shipwrecks which had occurred the winter before that the amiable pasha ended where he ought to have begun, by assuring me that if I were really desirous of reaching Jerusalem by Easter, it was necessary that I should travel there by land.'

One point still remained to be settled: how to ensure her safety when crossing the perilous Djaour-Daghda. To solve the problem the Pasha provided her with an escort of twenty men and a letter of introduction to Mustuk-Bey, Prince of the Mountain. When they reached the latter's residence in the village of Bajuz, she found to her relief that the Bey was a pleasant, good-natured man with keen smiling blue eyes, who, to her further relief, did not suggest she should sleep in the harem but placed a large apartment at her disposal, informing her at the same time that his wives would receive and return her visits whenever it would be most convenient to her.

'The aspect of the *dame-en-chef* impressed me peculiarly; she reminded me involuntarily of a retired acrobat. This sultana had once been beautiful, and her beauty was not yet entirely gone. Her complexion presented a curious mixture of something like sun-tan and of various layers of paint, under which the original tint was scarcely perceptible.

'During her husband's stay in the room she appeared to be as timid as a young bride on her wedding day, only answering questions in monosyllables. Turning her face to the wall, she would indulge in little nervous spasms of laughter, and then show herself ready to melt away in tears at the first favourable opportunity, repeating, finally, all the petty manoeuvres which I had so often seen practised by women in the same position, and with which their oriental husbands are always so greatly flattered. It is, they say to themselves, a feeling of their inferiority which thus troubles them. The inferiority of those who surround us necessarily implying our own superiority, the masters of the harems are led to regard the embarrassment caused by their presence as a compliment.

'After enjoying for some time the charming emotion which he had excited, and after repeatedly begging me not to mind his wife, who was only a Turk, the Bey left us, informing me that I would not obtain a word from her as long as he remained there.'

When he had departed, Cristina turned to his wife. She thought at first that the woman had disappeared through a trap-door, leaving nothing to represent her but a bundle of clothes. A slight movement of this shapeless mass convinced her of her error. 'There soon came forth, as if from a cloud, the smiling face of my hostess. The emotions caused by the fond adieus of her dear husband had thrown her into such a state of beatitude that she could do no less than bury her head between her knees.'

Now that they were alone, the wife threw off her timid mask and became perfectly at ease. She asked a great many questions about European manners and customs which seemed to her as peculiar. She did not appear as stupid as her husband imagined her to be, and was interested in everything she was told. 'She demanded the *why* of every statement I made. It would have been very difficult for me to have given a categorical answer to all these questions, in a mode that could have been understood by her, but I already possessed the magic words which quickly paralyse all oriental curiosity. All you need reply is: "It is the custom of our country." Orientals regard custom as an unchangeable, inexorable divinity, supreme above all others, and against which it is in vain to contend.'

Four hours' travel separated the then little town of Alexandretta from this Bey's palace. The scenery through the mountains and then along the sea coast Cristina described as being the most picturesque in Syria. Alexandretta itself, though beautifully sited on a verdant plain, bounded on three sides by a vast amphitheatre of mountains and on the other by the sea, she found a disappointing huddle of a few tumbledown houses. She stayed in the home of the English consul, who was absent on leave. Its green blinds and covered balconies 'transported me back, as if by enchantment, to the charming habitations of Brighton and Cheltenham.'

Unfortunately the interior did not live up to the promise of the exterior. 'The consul being several months absent, a crowd of Arab domestics had established themselves in every room, leaving only too evident traces of their occupancy . . . I selected a chamber with a northern aspect, in order not to disturb those microscopic beings who prefer to establish themselves in chambers exposed to the south, and for the rest of the day set to work with brooms and brushes, and eventually went to sleep in a varnished iron bedstead.'

She took every opportunity to be absent from the house in these circumstances, and spent most of her time walking on the sea-shore. 'How much I regretted my ignorance of natural history! I walked about on a mosaic of precious marbles and glittering pebbles, cast up by the sea with a multitude of exquisite shells, the waves still lending them the lustre of their humidity, and the rays of the Syrian sun making them sparkle like diamonds. I gathered several handfuls of these pebbles and shells, and made many journeys to and fro between the sands and my room to store what I had collected; but it was not long before I said to myself, those pebbles, so precious in my eyes, a savant would regard as ordinary stones; so I got up and flung my collection out of the window.'

The next large town they reached was Antioch, the ancient capital, where everything pleased Cristina from its 'fine ruins to its delightful gardens and fountains.' But she was unable to linger there as she had made up her mind to reach Jerusalem by Easter.

It remained for her to decide whether or not they would set out from Antioch alone. An Arab tribe was in revolt and the Pasha of Aleppo was about to send troops against them. They were advised to join the soldiery. 'I, on the contrary, reflected that to travel with soldiers was equivalent to running into the jaws of the enemy, and decided therefore to remain as isolated as possible, and to place myself under the protection of no one ... My resolution was more easily formed than executed. When two parties set out from the same place, march in the same direction and nearly at the same speed, it is not easy to keep apart. We might have remained one or two days in the rear, but that would have meant losing time. We resigned ourselves, accordingly, to the necessity of passing the soldiers and allowing them to pass us in return, often more than ten times a day, promising ourselves, meanwhile, to neglect no opportunity to assure the people amongst whom we travelled that our encounter with the troops was accidental. Every time the soldiers rejoined us the whole regiment fired at us a salvo of Turkish maledictions, which tried my patience sorely.'

After several adventures she reached the town of Gild, where for the first time since her arrival in Syria they encountered European travellers – a Church of England clergyman and his wife.

'The husband was dressed entirely in black, as if ready to ascend the pulpit. He wore a close-fitting white cravat, and a white felt hat encircled with a band of black crape. His wife seemed to be dressed as if about to promenade in an English park, only she wore over her hat a kind of complicated hood, composed of pasteboard, linen and whalebone, intended to protect the head from the sun's rays. A parasol, however, asserted its prerogative, and towered above the hood. This couple were engaged on a mission. Speaking no other tongue than English, armed with several Bibles, an Arabic grammar and dictionary, they were scouring towns, villages, mountains, plains and deserts, converting or trying to convert *pell-mell* to Protestantism, Turks, Arabs, Mussulmans, idolaters, Jews and Catholics.'

Tuesday of Holy Week found the Princess and her party on their way to Nazareth in a driving rain. They reached their destination at night and stayed in a guest house belonging to the Capuchin Fathers. Next morning one of them conducted her first to the Church of the Annunciation, and then to the various sanctuaries erected on the sites mentioned in the Scriptures.

Cristina records her doubts thus: 'One repudiates the idea of assigning the scenes of the infancy of Jesus to such places. Authority, in fact, for the localities here designated as illustrating the various scenes of the New Testament dates no further back than the establishment of the Fathers at Jerusalem in the Holy Land. These good monks were great collectors of local traditions. At every spot which their veneration sanctified arose shrines and convents. Can they be blamed for an excess of credulity which, after all, attests an ardent faith?'

Jerusalem itself she reached on the eve of Easter Sunday. When she first saw from a distance the city's crenellated walls and beyond them a bluish line mingling with the horizon indicating the Sea of Galilee, she was very moved. 'Strange to say, this sense of joy remained with me during the whole of my stay there.'

The following morning she visited Calvary, which she had supposed to be on a height and was surprised to find it now the site of a church, reached by a street on a descending gradient. She describes in detail her visits to all the Holy Places and her impressions of them. About the Garden of Gethsemane she writes: 'For once, nobody could dispute that this garden is what it is asserted to be. Although the wall is of modern construction, and it may not be built on the precise perimeter of the ancient garden, the whole of this portion of the hill is covered with fine old olive trees, and if it be not under one of these that Christ sat down and wept over Jerusalem, some of those now existing are certainly descended from them.'

Later she proceeded to the gardens of Solomon. 'Never, indeed, have richer clusters of fragrant flowers gladdened my eyes, never have sweeter melodies of birds greeted my ears! Were the King and the fair Shulamite about to appear before me in the midst of this fairy landscape? I was almost tempted to believe so, when something happened to dispel whatever visions of this nature I was striving to evoke. I found myself in the presence of an English "party". A Britannic colony, such as one encounters in every quarter of the universe, had possessed themselves for the summer of Solomon's gardens; they had rented them just as they would rent a country house at Saint-Cloud. A few tents of diverse colour and form constituted their domiciles; these remained unoccupied during the day, while the group frolicked about amid the surrounding fields and shrubbery.

'There were ladies among them in morning toilettes, as neatly arranged as if they were sojourning in one of the castles in the heart of England, and also a swarm of young girls dressed in white frocks, with long, braided hair tied with blue and red ribbons, and falling down over their bare shoulders. A little further off I noticed a group of gentlemen in hunting costume, engaged in some rural occupation.

'On making some inquiries about this group, I learned that they consisted of a colony of missionaries, who had imposed on themselves the task of showing Arabs, and principally Jews, the salutary effect of Bible societies and patent plough-shares.'

Whilst in Jerusalem, Maria, Cristina's daughter, made her first Holy Communion, which surprised 'some of the brethren and sisters, who regarded me as pledged to the worship and practice of the doctrines of Voltaire and Rousseau.'

She visited the lepers' asylum and commented: 'Nobody considers leprosy in the Orient a contagious malady, or a shameful or disgusting infirmity.'

She spent a month in Jerusalem, then left. 'I had no time to lose if I would regain more temperate regions before the approach of the Syrian dog-days. I set out accordingly. I left the ancient walls behind me, within which my feelings had been so deeply stirred, and on the summit of the hill where, a month before, Jerusalem first broke upon my sight, I turned and last looked upon the sacred city of Judea.'

The places she visited next – Damascus, Aleppo, Mount Lebanon – she found differed but little as regards nomadic and domestic life from those she had earlier observed at Angora and elsewhere.

RETURN TO CIAQ-MAQ-OGLOU

The return journey began badly. On the second day the Princess became very concerned over her horse, Kur, whose white coat had been sadly disfigured through vicious fly bites. Whilst about to tend the animal's wounds she noticed a large pest busily attacking it. Taking out a handkerchief, she drew nearer and dealt the fly several slaps.

'Through my being behind him, Kur could not see what I was attempting to do. Exasperated by the stinging bites and by my blows, the horse suddenly gave a violent kick which caught me just below the left knee. I feared my leg had been broken. I lost all sensation in it, and fell into the grass. Slowly, however, feeling returned, but my suffering then became so intense I could scarcely refrain from crying out.'

This was but the beginning of that day's troubles. The pain, fatigue, heat, and the dry desert wind brought on a fever. She lay upon some shawls and cloaks under the shade of an immense mangrove tree, waiting for the cool of evening.

'It seemed as if flames were rising up from the ground around me, and my chest became tight as if it were refusing to breathe in the scorching air. With my head so hot, my temples throbbing, and a stunning noise in my ears, my whole body seemed to be on fire. I fell, then, into a sort of coma.'

Later she heard voices and, opening her eyes, found herself surrounded by Arabs 'with swarthy faces, black beards and eyes, and robed in white.' They were all regarding her with obvious concern. One gave her water to drink, others fanned her with large leaves obtained from the neighbouring trees, and another drove away the gnats and flies that tormented her, whilst telling her that she possessed twenty-three out of the twenty-seven points that the Prophet Mahomet had declared the perfect woman should be blessed with.

'It did not even occur to them to demand the inevitable baksheesh for every new service they performed. We were their guests and not their enemies. I know of Europeans who, seeing me in such a state, would have stepped swiftly by on tiptoe.'

Towards evening, both the sirocco and her fever abated. Although her limbs still hurt her, she succeeded in mounting her horse, and late that night reached Nazareth, where she managed to find accommodation in a cool, dark room with a comfortable bed, where she remained for eight days recovering.

They next set out through the desert for Damascus with an experienced Arab guide. On the way they pitched their camp near a bathing establishment on the side of a lake outside Tiberias. There she had an opportunity to admire the way in which English people resigned themselves to the discomforts of Oriental travel.

'On reaching Tiberias, towards nine o'clock in the morning, and whilst I was sighing for a shady camping-ground where I could pass the hot hours of the day, I met an English family about to start out for Safed. Milady sat in a litter suspended between two mules, the most uncomfortable of all means of transportation yet invented for the punishment of travellers.'

Another English family had set out from Nazareth on the same day as Cristina, following the same road and stopping at the end of the same stages. They would resume their journey, however, at the very times of day which she would choose for pausing and resting in order to avoid travelling when the heat was most oppressive. 'We could see them from our cool retreat ambling gravely along at a slow pace, the ladies protected by immense funnel-shaped bonnets and white calico parasols, and the gentlemen with umbrellas only, their faces purple and the perspiration streaming down upon their vests and cravats.'

She made repeated attempts to induce them to arrange their schedule differently, to rise early and rest themselves during the hottest part of the day. The husband declared that his wife and daughter were not fond of early rising, and that they could not possibly complete their toilet and pack their trunks by nine o'clock in the morning. 'Besides,' he told Cristina, 'we are not too warm. We find it very pleasant travelling when the sun is overhead.'

Cristina comments that the temperature was then 106 degrees Fahrenheit in the shade. 'What is still more astonishing is that neither the gentlemen nor the ladies suffered from refusing to change their routine. What stamina these English have!'

At noon, Cristina retired into the interior of the bathing establishment and was resting on a mattress when a celebrated beauty arrived, accompanied by numerous attendants. She sent her slaves to wake and bring Cristina to her, saying that she wanted advice on an important matter.

'Although in bad humour from being disturbed, I stood dumb with astonishment on appearing before my beautiful client. If ever a woman's face could be compared to a bright clear moon, if ever fresh complexion, rosy cheeks and lips, luxuriant hair . . . if all these were found combined to the highest degree of perfection in a single woman, it was assuredly in the one before me.'

The beauty was the wife of an old and wealthy Arab, but had lost her hold over him owing to her sterility, which was all she could think and talk about. She wanted Cristina to help her, and was very disappointed and angry when the Princess said she knew of no cure for barrenness.

News now came that the mountain Arabs were in revolt. Terrible travellers' tales were in circulation of massacres and robberies, and their route was said to be completely blocked by bloodthirsty hordes. Cristina had difficulty in persuading her guide, Mohammed Zaffedy, to continue the journey. They next camped on the heights of Safed, north of Tiberias, where an old Arab who acted as English Consul called on her. When she told him her intended route, he asked if she were aware of the condition of the country.

'Only by hearsay,' was her reply, 'and I should be happy to know from yourself if the reports I have are reliable, for my guide has made every effort to induce me to abandon the route through the desert. The stories of Arabs and brigands don't frighten me.'

'You are right,' returned the Consul. 'When one trusts in God, as you seem to do, there is nothing to fear from the wicked. Whichever road you take, you will find brigands on all. They cannot deprive your soul of its trust in God. I have not seen such faith for a long time, and far be it from me to think of opposing it by any of those miserable suggestions which grow out of a love for one's life, or for the perishable goods of this world.'

Cristina wrote that she was somewhat embarrassed by this. 'There was, nevertheless, something bordering on the comic in the expression of respectful admiration which lit up the worthy man's face. My motives for choosing the most direct and the shortest route were not based on belief that God would intervene in a crisis in my favour. But I felt myself unable to confess this to the worthy Consul. I tried to obtain from him, indirectly, some information on the state of things, but without success. Whenever I led the conversation to the perils of the desert, the pious Consul stopped me short with exclamations like: "Of what concern is that to you, madame? Have you not the God of battles with you? Oh! if everybody possessed your courage and your faith, the highways would not be so quickly abandoned, and the wicked would not so readily make themselves masters of them."

'"Am I to conclude from what you say that they are actually in possession of these roads?" I enquired.

'"And what if they are – they could never get the advantage of one who relies upon the God of the strong. Etc."'

Seeing that she would get nowhere with the Consul, she asked one of her companions to take his turn in sounding the man, and in procuring from him, if possible, letters of recommendation to some of the Arab chiefs through whose territories they would pass. But this approach met with no better success. All the sheiks the Consul knew appeared to be either away or dying.

She tried again to persuade Mohammed to set out. But he said he had forgotten the way, so she engaged a guide. Then Moham-med said he couldn't think of venturing into country occupied by the enemy. Cristina comments that she never succeeded in ascertaining whom he called an enemy but that she believed he regarded as an enemy everybody of whom he was afraid.

He then demanded that some strong well-armed men be recruited to protect them. Cristina agreed to this, on condition that the entire troop should not exceed ten men, and that nobody should be paid before they reached Damascus. At first Zaffedy made no objection to this arrangement, but just as they were on the point of leaving, he said that the local 'strong-arms' he had taken on demanded three-quarters of their pay in advance.

'Monsieur Zaffedy reserved this *coup de théâtre* for the last hour, presuming, doubtless, that I would agree to anything in order to save both time and money.' But she had no money with her, and could not obtain any until they reached Damascus. Necessity compelled her to be firm.

' "It is time," I said, "to set out. If Mohammed and his men are willing to follow with or without reinforcements, according to existing arrangements, well and good. If they decline, although I am entitled to refuse to pay them since they have not fulfilled their engagements with me, I am willing to remit the sum due them into the hands of any person at Damascus they may choose to name. And now I am going. If you are disposed to follow me, you will all meet me at the bridge of Beni-Jacob. In case you are not, appoint one of you to act for you and let him come to me and make arrangements for your pay."

'With these words I mounted my horse, and my companions likewise. It was then that Mohammed Zaffedy threw off the mask. He became frightfully pale, and his fine form shrunk to such a degree to be almost unrecognisable. Darting at my horse's head, and making a menacing gesture he cried out, trembling with rage: "You shall never move one step till you pay me!"

'He thought this would intimidate me. But he was unaware that threats always have the opposite effect with me. Besides, I understood my horse perfectly, and I well knew that no sign or motion from any Arab hand would stay him. I accordingly gave him the rein, crying out to the impudent Arab to touch me at his peril. His comrades ranged themselves all on my side, for I was a woman, and an Arab must be the very meanest of his race to forget this.'

Some threw themselves on Mohammed and forced him back.

Others sprang into their saddles and shouted that they were prepared to follow Cristina wherever she wished. Mohammed, seeing himself abandoned, burst into tears and begged to be forgiven. A reconciliation was effected and off they set.

The custom-house man at the bridge of Beni-Jacob over the Jordan confirmed the bad news. Not a traveller had passed over the river for three weeks, and the only news from the interior was that of armed brigands' robberies and massacres.

But this did not worry Cristina. Why should these Arabs do them injury? They were not allies of the hated Turks, were almost moneyless and carried no valuables. The only danger was that the guards she had hired might flee on encountering any Arabs they thought might be bandits, in which case she might find herself held up to ransom. So she kept reminding her escort that she had no wish to fight any Arabs, but of 'maintaining with them a friendly and cordial intercourse.' Every time she said this the guards replied: 'We will defend you – fear nothing.'

At last, four days later, after several false alarms they reached Damascus, about which she wrote extensively and entertainingly. 'Time glided away at little cost to me in this beautiful region, surrounded as I was with friends and curious and interesting objects. The conversation one day turned on a celebrated Arab danseuse (Armenian by birth), whose charms and talents approached the marvellous. I was not a very ardent admirer of the oriental dance, but my friends insisted that I could not really appreciate these dances unless I saw the illustrious Khadoun perform.'

So it was arranged that this exponent of the art should for a fixed sum entertain Cristina, whose curiosity had been aroused when she learned that one of Khadoun's troupe though having only one eye had captivated and married an aristocratic English colonel, to become a milady with her own salon.

News of the soirée swiftly spread, and on the appointed evening Cristina's house was packed with guests and many self-invited ones. But just before the entertainment was due to begin there was trouble, she records. 'An old ragged woman, the mother of my Terpsichores, sat in front of them talking excitedly, whilst

servants bearing cymbals, tambourines, castanets and innumer-
able boxes kept coming and going. I saw at a glance that something was wrong, so making myself known as the mistress of the
house, I asked these nymphs if anything had occurred to displease
them. Khadoun's dancing partner, Zobeide, acted as spokes-
woman. She declared that the presence of such a large assembly
intimidated them, and that they did not feel able to take a single
step until they were satisfied regarding how much I intended to
pay them.

'I was about to appeal to my friend, the Arab, who had conducted negotiations with these ladies, when suddenly somebody
glided behind me and whispered in my ear: "Give them some
brandy. They won't dance unless they're drunk!"

'Being, fortunately, well supplied for the soirée, I hastened to
take this advice, and put into the hands of each danseuse a well-
filled bottle, which they immediately raised to their lips, making
constant use of it while the discussion lasted. The brandy, however, did not take immediate effect, and they retained enough of
their sang-froid to declare that they would not raise a foot short
of a guinea for every spectator.'

This exasperated Cristina. 'The door is open,' she told them,
'and you will oblige me greatly by taking advantage of it. As to
the people assembled, I will send for a Punch and Judy show and
some dancers from a neighbouring café, who will give them as
much satisfaction as your contortions.'

The indignant ladies rose and donned their wrappers and
departed with their suite, but they went no further than the street
door and then sent one of their companions on a peace errand,
saying that they would perform for twice what Cristina had
agreed to pay them if she also allowed them to circulate a pewter
dish and make a collection from the company. She agreed and
the spectacle began.

Neither music nor dancing appealed to Cristina. The dance
resembled what she had previously watched in Asia Minor.
Khadoun placed herself in the centre of the carpet, erect and
motionless, and then, as the music prompted her, extended her
arms, agitated her feet, and gave a quivering movement of the

thighs which continued uninterruptedly, whilst without any other motion she apparently glided along from one extremity of the carpet to the other, and again returned in the same manner.

'I do not consider myself a judge of the grace inherent in such movements, nor of the effect which they are apt to produce in spectators of the opposite sex. Certain it is, the effect is violent and almost universal. All the men, save a few rare exceptions, seem to be sent into a state of ecstasy by it.'

If Khadoun had been a young and beautiful woman with a pliant, graceful and symmetrical form, the Princess felt she might have understood why some found her attractive. But this danseuse weighed at least one hundred and twenty pounds. 'Her flesh, unconstricted either by corset or whalebone, voluptuously swelled her light and ample drapery. Diamonds hung down over her cheeks and even over her eyes, while her skin was so painted that it was impossible to detect its natural colour. Her eyes were such as Homer would have compared to those of an ox, reddish black disks, swimming on oceans of yellow white, overcast with a network of veins.'

Zobeide followed Khadoun and repeated 'the same antics with similar effrontery.' After this, both performers executed a dance differing but little from what had preceded it – 'except that the signs and invitations, which were at first addressed sometimes to the spectators and sometimes to an imaginary being, were now exchanged between the dancers, thereby becoming much more clear and intelligible. The last dance executed, the odalisques allowed themselves to fall upon the carpet apparently in a state of exhaustion which, to my eyes, was not the least repulsive part of the performance.

'This tableau, however, only lasted a few moments, for the pewter dish had not yet circulated, and it was important to profit by the spectators' enthusiasm. After the collection the troupe withdrew into a room, where they drank as much coffee and brandy as I could furnish, and then wrapping themselves up in their veils, they retired, stepping along as steadily as possible, considering the way in which they had spent the half-hour preceding their departure.'

Cristina wrote that if she were not destined to see the best aspects of human nature at Damascus, she did see many of its strangest aspects. She had often heard accounts of hashish and its consumers. She had even tried the drug herself, but had experienced only intolerable physical distress, unaccompanied by those wonderful visions and other symptoms which it was said hashish produced in a hundredfold greater degree.

She became acquainted in Damascus with several persons who made the consumption of hashish their chief pleasure, and even business. These people urged her to join their circle, and although the recollection of what she had once suffered was by no means encouraging, she, however, made no strong resistance, for she was sure of not becoming an addict.

The day being fixed, her initiators assembled at her house and the ceremony commenced. 'I smoked hashish, I ate it, I drank it, but all in vain. My brain (I will not say my mind) being exempt from vertigo, I remained almost impassible. My eyes grew heavy and my lips dry. I had an impression of doubt, as if I were not perfectly sure of being able to say what I desired, a symptom, but temporary, and which did not manifest itself externally; such was the *ne plus ultra* of the effects of hashish on myself. But my initiators were not so fortunate. One of them, perceiving the danger of too great an expansion of sentiment, prudently kept silent, and confined himself to an inner enjoyment of bliss, giving way, now and then, to spells of suppressed laughter and immediately falling back into a state of beatified taciturnity. Another seemed more confident. He had been told repeatedly that hashish rendered him exceedingly eloquent – this led him to declaim, in an emphatic tone a series of disconnected phrases, which separately taken, were of no unusual significance, and which, if any mysterious thread of meaning held together, had no place in his mind before.'

The sitting lasted some time, and ended to the great discontent of her initiators, who attributed her insensibility to numerous causes, all of which might easily be made to disappear. They insisted on repeating the experiment on a larger scale at another house, and in the company of other novices. Among them was one of her travelling companions. Cristina yielded.

But she was as little affected as before. Her companion's experience was different. After absorbing a considerable quantity of the drug he began to howl like a wild beast. 'Never in my life shall I forget the spectacle presented to me. His features exhibited that *facies hippocratica* with which physicians are so familiar. His clothes were in disorder, his hair stood erect. He struggled in the arms of two servants, both of whom were striving to force him backward on a sofa, whilst the professor, half-scared and half-triumphant, sought to calm him by assuring him in a low voice that such sensations were well-known to himself, and that in a few moments they would be succeeded by a state of infinite bliss.

'But these assurances had no effect on the sufferer. He renewed his frightful cries, and demanding a confessor, without awaiting his coming, began to avow the most unheard-of acts. The crisis terminated at length in swoons of an alarming character, his pulse becoming slower and slower every second, as if the eater of hashish had really succumbed and fallen into a state of syncope.

'This lasted several hours, and it was not without some trouble that I persuaded my professor friend, the master of the house, to send for a physician, for he pretended that such symptoms were not extraordinary, and that every amateur of hashish had been obliged to cross a similar Rubicon.

'After this declaration I felt, for my own part, but little disposed to be grateful for the strenuous efforts he had made to attach me to his circle . . . The end of the matter is that my companion did not die, but recovered in good time – but neither he nor myself again exposed ourselves to such an adventure.'

Cristina was about to leave Damascus when her daughter, Maria, fell ill with a fever which grew daily worse and defied all medical treatment. In despair the mother 'after having wept much and prayed much, put aside all medicaments, and letting the child sleep for several hours only concerned myself with the means of calming her irritated nerves, and accordingly administered narcotics in very small doses. God be praised, the alarming symptoms disappeared; sleep, appetite, and curiosity all returned. I was no longer obliged to see her stretched for hours upon her couch

DRAWING OF COUNT CAMILLO DI CAVOUR
by Princess Cristina

PRINCESS CRISTINA'S TOMB AT LOCATE

indifferent to everything passing around her, and expressing no other desire than that of quitting Damascus.'

After passing through the mountains of the Lebanon, they entered flat lands and travelled through stifling heat to Aleppo, where she learned that any stranger visiting the town and remaining but a short time would get the Aleppo Button. Twenty-four hours spent there convinced her of the contagiousness of the illness, for she encountered no one in the streets or in the houses she visited who did not exhibit the traces of it in a very disagreeable manner. 'Foreigners seemed to be no more exempt from it than the natives, and among other victims, I made the acquaintance of a Polish Colonel, on whose nose thirteen of the Aleppo Buttons were then flourishing. What this nose was before it was invaded by this avalanche of boils I know not, but I dare affirm that in the year 1852 it was the most extraordinary nose in either hemisphere. The prevailing opinion is that this malady is due to the water that supplies the town. We passed but one month at Aleppo, and two of my travelling companions and myself each developed a genuine Aleppo Button.'

Whilst at Aleppo she attended a ball at the country residence of a French physician, and was horrified to find that although the company assembled consisted entirely of Christians, no minuets, waltzes, polkas or any other occidental dances were performed. 'No, instead the company spent the entire evening repeating the dance which I witnessed being done in Asia Minor by miserable boys disguised as women, and at Damascus by the celebrated Kadhoun and Zobeide. The Aleppoites pretend, however, to execute these strange figures without departing from the strict line of decency. They have succeeded in solving this difficult problem, and those present with me at the doctor's ball agreed that the oriental dance thus westernised could not offend feminine modesty. It is true that the dance itself does not gain much by this somewhat unnatural alliance. Hitherto I had seen contortions of the arms and of the shoulders only accompanied with the fluttering of the thighs, of which no account can be made within the confines of propriety.

'The ladies of Aleppo have thus wisely suppressed that which forms the body and soul of the oriental dance, and not having pushed matters far enough to substitute something better, the oriental dance is about reduced to a nullity. The entire merit of the danseuse consists of an imperceptible movement of the foot, the point of which never penetrates outside the clouds of drapery belonging to the long skirts and ample trousers. The title of perfect dancer is nevertheless one of eager ambition, and on this occasion, the prize was awarded to a respectable and very amiable matron of the mature age of ninety-one years, who, I was informed, had never found her equal since she first began to shake her feet in this manner.'

A few days after this, Cristina attended a wedding. The young couple had never seen each other. As their families were among the wealthiest and most prominent of Aleppo, and as their relatives consisted of about half the Christians of the city, there was a vast number of guests at the wedding. Cristina says that 'the toilets displayed on the occasion surpassed anything the imagination can conceive of. Having no room in my carpet-bag for any but travelling dresses, I was obliged, in order not to appear as a blot on this brilliant canvas, to accept my hostess' offer, and exchange for one day my plain long skirt for the complicated habiliments of a Syrian lady – expansive trousers, dress open on the front, back and sides, the corsage over this, the fez and blue tulle handkerchief around the head, diamond clasps, pearl necklaces, etc., etc.'

The Mussulman authorities of the city also treated her very well. Aleppo had both a civil and a military pasha. Hearing that Cristina had searched in vain for ice, the former arranged for her to be sent some. The old man had been ill and next day he died. 'This death caused a great excitement,' Cristina writes, 'and some attributed it to the malevolence of the Mussulman priesthood who were incensed at the numerous marks of sympathy manifested by this pasha for the Christians.'

His military colleague was not intimidated by this, for he sent his son to invite her to a garrison review which he had ordered in her honour. They had all heard of her activities in Italy and how she had been in command of the Neapolitan volunteers who had gone to the aid of the Milanese. So she had gained the reputation of being a female warrior, a veritable Amazon. When Cristina denied that she had actually indulged in any fighting, they did not believe her, ascribing her denials to modesty or to secret diplomatic reasons. She had ended by accepting the part assigned to her, contenting herself with maintaining silence whenever any warlike exploits were alluded to.

'But never, as at Aleppo, have I been treated as an actual general, which was the case the day I repaired to the residence of the military pasha.' On entering the vast court in front of his palace, the entire body of troops presented arms, a honour to which she responded by giving them a smart military salute. She then took up a position at a window in the pasha's reception hall whilst the troops filed past saluting her to military music.

When the review was over, she happened to tell the Pasha how much she admired Arabian horses. This delighted him and he presented her with a colt for her daughter, which later became the glory of her stables.

Before leaving Aleppo the Princess visited a lunatic asylum. She entered a kind of dingy, dirty court, on the left hand side of which in the midst of some rubbish were three or four cells hollowed out of a standing wall, or rather, out of the ground behind it, in front of which a wall had been constructed. A heap of straw formed the entire furniture of the cells.

The keeper told her that he accepted such patients as were sent here by their relations. Some celebrated Santon was buried on this spot, and the proximity of his ashes was a sovereign remedy for madness. The treatment of the patients consisted in placing them on the Santon's tombstone, which remedy repeated several times a day for three days, she was assured, rarely failed to produce the required effect. The patient during these three days would be fastened down on a litter of straw, left quite alone, and subjected to a very meagre diet, until he said he was cured. His word would be accepted and he would be returned to his relations.

The establishment, such as it was, wrote Cristina, was the only one of its kind in Syria, and its cells were often empty. One must not conclude from this that there were no maniacs in Syria. She was personally acquainted with more than one, but the cells of Aleppo did not appear to attract them.

At last, in December 1852, the Princess and her party returned to Ciaq-Maq-Oglou. She has recorded her feelings when she saw her peaceful valley shimmering in the sunshine as she reined in her horse on the brow of the hill above. 'Although I had not come back to my native land, to the home of my ancestors, after so much travelling in unknown territory during which I had experienced social conditions quite unlike anything I had known before, I felt that it was pleasant to be able to tell myself: "This house is mine – my food sufficient for all my needs is grown on that land. Those who labour on it are loyal to me, if not through love certainly through self interest!"

'An exile in a foreign country, I had returned after eleven months to a place which had given me happiness and which had done much to remove the bitterness of exile. I had also enjoyed my adventures during those months. My health had not suffered through the arduous conditions I had had to endure, and I had brought back with me a number of important memories. This was something for which I ought to thank God as eloquently as I could. But when I went into my room and knelt down to pray, I found all I could say was: "Thank you, my God, thank you."'

On 13 January 1853, she wrote to Augustin to say that towards the end of her travelling she had lost all enthusiasm for it and had devoted what energy remained to her to the task of completing her journey, fearing that she might not have the strength left to do so.

But despite her weariness, she had achieved much of which to be proud. Few Europeans had explored Asia Minor, Syria and Palestine as she had. Indeed, there were parts that probably none had visited before. In an earlier letter to Thierry she had written: 'At school we learn geography and believe implicitly in the truth of what we are taught. Please take out the most detailed and recent map of Asia Minor you can find and study the two provinces of Galatia and Cappadocia. You'll notice that a chain of mountains called Elma Dagh separates them a little below Angora, but beyond this range as far as the outskirts of Caesarea where the

Anti-Taurus commences, you will see the map coloured to suggest that the land is all desert. I have just crossed this territory and I am writing to you today from a town with a population of nearly forty thousand souls, situated in the heart of this supposed desert.

'I can also assure you that there is no country less flat than Cappadocia. We have travelled for seven days across mountain after mountain covered with snow, and not one is shown on any map. As for the people of these parts, they'll tell you that this mountain is called the "Wolf's Back" and that one is known as the "Hound's Tooth". If you speak to them about mountain chains, they look blankly at you and say mountains aren't chains.'

Whilst she had been on her tour, things had worsened from her point of view in France. On 2 December 1852, the Prince President had been proclaimed Napoleon III, Emperor of the French. 'The form of government now established in France,' she told Augustin, 'is entirely repugnant to me, and the means employed to bring it into power are as bad as can be.'

On returning to her farm, Cristina found to her dismay that the Alsatian overseer she had left in charge during her absence had failed her in every possible way. He had mismanaged everything. The crops had been a failure. Cattle had mysteriously vanished, and the farm was heavily in debt. He had clearly been systematically swindling her in a very cunning manner.

To add to her troubles, following an abortive rising in Milan, fomented by Mazzini, the Austrian Emperor by an edict dated 18 February 1853, confiscated the property of all Lombards living abroad, such as herself, and banished them for life. It now became impossible even for her astute lawyer Pastori to send her any money from Italy. This made her very dependent on her writings. She sent articles describing her travels to Augustin Thierry, asking him to submit those he regarded as suitable to Buloz, the editor of the *Revue des Deux Mondes*. All were in fact published and were so well received that they were later printed in book form, and reproduced in American newspapers.

Cristina also put up for sale her houses in the Rue du Montparnasse, much to Augustin's sorrow, for he feared this meant he would never see her again. Certainly her letters showed her content enough not to leave Ciaq-Maq-Oglou for many years to come. She wrote to Caroline Jaubert: 'You say I must be lonely. I have never been a chatterbox, and I have learnt the value of silence living here in my valley. Most people talk too much and say a hundred words where one would suffice.'

But Cristina was not destined to spend the rest of her days happy in her Eden.

CHAPTER 12

ATTEMPTED MURDER

On 30 June 1853, the Princess narrowly escaped being murdered by a Lombard from Bergamo, who had been in her employ as a warehouseman for two years. He had actually been very ill soon after arrival and owed his life to her nursing.

In a letter dated 5 July 1853, she gave Caroline Jaubert a very full account of what had happened. 'If you love me, whatever may be your doubts and opinions, kneel down when you receive this letter, and thank God for having miraculously saved me from death. An attempt was made on my life five days ago. I have seen many wounds and many wounded, but never anything to equal my condition. I ought to have died twenty times, and yet I am now well on the way to recovery . . .

'I have told you about a storekeeper who has caused me a great deal of annoyance and whom Mrs Parker said was desperately in love with her, but whose eyes told me quite another story. For some time he had been getting increasingly ill-tempered, and I knew that all he could talk about was killing and destroying, but nobody took his threats seriously and they were regarded as being brought on by some passing brain storm.

'His anger was principally directed against Mrs Parker, one of whose eyes he had bruised and whose nose he had broken with a savage blow one morning. It was clear that her relations with him had been improper or he wouldn't have dared treat her like he did. That is what I told her when she came to seek my protection. I refused to help her so long as their discreditable love affair continued. She then said that she would be only too glad to end it, providing I defended her against the man's brutality.

' I had him brought to me and told him that up till then I had refused to interfere with his philandering, but since Mrs Parker had told me she wanted to mend her ways and had sought my aid in the matter, I had to do something about it. He must remember that Mrs Parker was not his wife, that if she wanted to end the affair she had a perfect right to do so, and if he tried to make her relent either by pestering or ill-treating her, he would be offending me. He appeared to agree to behave himself in future, passing it all off as a joke and finally saying: "I give you my word not to lift a hand against her and to leave her in peace."

'But his behaviour soon belied his promise, and he showed signs of becoming more and more mentally unbalanced. He started spreading false tales about me and complained bitterly to several people that I was taking sides against him with a young Pole, who lives here, and that I had written to Constantinople without his knowledge for another storekeeper to replace him. This was untrue, but he was convinced that I would have dismissed him if it had been possible for me to have paid his wages. He had discovered that I was short of money through Pastori not having sent me any for four months. At last he decided to give me notice himself, and told others that before he left he would kill those who had persecuted him. Unfortunately nobody reported his threats to me.

'Last Wednesday he called my personal servant, a good and honest Armenian boy who is very much attached to me, and holding out a cup full of wine with one hand and brandishing a dagger in the other, ordered him to drink. The terrified boy, who had seen him dissolve some arsenic in the liquid, had no option but to obey and consequently narrowly escaped dying. He was sick for several hours and recovered only through drinking a great deal of sour milk.

'Whilst he was so ill, the wretch who had tried to murder him knocked on my door and asked to speak to me. I had seen him that morning looking so distracted that I did not want to listen to any more of his crazy talk, so I called through the closed door: "When you haven't drunk any brandy for a whole day, then I'll listen to you."

'At dinner time he appeared dressed with studied elegance and with long, flowing ruffles to his sleeves which almost covered his hands. His first act was to knock over a candle. I automatically exclaimed: "Mind what you're doing!" At this he flew into a rage and asked why I had reprimanded him. "Because you knocked over the candle," I returned. "I won't have you say mind what you're doing when I do something accidentally," he shouted back. "If you repeat that, I'll say something that you won't like."

'Never had I seen him in such a state. Usually he is so diffident in my presence that he doesn't say a word or even look me in the eye. I told him that I wouldn't allow him to address me in such an insolent way and that if he were going to continue, he had better leave. "You're going to listen to much more," he retorted. Then he stopped and for some moments became gloomy and deep in thought. But the mood passed and he smiled to himself and ate like a wolf.

'After dinner I usually go up into my bedroom followed by my Armenian, who carries the candle and my narghile, and who after lighting the latter leaves whilst I undress and go to bed. I spend my time reading till I tire and fall asleep. This evening as I was going out of the dining-room, my problem employee mumbled: "That's the end." Then he seized the candle and followed me as if to light my way, feeling sure no doubt that the Armenian he had poisoned that morning was dead. I had mounted three or four steps when I happened to turn round and, seeing him on my heels, candlestick in hand, I took it from him, saying: "I haven't any light up in my room, so I'll need that."

'He didn't stir and seemed hardly to have heard me. I thought that his fury was beginning to subside and that he was already regretting his misbehaviour, for I knew him to be a coward. I judged him well! At that moment the Armenian, who had partly recovered, appeared with my narghile. He slipped swiftly between the man and myself, took the candlestick from me with his free hand and followed me upstairs.

'The other remained behind for a moment, waiting no doubt

for the stairs where he stood to become hidden in the shadows as
the Armenian moved upwards, so that we would not know that
he was following us.

'On entering my room, as it was very hot, I walked straight
over to the window whilst the Armenian went to place the
narghile in a corner. I had reached the window, when I heard
the man's footsteps in the passage and he came in. He moved
right up to me and said: "Madame, you have insulted me by
telling me to leave your employ." Then he dealt me four blows
with a dagger which he was holding hidden in his sleeve, and
shouted: "Die, you heartless woman! Die!"

'I received the first two blows without realising what he had
done to me, for I couldn't see the weapon which was concealed
by his ruffles, and I had never expected such an attack, but when
he stabbed me in the left breast, I saw the blade. I started back
and broke a window pane, which shattered below making a
tremendous noise. I held my left hand in front of my chest, but
that did not prevent him stabbing me there a fourth time. Then
slipping away to the right, I went round a table and took refuge
behind the Armenian, who, having his back turned at the time,
hadn't witnessed the attempt on my life (I had been so stunned
that I hadn't uttered a cry). But when the boy saw the assassin
coming towards us with raised knife, he made off and I followed,
pursued by the killer.

'The noise of the shattering glass had raised the alarm and I
found the staircase crowded with people rushing up. They
blocked my way and I had to stop. My attacker took advantage
of this to deal me a fifth blow. The others seized him. He struggled
to free himself, and after receiving some punishment managed to
break loose and jump from a balcony into the courtyard and
escape.

'I still did not feel weak, though I was bleeding profusely. I
went quietly back in my room and lay unassisted on my bed.
My poor little Maria had awakened and now ran to my side.
She kept crying: "Don't die! Mother, don't die! What must we
do? Think! Tell us!" But she wasn't the only one to weep. The
house echoed with the sobs and wailing of all who worked for

me. They sounded more upset than I was. How I wished they would be quiet!

'Maria was now kneeling and praying. I watched her and I, too, prayed, saying: "My God, if it be possible, don't take away from that child her only support." What I felt at that moment is indescribable. It seemed to me that I was coming out of a bad dream, that my strength and intelligence were increased three-fold, and that there was nothing I could not do. I called the pharmacist and told him how to bandage me.

'I had a huge wound in my thigh and a smaller one in my groin, but I was relieved to find that no arteries had been severed. I managed to staunch the bleeding with cold water. The thigh wound was soon bandaged, but the other worried me more because I feared that it might have penetrated my abdomen, but on examination I was relieved to find that the tip of the knife had been deflected by my hip-bone. The wounds which now gave me the most concern were the ones in my breast. Half-an-hour had passed and little blood was now coming from them. My heart-beats though loud were regular. My pulse was steady. I could breathe without difficulty. There were no signs of my lung having been pierced. So I told myself, I am not without hope, and if death does not come in two hours I may live.

'Maria ran out to tell those waiting outside my bedroom what I thought, and this calmed them. I said that I wanted to be bled in the left arm. "But, Princess," said the young Pole, "think of all the blood you have lost." "I shan't die from loss of blood," I returned, and I made him open a vein. The blood flowed freely. Further cause for hope. Fortunately we had some leeches in the house. I had them applied to my chest and abdomen. Then I ordered more to be fetched from the pond, for I feared the inflammation which might result from all these wounds, and internal haemorrhage. I also had some aconite pills made, and when the dressing of my injuries was completed I kept very still.

'But I was unable to rest for long as I started suffering from nausea and intestinal pains. Now I knew well that these can be fatal symptoms following being stabbed in the abdomen. Nevertheless it was possible that loss of blood coming immediately after eating might be responsible for them. I felt sure that this was so when I saw that I was bringing up only what I had eaten and that there were no traces of any blood.

'Thanks to some laudanum poultices, after two hours these pains subsided, but were succeeded by shooting and stabbing ones in my chest and I breathed with difficulty. I had recourse again to leeches and aconite, and repeated this treatment three times. At last I ceased suffering and my breathing became easier. I was able to lie on my right side without discomfort. The fever vanished and after twenty-four hours all that troubled me was a sensation of soreness round my wounds.

'Maria and the others were delighted that I was better, but I hesitated to declare the battle won. I told them: "We must wait and see what I'm like in two or three days' time." But when the sore feeling faded away, when my breathing improved, when the wounds in my breast showed signs of beginning to heal, I rejoiced with the others.

'Three days after the attack I left my bed, and although walking was forbidden me I spent part of each day seated in my garden. On rising I discovered by chance a fifth wound in my shoulder near the spine, but the folds in my dress had prevented the dagger from doing me serious injury.

'I came to the conclusion that my assailant must have dealt his blows from below upwards, thus failing to pierce through to my heart or stomach, as intended. This explains why the wounds not being deep began healing so soon.

'I should like you all the same to consult some able surgeon on my behalf to find out if I have any after-effects to fear. For example, if the pleura has been damaged, what are the symptoms that would indicate this to me? .

'The first day after being stabbed I had a slight cough, but I cured this by taking some kermes. Then on the fourth day I started smoking my narghile again, more as a test than for pleasure. It did not have any ill effects . . .

'Yesterday was market day in a town two hours' journey from

here. My servants went there as usual to buy provisions. Almost the first person they saw was the man who attempted to murder me. He was lying on the ground in a corner of the market. Madame Stroset went up to him and cried: "You wretch, what devil possessed you yesterday?"

'"How is the Princess?" he enquired.

'"You narrowly missed killing her!" she retorted.

'He made no reply and my people went to the magistrate and made a charge. Guards were then sent to arrest him. When this was done, he asked them to beg me not to do him as much harm as he had tried to do me, and that whatever I decided, would I order it to be done quickly.

'Meanwhile Maria had sent the Pole to Sofran Bolo to inform the Turkish Governor what had happened. The worthy man nearly had a stroke. "God help me," he cried, "is he a Turk?" "No, your Excellency, he is a European." "God be praised, if he had been a Turk, I should have lost my governorship."

'He ordered the man to be taken to the town gaol. On the way there he and his guards passed through my estate, and all the women and children came out of their houses and followed him, jeering and shouting: "There goes the man who tried to murder our mistress! She fed him and nursed him when he was ill and he tried to kill her. Curse you for trying to kill our mother!" They spat in his face and threw stones at him. Then the men joined in shouting in their turn: "You faithless one – you were treated too well. Your bed was too soft – your coffee was too sweet – and the mistress too indulgent!" ...

'The Governor insists in believing that he is a hired assassin in the pay of Austria, but I don't believe it. My peasants do not seem at all astonished to see me alive. "We knew you wouldn't die," they all tell me. "How could the poor exist if you were not here to feed them?"'

In a letter[1] dated 3 July Cristina gave Augustin Thierry a somewhat shorter account of the attempt on her life, and added that she had sent a more detailed report to Madame Jaubert who would read it to him.

To people of today it must seem extraordinary that Cristina

should have survived not only the attempt on her life but her own method of trying to save it. Bleeding was then the invariable cure for all ills. Maxime du Camp in his *Souvenirs littéraires* wrote that at school he was bled for a headache and that when he had typhoid fever, he was bled three times in a week and had sixty leeches applied to him.

CHAPTER 13

FOR THE SAKE OF MARIA

Cristina's morale was severely shaken first by her Alsatian over-seer's malpractices leaving her in debt and jeopardising her hopes of earning a livelihood from the farm, and now by this attempt on her life. Although she bravely made light of her injuries, she never really recovered from them and she became prematurely aged. Thinking of her daughter's future, she decided to try and make her peace with the Austrians so that Maria might one day enjoy the family estates.

Thierry had become so worried about Cristina's financial position that he sold various valuables she had given him and sent her three thousand francs. Acknowledging this on 2 August, she wrote that it was very welcome as 'the last three months that I have spent here will for long be burnt into my memory as among the most distressing of my life.' A certain matter is giving her further anxiety and she would like his advice, together with that of Caroline Jaubert and François Mignet. She has heard that failure had met all her lawyer Pastori's representations on her behalf to Marshal Radetzky to obtain either the lifting of the sequestration order on her property, or to be allowed some of the income from it.

The Marshal had said that before anything could be discussed she must first petition to be permitted to return to Milan. This would probably be allowed, then when she was once more under Austrian jurisdiction they would go into the matter. She did not know what to do. Even if she obeyed and the Austrians did not ill-treat her on return, what guarantee had she that at the least sign of another rebellion they might not make an example of her and imprison her in some fortress in Silesia. On the other hand, if she remained abroad might not the sequestration of her estates be followed by complete confiscation?

'It isn't the present which worries me the most, it is the future. What will happen to us? After much painful thought I decided to wait a little before making a final decision. So I have written to Pastori that nothing in the world would give me more pleasure than to see Locate again, and that if the Austrian Government would agree to overlook my political activities prior to 1848, I should raise no objections as to placing myself in their power. But I added that to undertake so long a voyage, I must have both health and strength, and that one could have neither after having being stabbed in so many places. I regretted I could not send a doctor's certificate to confirm this, not having the money to consult one, but that if the Government wished, they had only to order their internuncio at Stamboul to send one to me, at their expense, naturally. I said that it was impossible to give an exact date as to when I should be well enough to travel, and that this would be delayed if the Government persisted in withholding from me the means to pay for proper attention and careful nursing.

'That is what I wrote, not knowing what better to say, but this reply restricts my future movements, for my relations with Austria will become even worse if I should leave here to go anywhere else than Milan ...'

She continues in her letter to Thierry that whilst awaiting a reply from Pastori she was busying herself preparing short stories based on Eastern folk tales. These were later published as a series in the *Revue des Deux Mondes* and, following that, in book form under the title of *Récits turco-asiatiques*.

Pastori, however, did not have any success with the Austrians. Radetzky – the 'octogenarian pandour' as Cristina called him – would make no concessions. Heinrich Heine, who had loved her in his youth, now paralysed and nearly dying, used his considerable influence in diplomatic circles to try and persuade the Austrians to show Cristina some indulgence.

But time passed and nothing happened. In fact the Princess's return was destined to be long delayed. Nobody offered to buy her houses in the Rue du Montparnasse at a fair price, which worried her because, as she wrote to Madame Jaubert: 'I don't feel like setting foot in Europe without a penny to live on.'

Now impatient to be gone, she decided to raise a mortgage on her Paris property. Writing to Thierry on 27 February 1854, she gave her probable date of departure as that July. Before handing over the management of the farm to someone else, she felt she must leave everything running as smoothly as possible, supervise the gathering in of the corn, harvest the opium poppy crop, be present when the lambs, the colts and the foals were born. When the granaries were filled and the sheep sheared, she would feel able to depart without dreading to leave her people in short supply or in danger of famine. All this would occupy her well into the summer, but she would take care to make the sea crossing before the equinox, so she would probably arrive in Europe towards the end of August or at the beginning of September.

She could make no plans before learning what was going to happen to her property in Paris. She had written to her agents there authorising them to sell for less than the price fixed by Pastori. She had also asked them to raise a small mortgage on the property so that she would have enough to pay for travelling back, which was going to cost her a great deal.

Later that year in a letter dated 22 July, Thierry was able to give her the news that Pastori had been in Paris a week, and had arranged for the sum of money she required to be made available to her.

If she decided to save herself from complete financial ruin by making her peace with the Austrians, he could guarantee that all her friends in Paris would unreservedly approve her action. Heinrich Heine from his sick bed had asked him to send her a message begging her to think of her future and, above all, that of her daughter. He had made use of his contacts to sound both the Austrian Emperor and his Chancellor, Prince Metternich, on her behalf, and the response received was: 'Unless the Princess formally asks permission to return to Lombardy, nothing will be conceded. Once she pleads to be allowed back in her country, all will be arranged.'

A few years earlier, Cristina would not have yielded on these terms, but her physical ills and mental depression now inclined her to do so despite the misgivings of her conscience. But it was going to be very difficult for her to take an oath of submission and loyalty to the Austrian Emperor, which her half-brother wrote to warn her she would have to do.

Then at the beginning of November she left for Constantinople. She had written to her eldest half-sister, Theresa (who had married a cousin, the Marquis Charles d'Aragona), saying that she intended to board a ship for Marseilles, which she hoped to reach by the end of the month. But she did not arrive, causing them all great anxiety as to what had happened to her.

It was not until some seven months later on 2 July 1855, that she wrote to Thierry from Constantinople[1]: 'Don't be angry with me. The reason for this long silence was my reluctance to make you share the fears and doubts which have disturbed my days and nights. Each time that I tried to express these in words, the pen would fall from my fingers and I would tell myself: "No, I'd rather say nothing."

'At last, today, my departure is fixed, or as fixed as anything in this world can be. Barring an earthquake, an outbreak of cholera or other calamity, I am sure to leave (since I have sufficient money now in my purse) in ten or twelve days' time.

'Where shall I go first? I don't know. If I leave here without having received any news from Vienna, I shall disembark at Marseilles and there I shall consider what to do next. Shall I have enough money left to visit Paris? That remains to be seen. If before departure, I receive permission from Vienna to go home, I shall make first for Genoa and then travel on to Milan. Once I have installed myself in Locate, I shall visit France, pausing to stay a few days with my sister before being reunited with you. Won't that be pleasant? I shall have much to tell you about Stamboul. We shall spend many fine days together if God so wills it.'

In due course the Princess arrived in Marseilles accompanied by Maria, Mrs Parker, two Turkish men-servants, an Arab horse, four Salukis, and two long-haired Angora cats. Not having heard from Vienna, she went to stay with Theresa at Salies, near Albi. Time and fate's buffets had blunted her resolution not to return to Paris whilst Louis Napoleon was in power. Now as Emperor he was more secure than ever. If she refused to sacrifice her scruples, she might never see Augustin Thierry again. The appeals of affection won, and she made her way to Paris in November 1855.

Six years of the severest strain and of near death had cruelly changed the looks of the former star of the salon, famous for her unusual beauty. She was now forty-seven, but looked very much older. Although in her letters she had courageously claimed to have completely recovered from the attack on her life, it was far from true. The wounds in her chest had done more harm than she had thought. She began to have difficulty with her breathing. The once proudly erect head fell more and more forward, until by the time she reached fifty she appeared from behind to be without a head. Only her eyes retained their beauty and fire.

But her old friend had become completely blind and was spared seeing her like this. Her voice, however, retained its charm and attractive tones. He had completed a work on the Third Estate. She read the manuscript aloud to him. In his joy at their reunion he dedicated it to her.

Suddenly, in December there was a dramatic change in the Austrian Government's policy. Her old enemy, Marshal Radetzky, died and the popular Archduke Maximilian and his charming wife, Princess Charlotte, became Viceroy and Vicereine in Milan. Now there was proclaimed a general amnesty and the restoration of confiscated estates. As a result, all was restored to Cristina without her having to take any oath of loyalty to the Austrian Emperor. This had been the real reason for her procrastination and which had made her continue putting off the return to Milan. At the end of January 1856, she travelled there. On 9 February she wrote to Thierry to tell of her safe arrival and to say that when she had called on the Governor he had received her 'with emotion and tenderness.'

Sad news came back from Paris telling of the death of Heinrich Heine, and shortly afterwards, on 17 February, her husband,

Prince Emilio, whom she had not seen since his last desertion, suddenly died in Milan.

In May, 1856, Cristina went to Paris intending to spend the summer with Augustin Thierry in a country villa at Port Marly, but to her sorrow he was struck down by a cerebral haemorrhage and in a few days passed away.

In their letters to each other over some twenty-five years they had signed themselves 'brother' and 'sister'. It was a mixture of pity and admiration that had first drawn Cristina to Augustin. His wife, recognising this, had never objected to their friendship; indeed, on her deathbed she had asked the Princess to look after her husband. It had been an association based not on evanescent sex but on a deep affection, and for this reason Cristina felt the loss more intensely.

Three men who had played important parts in her life had died in the space of a few months. She was suffering, too, from the after-effects of the murderous attack on her in Asia Minor. Her morale was very low that summer. Friends invited her to stay with them in their country homes, but such visits failed in their purpose.

In August 1856, she was the guest of the Marquis de Marbois in the Château de Noyers, Tilliers-en-Vexain, Eure. From here she wrote to Caroline Jaubert: 'I am in a little hell. The only other women look like three witches. The men consist of Victor Cousin and François Mignet who are my sort, then there is the excellent M. de Marbois, one of his contemporaries and a secretary who is a nonentity. So the company is not very congenial. All this would not matter if I were not tortured by neuralgia caused by those dagger wounds. But I am bored during the day and I suffer at night. It really is too much for me to endure. I took M. Pétroz's powder and I felt better for two nights running. But on the third – that is last night – the agonising pain started again. I have come to the end of the powder and I still have eight deadly days to spend here. Please, dear Mme. Jaubert, send a further supply. Tell M. Pétroz that I suffer the moment I lay my head on the pillow. If I sit up, the pain goes from my neck and eyes. Last night's attack was of shorter duration than usual and lasted for nearly two hours ... Anything which suddenly jolts my head racks me, and travelling here I had plenty of jolting. Perhaps you would be good enough to ask M. Pétroz if he could prescribe something which I don't need to take four hours after a meal and four hours before an attack. He would be doing me a great service for the trouble commences the moment I go to bed at 9 p.m. This means I cannot eat after 1 p.m., which causes quite a stir in the kitchens here ...'

In September Cristina returned to Locate. Her two youngest half-sisters were married to Piedmontese noblemen and residing in Turin. The youngest, the Marchese di Rorà, was already reigning over a brilliant salon which Count Cavour often attended. Cristina now accepted an invitation to pay her a visit.

CHAPTER 14

FULFILMENT

Plump little Camillo Cavour had first met the Princess in Genoa in 1829 and again in 1838 when visiting Paris. He then wrote in his journal that she was talented and knowledgeable, but that her attitude towards his master, King Charles Albert, had irritated him. One day she was opposed to the King, another day his supporter. Then she would change again and attack him. She bewildered the Count, too, as he puts it 'by advocating the most fantastic schemes.' At last on 27 January 1838, appears the entry: 'I shall not go back there again.' He had left her salon early after a disagreement with her and had finished the night at the Opera ball. However, five years later, on a visit to Paris in March 1843, he called on Cristina and they were reconciled.

Cavour would have made his name as an agriculturist had not the revolution of 1848 attracted him into the political arena first as a newspaper editor and later as a minister. His policy had become to establish Piedmont as the most progressive state in the peninsula and the hub round which the other states would attach themselves to form a united kingdom. He reformed the law and welcomed political exiles. 'You will see, gentlemen,' he told the Piedmontese Parliament, 'how reforms carried out in time strengthen it, instead of precipitating revolution they prevent it.'

Industry had languished in Piedmont through lack of capital. Cavour was instrumental in starting up a bank to provide the necessary credit at reasonable terms. To stimulate trade he reduced tariffs. He took such an interest in railroad construction that by 1859 Piedmont could boast of more track by mileage than the rest of Italy, and they stretched to every frontier, which proved of immense value when the war with Austria erupted. It was thanks to his foresight that the Mont Cenis tunnel was bored bringing Paris within easy reach. To wage a successful war he believed Piedmont must make its own munitions as far as practical, so he sent men to England for training.

Since 1852 the Count had been the Prime Minister of the new King, Victor Emmanuel. In January 1855, he had enhanced the prestige of his country by entering the Crimean War on the side of England and France, and by sending fifteen thousand troops under General Marmora to the front, where they distinguished themselves by winning the Battle of Tchernaya in August. It cost the taxpayer some fifty million lire, but as a result, when in March 1856, Cavour attended the Congress of Paris to make the peace, he was able to insist that Piedmont be treated as the equal of the great powers.

Now, also in 1856, in Turin, Cavour and Cristina became close friends. They would meet for talks that continued into the early hours of the morning, and he would go as far as the Roràs' country house at Oleggo Castello on Lake Maggiore to see her. He tried to persuade her to use her pen in propaganda to enhance Victor Emmanuel's popularity throughout the peninsula.

As a man the King did not appeal to Cristina for his morals reminded her of Emilio's. He boasted of his affairs, claiming that all the beautiful women in Turin had been to bed with him, both mothers and daughters. What he liked most about Paris, he declared, was to discover that fashionable women no longer wore *caleçons*. His enemies said that he looked and behaved like a sergeant-major, and flavoured his conversation with coarse epithets.

Lord Clarendon, at one time British Foreign Secretary, thought Victor Emmanuel intelligent and liked him on his visit to England in 1855. Greville in his *Memoirs* wrote of him then that he appeared to be 'frightful in person' but was a great strong, burly, athletic man, brusque in his manners, unrefined in his conversation, very loose in his conduct, and very eccentric in his habits. 'When he was in Paris his talk in society amused or terrified everybody, but here he seems to have been more guarded. It was amusing to see all the religious societies hastening with their addresses to him, totally forgetting that he is the most debauched and dissolute fellow in the world; but the fact of his being excommunicated by the Pope and his waging war with the ecclesiastical power in his own country covers every sin against morality, and he is a great Hero with the Low Church people and Exeter Hall. My brother-in-law said that he looked (atWindsor) more like a Chief of the Heruli or Longobardi than a modern Italian Prince, and the Duchess of Sutherland that, of all the Knights of the Garter she had seen, he was the only one who looked as if he would get the best of it with the Dragon.'

Certainly on this visit though he may have looked like a bull he behaved like a lamb. Queen Victoria was very taken with him and rose at four in the morning to see him depart. She wrote in a letter that he was 'more like a Knight or a King of the Middle Ages than anything one knows about now.'

Victor Emmanuel was undoubtedly popular with the masses with whom he had the reputation of always keeping his word. They called him 'Il Re Galant 'uomo' and enjoyed hearing tales of his philandering. 'He is truly the father of many of his people,' a wit said. It was widely rumoured that Queen Victoria had offered him one of her daughters but that the young Princess knew too much Greek and Latin for his taste.

Cristina still believed that Italy when united should be a kingdom. She decided to write a history of the House of Savoy in which she would present as strongly as possible the case for Victor Emmanuel's becoming the first King of Italy.

The Piedmontese capital, attractively built out of amber-coloured stone, was crowded with refugees from all over the peninsula who argued excitedly in the Cafés San Carlo and Fiorio in the principal piazza. Accompanied by her secretary, Cristina would occasionally visit them so as to hear what their frequenters had to say.

Sometimes she would go to look over the mills and factories that were being built on the outskirts of the town. She would regard them from the point of view of the work-people and suggest improvements for their health and comfort.

These were the least of her activities. Later the *North British Review* was to write of Cristina's work at this time: 'She was one of Count Cavour's most indefatigable agents, travelling from place to place holding conferences, reconciling republicans and constitutionalists and gaining friends and allies.'

The new Viceroy in Milan was courting popularity through tempting promises of constitutional reform. This dismayed Cavour, so he changed his policy of 'revolution by evolution' to one of secret political agitation. If Austrian appeasement were to succeed, Lombardy would never want to revolt again. So the Milanese must be made to provoke their masters so that they would be forced to mete out harsh punishment. *Agents provocateurs* and *saboteurs* in the Count's employ stoned and sniped at the 'White Coats' and painted patriotic slogans on the walls of barracks and government buildings. They stirred up ill-feeling among the young men against Austrian officers, who through being plentifully supplied with money were able to pay for the company of beautiful Lombard girls.

It became Cristina's role in Cavour's campaign to do all she could to popularise Victor Emmanuel, stressing his honesty and sincerity. Her journalistic gifts were employed acting as deputy to Carlo Tenca, editor of a new Milanese journal, the *Crepuscolo* aimed at influencing the more intelligent Italians through quality reading matter. This deliberately omitted mentioning anything associated with Austria.

When, in 1857, the Emperor came from Vienna to Milan, the *Crepuscolo* made no reference to his visit, despite police pressure demanding that a welcoming editorial be published. The Emperor found all blinds pulled down and curtains drawn in the houses of the streets through which he passed, and Milanese society avoided attending any of his receptions.

Cristina's main undertaking was the writing of the *History of the House of Savoy*, which took several years and was eventually published in Paris in 1860. Although her writing occupied much of her time, she still devoted some of it to social activities, in particular for the launching of her daughter. Maria enjoyed amateur theatricals, so the Princess had a large room in her villa at

Locate turned into a theatre, and even played a part herself occasionally.

Despite the trouble fomented by Cavour's agitators, Archduke Maximilian persisted in pursuing a conciliatory policy. The Count then had rumours spread that the Archduchess had forced her husband to court popularity because she wanted to become Queen of Italy.

It was the Emperor himself, however, who unwittingly provided Cavour with the fuel to inflame the people. Resenting the way he had been snubbed during his state visit, he authorised export restrictions to be imposed on Lombard produce so as to favour Austrian trade. But what angered the working class was the extension of the period of service for conscripts, and that they were forbidden to marry until the age of twenty-three.

The Count realised that making the people of Italy anti-Austrian was not sufficient, he must be certain of the support of a major power in a war with Austria. Despite the new French Emperor's crushing of the Roman Revolution in 1849, he believed that if it were made worthwhile, Napoleon III would find the temptation irresistible to follow in the footsteps of his great-uncle by winning military glory and extending the frontiers of France.

Cavour astutely tried to influence Napoleon III through the Emperor's closest friends and advisers, Count Arese and Dr Conneau, who were sympathetic to the Italian cause. He sent his own beautiful and amoral twenty-year-old cousin, the Countess Castiglione, to Paris on a mission – to become the Emperor's mistress and then make him militantly pro-Piedmontese. 'Succeed, my cousin, by whatever means you like, but succeed.' She was an extremely vain woman whose chief distraction was admiring herself in the nearest mirror. She certainly had a remarkable effect on Napoleon. After becoming her lover, instead of leaving his carriage by the door he jumped nimbly out of the window.

The Countess first met the French Emperor in November, 1855, when he and the Empress Eugénie held a ball at the Tuileries. Cristina who had just arrived back in Paris from the East learnt through her close contacts with the Italian exiles of the secret reason behind the Countess's visit. The thought that the man whom she despised for duping the Roman revolutionaries might now himself be duped pleased her, and when she heard that Virginia de Castiglione planned to aim her first arrows at Napoleon III's heart on the occasion of this ball, she, too, accepted an invitation to be present.

The fame of the Countess's beauty had so spread that when she arrived deliberately late both orchestra and dancers paused to look at her. When she was presented to the Emperor, he immediately asked her to partner him in the quadrille and so the affair started. But her reign was not to last long, for Napoleon's ministers became alarmed by this Italian infiltration and engaged the most attractive French *horizontale* they could find, Marguerite Berranger, a former circus rider, to wean their ruler away from the Florentine woman. They hoped that he would be completely captivated by a charmer who could turn somersaults on her horse. She succeeded at their very first meeting by making an impressive entrance walking on her hands.

In her will the ousted Countess gave instructions that she was to be buried in the gray batiste and lace chemise she had worn when Napoleon first succumbed to her. However, the house he rented for her did provide the means whereby Cavour's agents could meet and become friendly with the French ruler.

What influenced Napoleon more than anything was Orsini's attempt on his life. The Italian patriots had never allowed him to forget that he had become a sworn member of the Carbonari in his youth and that the penalty for breaking the oath was death. Orsini wrote him a letter in January 1858, threatening assassination unless he made a positive move to further Italian unification. 'I beg Your Imperial Highness to restore to the Italians the liberty they lost by the deeds of the French themselves in 1849 ... Set my country free, and the gratitude of twenty million people will be with you for ever.' But the Emperor made no response.

On the 14th of the same month Napoleon and Eugénie attended a gala performance at the Paris Opera in honour of Duke Ernest of Saxe-Coburg. The programme consisted of an act from *William Tell* which, of course, tells of the Swiss fight for independence from the Austrians, followed by an excerpt from *La*

Muette de Portici so associated with the Belgians' rising against oppression. The evening was to end with part of *Un Ballo in Maschera*, which rather ominously concerns a King's assassination.

On the night the directors of the Opera stood waiting anxiously with lighted candles by the entrance to greet the Emperor and Empress and escort them to their box. They were late, and the Rue Lepelletier was lined with impatient sightseers. At last fourteen lancers in silver breastplates with pennons flying clattered up ahead of the imperial berline to shouts of '*Vive l'Empereur*'. A minute later Orsini and his fellow conspirators threw their bombs at the cobbles beneath the wheels. The coachman was blown to pieces, so too were many of the horses, but Napoleon and his consort escaped unhurt.

The Emperor's conscience must have been disturbed by the shock, for he not only tried to save Orsini from execution (though in vain) but from then onwards paid more serious attention to Cavour's overtures. In the middle of July it was officially announced that Napoleon had left the capital to take the cure at Plombières, the spa in the Vosges he had made fashionable. Here, too, came a fair bullet-headed bespectacled man wearing a broad-brimmed hat who looked like a German professor but who was really Count Cavour travelling under an assumed name.

The two men met in the gloomy *Pavilion des Princes* and made a secret agreement that when the time was propitious the two countries would declare war on Austria. In return for French military assistance, Victor Emmanuel was to cede Savoy and Nice to France. To strengthen the links between the two countries, the latter's fifteen-year-old plain daughter, Princess Clotilde, was to marry Prince Jerome Napoleon (known as 'Plon Plon') an ageing roué cousin of the French Emperor, who whipped his mistresses and who was promised a new Kingdom to be set up in central Italy after a successful war.

When he returned to Turin, Cavour confided in Cristina what had been agreed, and she was pleased by the news that the friend of her youth was now prepared to make some amends for his betrayal of the Roman revolutionaries in 1849. The Count's first move was to summon Garibaldi from his farm at Caprera and tell him to prepare for war by raising a corps of volunteers from all over Italy to be known as the 'Cacciatori delle Alpe' – the 'Hunters of the Alps' – so that when hostilities began it could be truly claimed that it was a national uprising. Next he recalled men belonging to the 1828–32 classes to the colours.

On 10 January, Victor Emmanuel in his speech from the throne said: 'I cannot remain deaf to the cries of pain that have reached me from every part of Italy.' Though it was not known at the time, these words had been suggested by Napoleon III himself. The Piedmont Parliament then passed a vote of credit for fifty million francs, so that the country could be placed ready for all emergencies.

In the secret agreement it had been stipulated that France would help Piedmont only if that country were first invaded by Austria. Cavour therefore did all he could to goad the ancient enemy into doing this. Already public opposition to war with Austria was mounting in France and Napoleon was vacillating, but nevertheless he made all necessary preparations and instructed his War Minister, Marshal Vaillant, to move four divisions to where they could at short notice invade Italy. Nine days before Victor Emmanuel had uttered the inflammatory words he had inspired, the French Emperor at a reception of the Diplomatic Corps on New Year's Day, 1859, had turned to the Austrian Ambassador and all present heard him say: 'I regret that relations between our two countries are so bad. All the same, would you tell your Emperor that my feelings for him remain unchanged.'

On Sunday, 16 January, Prince 'Plon Plon' arrived in Turin for his marriage. Acting on behalf of Napoleon III, he signed a treaty of friendship between the two countries to the effect that in the event of war France would come to Piedmont's aid with 200,000 men on condition that the latter state provided half that number of troops. The combined forces were to be commanded by Napoleon.

All now depended on how successful Cavour was in provoking Austria. Then the Czar of Russia surprised the world by proposing that the Italian question should be settled by a congress of great powers. England supported the plan, but wanted all Italian states to be represented. The Count was dismayed by this turn of events, but Austria foolishly insisted that Piedmont must demobilise before sending a representative to the congress, and then on 23 April imperiously demanded compliance within three days.

Realising that the time to take up the struggle again was near, young men in Lombardy were escaping across the frontier to join Garibaldi. Immediately she heard of the Austrian ultimatum, Cristina went to Paris and had a secret audience with Napoleon. On 26 April, Cavour informed the Austrian Chancellor that his terms were completely unacceptable, and the next day the Austrians invaded Piedmont.

Victor Emmanuel immediately declared war, and France, fulfilling the treaty obligations, came to his aid. On 12 May the imperial yacht, *La Reine Hortense,* steamed into the harbour at Genoa with Napoleon on board. He came he announced 'to free Italy from the Alps to the Adriatic'. The excited citizens told each other that at last the Veltro prophecies made by Dante six centuries earlier were going to be fulfilled. Everywhere the French and Italian tricolours flew side by side. Cavour came aboard to greet the French Emperor who was then conveyed in Victor Emmanuel's royal barge to the landing at his Palace. An eyewitness has described the water on the way as resembling an oriental garden so profusely was it strewn with flowers.

The new Commander-in-Chief issued a stirring appeal to arms. 'Soldiers! I have just put myself at your head to lead you to the combat. We are going to second the struggles of a people reclaiming its independence and to rescue it from foreign oppression. This is a holy cause which has the sympathy of the whole world.'

The Austrians were defeated first at Montebello, then followed the great victory of Magenta on 4 June, after which the two rulers made a triumphant entry into Milan to cries of '*Viva Napoleone! Viva il Liberatore!*' whilst in France *Te Deums* were sung in *Notre Dame* and every church. A relation of Cristina's husband, Count Luigi di Belgiojoso, became Mayor of the liberated city. Cavour spent little time at the official receptions. He preferred instead to be alone with Cristina in her Milanese home. Somehow in the midst of all the rejoicing she felt uneasy and had a premonition of trouble that was to prove correct.

On 24 June at Solferino another resounding victory was won by the French and the Piedmontese. But by now Napoleon was having second thoughts. Though personally brave, he had a horror of bloodshed and the aftermath of battle. He was genuinely distressed by the heavy French losses at Solferino – the piles of bloodsoaked corpses, the still living mutilated casualties. 'War is horrible,' he was heard to say as he rode away. His personal motives in embarking on this campaign had probably been selfish ones – to obtain Nice and Savoy for France, to have cousin 'Plon-Plon' his creature king in central Italy, and the whole peninsula under his influence. But this he now realised would not suit Cavour who had never intended the last two objectives to be achieved by Napoleon.

Since the outbreak of war Modena, Parma, the Romagna and Tuscany had revolted and had expelled their rulers. In each state Cavour's agents had engineered demonstrations where they shouted for Victor Emmanuel to become their king. As a result Provisional Governments had been set up ruling in his name. This was not at all what the French Emperor intended to happen. Alarming news, too, had reached him that Prussia was mobilising on the Rhine and threatening to fight in support of Austria. These factors made him decide not to continue the war.

On 9 July the startling news reached Milan that Napoleon III had met the Emperor Francis Joseph in secret on the preceding day. On the 11th a draft peace treaty was signed at Villafranca whereby Austria ceded Lombardy and Parma to Napoleon, who promised to hand them over to Piedmont. Venice was to remain in Austrian hands, whilst the other Italian States were to be grouped in a Confederation with the Pope as its President.

Cavour was stricken and at a stormy interview advised his King not to agree. When the latter attempted to argue with Napoleon and spoke of even continuing the war himself, the Emperor retorted: 'If you do so, instead of one enemy you might possibly have two.' With great dignity Victor Emmanuel kept his temper and signed the treaty, adding, however, the statement: 'I approve so far as I myself am concerned.' The Count when he heard raged at the King, then resigned. In France public opinion, which had never really supported the adventure, approved of the peace.

Cristina was always at her best in an emergency. She now started up a new paper, *L'Italie*, backing it with her own money and both editing and managing it. The paper was printed in French, because it was her aim that it should be read internationally. She wholeheartedly supported Cavour, who soon returned to office. She started holding a salon in Milan so as to stimulate interest in *L'Italie*, and to collect news for it.

The next few years saw swift progress towards the unification of Italy. Professor G. M. Trevelyan has called 1860 the decisive year in the making of Italy. In March the people of Bologna, Modena and Tuscany voted for union with Piedmont. In early April there was a rising in Palermo against the Bourbon ruler, King Francis II of Naples. A month later Garibaldi and his Thousand Redshirts sailed from Genoa and landed in Sicily to be welcomed with enthusiasm by its people. On 27 May he attacked Palermo.

Cavour had not expected Garibaldi to succeed and had therefore officially disapproved of the adventure. Like the rest of Europe he had not imagined it possible for a thousand undisciplined volunteers supported by a motley collection of Sicilians to defeat King Francis's twenty thousand regulars. In Naples the King so panicked when he heard the news that he telegraphed five times in a day for the Papal blessing, which even in fivefold strength failed to be efficacious. The British Minister in Rome wrote to Lord John Russell about this: 'Cardinal Antonelli, through whom the application had to be made, telegraphed the last three blessings without reference to His Holiness, saying that he was duly authorised to do so. The Convents are awfully scandalised at this proceeding.' The devout no doubt found in this the cause for the subsequent fall of Palermo.

The King had to allow General Lanza to capitulate with the one concession that the royal army was permitted to take ship for Naples. By 1 June Garibaldi was the island's dictator, and Cavour's fear became that he would cross to the mainland, conquer the rest of the Kingdom of Naples, and having achieved this unaided proclaim a republic. So, true to his opportunist rule of pursuing several policies at the same time, the Count sent agents to Naples to bribe all they could and stage a revolution that would overthrow the Bourbon King and lead to a 'popular' demand for Victor Emmanuel to take his place, but this failed. Whilst these subversive activities were in progress, Cavour's minister in Naples was officially assuring King Francis of his country's friendly intentions.

Meanwhile from every part of northern Italy the finest of its youth were eagerly volunteering for service with Garibaldi. Within three months of the capture of Palermo, some twenty thousand of these sailed southwards. Those who could not go to fight contributed money which came freely from both rich and poor. In Milan the Million Rifles Fund supplied the recruits with arms, and received in secret large sums from the Piedmontese Treasury. Cristina gave generously to this fund and also helped to raise money for it.

Cavour's motives for pursuing a policy of tortuous diplomacy were besides his fear of republicanism his other fear of Napoleon III's ultimate reactions to the course of events. With French troops based in Rome it would be easy for them to be reinforced by sea and should Napoleon suddenly decide to go to the aid of King Francis the whole Garibaldi adventure might come to nothing as it had in 1849. After the Dictator's victory at Milazzo all Europe waited to see if he would succeed in crossing the Straits of Messina. Whilst publicly discouraging him from doing this, Cavour in private urged him on.

Napoleon III now suggested in confidence to the British Government that the joint fleets of their two countries should police the Italian coast south of Rome to prevent any invasion by Garibaldi. But through the Empress Eugénie's indiscretion, Cavour learnt of this and sent a picked representative post-haste to London to plead so eloquently with the British Foreign Minister that Lord John Russell decided after all not to intervene and made it clear to the French Emperor that England would disapprove of his taking unilateral action.

The maritime threat removed, Garibaldi cleverly crossed the straits before the enemy was aware of it. On 21 August Reggio surrendered and seventeen days later he entered Naples to a wild welcome from its half-million inhabitants. But the regrouped troops of King Francis strongly based on the Volturno barred the road northwards to Rome.

Cavour decided the time had come for swift action. He told his cabinet colleagues that this was necessary 'to combat the influence of Garibaldi and to prevent the revolution extending into our kingdom.' They agreed that the Papal States should be invaded to this end, and an emissary was sent to Napoleon III to tell him what was intended. The Emperor said he had no objection to the Piedmontese restoring order as long as it looked like 'a response to a spontaneous insurrection reflecting the wishes of the people'. There remained the danger from Austrian intervention. Cavour knew that they could not risk military defeat with Prussia now threatening them, so to win Bismark's support he openly declared himself in favour of German unification.

As soon as he felt confident that France and Austria would not intervene, Cavour set about staging the 'spontaneous insurrection' which Napoleon had demanded. The North Italian army had little trouble in defeating the Papal forces and soon nothing stood between the Piedmontese and Garibaldi except King Francis's troops on the Volturno. The King's advisers concerned lest they should be attacked in the rear persuaded him to take precipitous action with the result that Garibaldi through superior generalship won a hard fought battle on 1–2 October and saved Naples.

On 9 October King Victor Emmanuel and his forces began their triumphal march from Ancona southwards and were acclaimed everywhere by the populace. Garibaldi meanwhile contrary to Cavour's earlier fears was doing all he could to establish Victor Emmanuel's authority in Naples. On 21 October the people were invited to vote 'Yes' or 'No' to the proposition: 'The people wishes for Italy one and indivisible with Victor

Emmanuel as Constitutional King, and his legitimate descendants after him.' The votes in favour totalled 1,734,117 and those against 10,979.

Five days later near Vajrano the King and Garibaldi met and the latter cried: 'I hail the first King of Italy.' Legal confirmation of this was given on 18 February of the following year when a newly elected Parliament meeting in Turin passed the shortest act in its history. It consisted of one sentence: 'King Victor Emmanuel assumes for himself and his successors the title of King of Italy.' Consequently he was proclaimed as such 'by the grace of God and the will of the Nation.'

During the debate Cavour stressed that the obvious capital for the new Kingdom was Rome. But there was little chance of this coming about whilst the Pope received military protection from the French. The Count attempted to find a solution to the problem by sending a Jesuit priest to negotiate with Cardinal Antonelli. He offered to guarantee the Papacy full ecclesiastical independence in return for the surrender of its temporal powers. But barely had the talks begun when Cavour fell critically ill. He had not much trust in doctors. 'They've given me up,' he told his nurse. When she refuted this, he retorted: 'Well, I have given them up.' They used the remedy Cristina had used on herself at Ciaq-Maq-Oglou. They applied leeches till no more blood would come. Next day he was dead. He was only fifty-one.

The Count's ministerial successors made no progress in reaching an agreement with the Pope. However, a step was taken in the right direction when in June 1865, the Italian Parliament was moved from Turin to Florence. An alliance with Prussia bore fruit when after Austria's defeat by the new Germanic power in the following year Italy received Venetia as her reward. This left only Rome as the missing piece in the jigsaw puzzle that would complete Italy.

Nearly all Cristina had fought for had now been gained. But ill-health soon made her relinquish the control of her paper. Nevertheless, she continued to entertain, and began spending more and more time in her villa at Blevio on the Lake of Como, not far from the Pliniana where her husband had lived with the young Duchess of Plaisance. Here she received a cosmopolitan society of all ages and classes, dropping out of the animated conversation now and then to make notes for her articles.

Guests were not only invited to her salon, but also asked to stay on for dinner as well. Her Turkish manservant would order them about, seating the most important round his mistress and the least noteworthy at the other end of the table.

Cristina would toy with the food on her plate, leaving practically everything, then she would fall asleep. Diners present for the first time were apt to be stunned into silence by such behaviour. Then she would open her eyes and in a reproving voice order them to talk to one another.

After the meal she would awake and lead the company into the music-room, and whilst they listened to some gifted musician she would sew or embroider, preparing clothes for children in orphanages, whilst she puffed at her narghile. Verdi came regularly to play for her. When she became ill, she rarely went to bed but lay in an armchair fully dressed and enveloped in shawls, occasionally dosing herself with medicine.

There are, of course, always those who gain a sadistic satisfaction to see beauty ravaged. Louise Colet was a French writer who for personal reasons detested the Princess, and who contributed sensational articles to Paris papers. Describing a ball held by the Duchess Visconti di Modrone on the occasion of a visit of King Victor Emmanuel to Milan, she writes[1]: 'What a glittering parade of goddesses in all their finery. It was in the midst of this divine crowd that the Princess appeared. As she approached, bent and tottering, the Turkish Ambassador said to us: "I can tell you all about the attempt on her life in Asia Minor."

'"Please spare us that," retorted a journalist who wrote for the *Perseveranza*. "Ghosts have a right to silence, if not to respect. She has ceased to aspire to love. She only wishes to be listened to. Every day she sends us reams of her writings which pack all our files. One needs a dam to stem the river of ink that flows out of her. The editorial staff have held a protest meeting. She is furious about it. Hide me!" He slipped behind the Turkish Ambassador. "Don't let her see me! They say she has the evil eye."

'Whilst the men were discussing her, this ruin of a woman passed us. She looked like a walking hunch-backed skeleton in her shroud-like white dress. Her toothless mouth was twisted in an envious, sinister smile. Her staring, sunken eyes glared about her. Diamonds gleamed ironically in her scanty hair, helping to cover the bald patches. The onlookers shuddered with pity and revulsion at the sight of her.'

Others, however, took a different view. Henri d'Iderville, in his *Journal d'un diplomate en Italie*, wrote that he had heard a great deal about the Princess's intelligence and energy, but he was far more impressed than he had expected. 'Though her back was stooped and her head twisted, the fire in her eyes, her distinguished face, her commanding gestures, her flair for the right word, and the compelling way she spoke, all made me realise that here was a woman of tremendous determination and passion.'

On 24 January 1861, her daughter, Maria married the Marchese Lodovico Trotti-Bentivoglio who was thirty-two and nine years older than his bride. Since 1859 he had been in the service of King Victor Emmanuel II of Piedmont, who made him a senator in 1891. It proved a very happy marriage.

The feminist movement was growing and becoming more militant. Cristina's sympathy with that cause is clearly stated in her excellent essay 'On the Present Condition of Women and Their Future,' published in the first issue of the *Nuova Antologia* on 1 January 1866. Society everywhere, she wrote, was based on the false assumption that women were inferior to men. It would be particularly difficult to change this in Italy where her sex generally accepted this as true. 'But surely it is time that the wives and mothers of the lords of creation were at least admitted to be intellectually on the same plane as men.' She goes on to suggest that for a start women should be allowed to qualify in all branches of the medical profession.

To the last she was fascinated by politics. Visconti Venosta wrote that even when she was nearing her end she retained this interest. 'I had called one morning to ask her how she was. She signalled for me to approach her and in a whisper, for her voice was failing now, she asked for up-to-date news regarding some important development. Italy was the great love in her life and its well-being was constantly in her mind.'

1870 saw the Franco-Prussian War and the downfall of Napoleon III. With this came the withdrawal of the French troops from Rome. King Victor Emmanuel was quick to take advantage of the changed position. He wrote the Pope a letter stating that in order to save 'the Papal tiara and the royal crown' from the revolution that was threatening them both he would be forced to enter Rome 'to maintain and occupy such positions as were indispensable for the preservation of order in the peninsula and the security of the Holy See.'

Pius IX was very angry and told the King's spokesman that his master was 'a whitened sepulchre and a viper.' But despite Pio Nono's protests Victor Emmanuel's forces bombarded the Porta Pia and marching through the breach thus made took over the city.

Many who spend their lives crusading for causes die with their hopes unfulfilled, but Cristina lived to see hers realised. The Italy on which she looked in the twilight of her days was one united country with the imperial city of the Caesars as its capital.

The following year she fell ill with dropsy, and when summer came she was too weak to be moved from Milan. Then on 5 July her head bent over her chest and moved no more. She was buried simply and quietly at Locate among the people she had cared for. She left her villa there for the use of the community. It is now divided into tenements and occupied by some twenty to thirty families.

Her distinguished ancestor, Marshal Trivulzio, Governor of Milan, victor of Agnadel, dictated on his deathbed his own epitaph. It is one singularly appropriate for her, too. 'A Trivulzio who never rested is now at rest. Silence.'

NOTES

CHAPTER I

1 Letter dated 14 February 1842, written from Locate, now in the Belgiojoso family archives in Merate
2 Archivio di Stato Milano, *Atti Segreti cart. I*
3 He left his wife for her. Greville in his *Memoirs*, volume IV, wrote in 1841: 'The other day died the Duchess of Cannizzaro, a woman of rather amusing notoriety ... She was a Miss Johnstone and got from her Brother a large fortune; very short and fat, with rather a handsome face ... Soon after her Brother's death, she married the Count St. Antonio (who was afterwards made Duke of Cannizzaro) ... He became disgusted with her, however, and went to Italy on a separate allowance which she made him. After a few years he returned to England, and they lived together again; but he not only became more disgusted than before, but he had in the meantime formed a liaison at Milan with a very distinguished woman there, once a magnificent beauty, but now as old and as large as his own wife, and to her he was very anxious to return. This was Madame Visconti (mother of the notorious Princess Belgiojoso) who, though no longer young, had fine remains of good looks and was eminently pleasing and attractive. Accordingly, St. Antonio took occasion to elope (by himself) from some party of pleasure at which he was present with his Spouse, and when she found that he had gone off without notice or warning, she ... set off in pursuit ... She ventured over the Strait and set on to Milan, if not to recover her fugitive better half, at all events to terrify her rival and disturb their joys.

'The advent of the Cannizzaro woman was to the Visconti like the eruption of the Huns of old. She fled to a villa near Milan which she proceeded to garrison and fortify, but finding that the other was not provided with any implements for a siege, and did not stir from Milan, she ventured to return to the City, and for some time these ancient Heroines drove about the town glaring defiance and hate at each other, which was the whole amount of the hostilities that took place between them. Finding her husband was irrecoverable she at length got tired of the hopeless pursuit and resolved to return home and console herself with her music and whatever other gratifications she could command. Not long after she took into keeping a strapping young Italian, a third rate singer ... this profligate blackguard bullied and plundered her ... and she managed very nearly to ruin herself before her death'
4 ibid. *cart.* III, 112. Rapporto 4797 P.S. Rapporto 4264 P.S. Also 1829 – *cart.* 115
5 Archivio di Stato Torino – *Gabinetto di Polizia*, Genoa, *Cart.* 1 and 2
6 V. Masuyer 'La Reine Hortense et le Prince Louis', *Revue des Deux Mondes*, 15 August 1914

NOTES

7 Madden – The Literary Life and Correspondence of the Countess of Blessington, Volume II, p. 429
8 G. Sforza – *Un fratello di Napoleone III morto per la libertà d'Italia*, R. S. R. vol. III
9 Letter to Bombelles, dated 15 February 1830, in the Collezione Piancastelli
10 La Cecilia – *Memorie storico-politiche dal 1820 al 1876*
11 A. S. W. R. de Berne, 21, XI, 1830, N. 38 B. St. K. *Schweis Berichte*, 1830, *fasc.* 255
12 Archivio di Stato Milano, *Atti Segreti*, 1830, cart. 126
13 ibid. *cart.* 130
14 ibid, *cart* 136
15 Archivio di Stato Torino, *Gabinetto di Polizia*, Genoa, *cart* 1 and 2

CHAPTER 2

1 State Archives Vienna. Central Information. *Protocoll.* n. 53/182. Also A. S. W. *Gabinetto di Polizia*, n. 5205, anno 1832, 347/1832
2 *Souvenirs du Marquis de Floranges (1811–1833)*, Paris, Ollendorff, 1906
3 The entire correspondence between Paris, Vienna, and Milan, quoted from in this chapter is available in the State Archives of Vienna and Milan

CHAPTER 3

1 Count Rodolphe Apponyi *Vingt-Cinq Ans à Paris* 1913
2 Marie d'Agoult *Mémoires*, 1833–54 (1927)
3 Duchesse de Dino *Chronique*, vol. II, p. 29

CHAPTER 4

1 Letter in *Collezione Piancastelli*
2 ibid
3 Balzac *Lettres à l'Etrangère*, p. 164
4 ibid p. 370
5 ibid p. 381
6 *Correspondance d'Alfred de Musset*, p. 181
7 Arsène Houssaye – *Les Confessions*, vol. I, p. 269

CHAPTER 5

1 This incident is recorded by the Comtesse de Bassonville in her *Salons d'autrefois*, vol. II, p. 161–163
2 Federico Confalonieri. *Memorie e lettere*, vol. II, p. 298
3 Albert Augustin Thierry, *Une Héroine Romantique*, p. 33

NOTES

CHAPTER 6

1 Count Hübner *Une année de ma vie*
2 Belgiojoso *Souvenirs dans l'Exil*
3 R. Barbiera *Passione del Risorgimento*

CHAPTER 7

1 *Revue des Deux Mondes* September 1848
2 Thierry, *op. cit.*
3 *Revue des Deux Mondes* September 1848

CHAPTER 8

1 Thierry, *op. cit*
2 Count Rodolphe Apponyi, *op. cit*
3 *Revue des Deux Mondes*, October 1848 and January 1849
4 H. Greeley. *Recollections of a Busy Life*, p. 188
5 Emilio Dandolo *The Italian volunteers and Lombard Rifle Brigade, 1848–49*
6 Henry James *William Wetmore Story and his Friends*, vol. I, p. 151
7 Howard R. Marraro *American Opinion on the Unification of Italy* p. 69

CHAPTER 9

1 Thierry. *op. cit.* Quoted from a letter to Augustin Thierry
2 ibid
3 ibid
4 ibid
5 ibid
6 ibid

CHAPTER 10

1 Belgiojoso *Asie Mineure* 1858 and *Oriental Harems* 1862

CHAPTER 12

1 Thierry, *op. cit*

CHAPTER 13

1 Quoted in Thierry, *op. cit*

CHAPTER 14

1 Louise Colet *L'Italie des italiens*

219

SELECT BIBLIOGRAPHY

ADAM, C. *La guerre d'Italie* (Paris, 1859)
AGOULT, MARIE d' *Mes souvenirs, 1806–1833* (Paris, 1877)
  Mémoires, 1833–1854 (Paris, 1927)
  Correspondance de Liszt et de la Comtesse d'Agoult, 1833–1864.
  2 vols. (Paris, 1933–4)
ALMERAS, HENRI d' *La vie parisienne sous Louis-Philippe* (Paris, 1911)
ANCELOT, MME *Un salon de Paris* (Paris, 1866)
APPONYI, COUNT RODOLPHE *Vingt-cinq Ans à Paris* (Paris, 1913)
ARRIVABENE, COUNT CHARLES *Italy under Victor Emmanuel* (London, 1862)
ARMANDO, W. G. *Franz Liszt* (Hamburg, 1961)
AUBERT, R. *Le Pontificat de Pie IX, 1846–1878* (Paris, 1952)

BALLEYDIER, A. *Histoire de la Révolution de Rome* (Paris, 1851)
BARBIERA, R. *La Principessa di Belgiojoso* (Milan, 1898)
  Passione del Risorgimento (Milan, 1903)
BEALES, DEREK *England and Italy, 1859–1860* (London, 1962)
BEAUMONT-VASSY, COMTE de *Les salons de Paris* (Paris, 1866)
BELGIOJOSO, PRINCESS CRISTINA di,
  Essai sur la formation du dogme catholique (Paris, 1842)
  Essai sur Vico (Paris, 1844)
  Etudes sur l'histoire de la Lombardie (Paris, 1846)
  Souvenirs dans l'exil (Paris, 1852)
  Asie Mineure (Paris, 1858)
  History of the House of Savoy (Paris, 1860)
  Oriental Harems (New York, 1862)
  Osservazioni sulla stato attuale d'Italie (Milan, 1868)

BERKELEY, G. F-H. and J. *Italy in the making: 1 January - 16 November 1848* (Cambridge, 1940)

BITTARD DES PORTES, RENÉ *L'expédition française de Rome* (Vannes, 1900)

BLANC, J. J. L. *History of ten years* 2 vols. (London, 1844–5)

BOULENGER, JACQUES *Les Dandys* (Paris, 1907)

BOULENGER, MARCEL *Souvenirs du Marquis de Floranges* (Paris, 1906)

BROGLIE, DUC de *Souvenirs* (Paris, 1886)

BROWN, ARTHUR W. *Margaret Fuller* (New York, 1964)

BUCHNER, A. *Franz Liszt in Bohemia* (London, 1936)

BUTT, I. *History of Italy* 2 vols (London, 1860)

CAMERINI, E. *Donna illustre* (Milan, 1870)

CAVOUR, CAMILLO di *Lettere edite ed inedite di Camillo Cavour* ed. Luigi Chiala (Torino, 1883–7)

CHAMBERS, LT.-COL. *Garibaldi and Italian unity* (London, 1864)

CLOQUET, JULES-GERMAIN *Souvenirs sur la vie privée du General Lafayette* (Paris, 1836)

DAVRAY, JEAN *George Sand et ses amants* (Paris, 1935)

DANDOLO, EMILIO *The Italian volunteers and Lombard Rifle Brigade, being an authentic narrative, 1848–49* (London, 1851)

DE GAILLARD, LEOPOLD *L'expédition de Rome en 1849* (1851)

DE LA RIVE, WILLIAM *Reminiscences of the life and character of Count Cavour* (1862)

DE LESSEPS, FERDINAND *Ma mission à Rome* (Paris, 1849)

D'IDEVILLE, HENRY *Journal d'un diplomate en Italie* (Paris, 1872)

DINO, DUCHESSE de *Chronique* (Paris, 1909)

DU CAMP, MAXIME *Souvenirs littéraires* (Paris, 1892)

GAILLY, EMILE GERARD *Les véhémences de Louise Colet* (Paris, 1934)

GASPARINETTI, ANNA *Quattro anni di attività giornalistica della Principessa Cristina Trivulzio di Belgiojoso.* Vol. XV, November 1936 and Vol. XVI, December 1937, of *La Vita Italiana* Rome

GIRARDIN, MME de *La Croix de Berry* (Paris, 1857)

GAUTIER, THEOPHILE *Souvenirs romantiques* (Paris, 1929)

GRIFFITH, G. O. *Mazzini: prophet of Modern Europe* (London, 1932)

HALES, E. E. Y. *Mazzini and the Secret Societies* (London 1956)

H., E. A. *The late melancholy events in Milan* (London 1848)

HINKLEY, EDITH *Mazzini* (London, 1924)

HOUSSAYE, A. *Les confessions: souvenirs d'un démi-siècle, 1830–1880* (Paris, 1885–91)

JAMES, HENRY *William Wetmore Story and his Friends* (London, 1957)

JAUBERT, CAROLINE *Souvenirs* (Paris, 1882)

KING, BOLTON *Mazzini* (London, 1902)
A history of Italian unity (London, 1898)

LISZT, FRANZ *Correspondance* 2 vols. (Paris, 1933)

MALMESBURY, JAMES, EARL OF *Memoirs of a ex-minister* (London, 1885)

MALVEZZI, ALDOBRANDINO *La Principessa Cristina* (Milan, 1936)

MARRARO, HOWARD *American Opinion on the Unification of Italy, 1846–1861* (New York, 1932)

MARTINENGO-CESARESCO, COUNTESS EVELYN *The liberation of Italy* (London, 1895)

MONSELET, CHARLES *Statues et statuettes contemporains* (Paris, 1852)

MAZZINI, GIUSEPPE *The life and writings of Joseph Mazzini* (London, 1891)

OSSOLI, MARGARET FULLER *Memoirs* 2 vols. (Boston, 1852)

POMMIER, J. *Variétés sur Alfred de Musset* (Paris, 1947)

RESTELLI, F. *Events in Milan* (London, 1848)

REVUE DES DEUX MONDES, September, October, December 1848, and January 1849, Paris

ROSTLAND, C. *Liszt* (Paris, 1960)

ROUSSELOT, J. *Franz Liszt* (London, 1960)

SALVADORI, MASSIMO *Cavour and the unification of Italy* (Princeton, 1961)

SCÉHÉ, LEON *La jeunesse dorée d'Alfred de Musset* (Paris, 1910)

THAYER, WILLIAM ROSCOE *The life and times of Cavour* (Boston, 1911)

THIERRY, A. AUGUSTIN *La Princesse Belgiojoso: une héroine romantique* (Paris, 1926)

WHYTE, ARTHUR JAMES *The political life and letters of Cavour 1848–1861* (London, 1930)

WHITEHOUSE, H. R. *A revolutionary Princess* (London, 1906)

WRIGHTSON, R. H. *History of Italy to 1850* (London, 1855)

VOGUE, E. M. de *Sous l'horizon* (Paris, 1904)

INDEX

Charles Albert, cont.
war on Austria, 102–3; Cristina's
letter to, 107–9; plan of campaign,
112; military defeats, 115; outside
Milan, 117–19; proposed capitulation, 120–3; forced to tear it up,
123, 125; deserts Milan, 124–5,
127, 130; Novara defeat and
abdication, 132–3
Charles Felix, King of Sardinia, 11
Chartreuse de Parme, La (Stendhal),
Cristina portrayed in, 39
Chateaubriand, Vicomte de, Cristina's
impressions of, 30–3
Chopin, Frédéric, 38
Ciaq-Maq-Oglou: Cristina's 'little
kingdom' at, 146–8, 150–4, 182,
183–4; overseer's mismanagement
of, 183, 193; attempt on Cristina's
life at, 185–92
Civita Vecchia, 135
Clarendon, Lord, 201
Clerici, General Giorgio, 121
Cloquet, J., 36
Clotilde, Princess, 206
Codogno, 115, 116
Coeur, Abbé, 78–9, 82
Colet, Louise: on de Musset's Ver-
sailles visit to Cristina, 62–4; on
Cristina's ravaged beauty, 214–15
Conciliatore (Nationalist movement), 3
Concordia of Turin, 141, 149
Conneau, Dr, 204
Constantinople, 145, 146, 196
Constitutionel, Le, Cristina's con-
tributions to, 18, 19, 20
Cousin, Victor, 45, 198
Cremona, 115
Crepuscolo (Milanese journal), 203
Cristina, Princess – see Belgiojoso,
Princess Cristina di
Croce di Savoia, La, started by
Cristina, 109

Crociato, Il, started by Cristina, 109
Croquet, Jules, 19

Damascus, 174–9
Delacroix, Eugène, 38, 71–2
Delaroche, Hippolyte, 38
Dickens, Charles, 139
Dino, Duchesse de, 44
Disraeli, Benjamin, 93
Djaour, Daghda, 162
Duras, Léopold, 148–9

Essai sur la formation du dogme catho-
lique, Un (Cristina), 53, 79–80
Essai sur Vico (Cristina), 80
Eugènie, Empress, 7, 204, 205–6, 211

Farina, Chevalier, 108, 109
Federazione secret society, 3
Ferdinand II of Two Sicilies (King
'Bomba'), 97–8, 103, 132, 137, 138
Ferrara, 95
Floranges, Marquis de, 5–6, 21–3
Florence, 7–8, 95, 96; declares war on
Austria, 102; Italian Parliament
moved to (1865), 213
Francis IV, Duke of Modena, 12, 13
Francis II of Naples, 210–11
Francis Joseph I, Emperor, 203, 204,
209
Fraser, Major, 34, 35
Fratelli d'Italia (Mamelli), 142
Fuller, Margaret, 133, 136, 137

Garibaldi, Giuseppe, 131, 132, 142;
defence of Rome (1849), 136, 138,
139, 140–1; war against Austria,
206–7, 208; attacks Sicily, 210–11;
expels Francis II from Naples,
210–12; resigns dictatorship to
Victor Emmanuel, 213
Gautier, Théophile, 40–1
Gazzetta Italiana: founded by Cristina, 81, 82, 86; ceases, 88